THE FLIPSIDE

FINDING THE HIDDEN
OPPORTUNITIES IN LIFE

Adam J Jackson

headline
business plus

First published in trade paperback in 2009 by
HEADLINE PUBLISHING GROUP
First published in paperback in 2010 by
HEADLINE PUBLISHING GROUP

1

Cataloguing in Publication Data is available from the British Library

ISBN 978 0 7553 1877 3

Typeset in Caslon 540 by Avon DataSet Ltd,
Bidford on Avon, Warwickshire

Printed in the UK by CPI Mackays, Chatham, ME5 8TD

Headline's policy is to use papers that are natural, renewable and
recyclable products and made from wood grown in sustainable forests.
The logging and manufacturing processes are expected to conform to the
environmental regulations of the country of origin.

HEADLINE PUBLISHING GROUP
An Hachette UK Company
338 Euston Road
London NW1 3BH

www.headline.co.uk
www.hachette.co.uk

'. . . the book is composed of heart-warming stories from celebrities and ordinary people alike, all overcoming adversity . . . this works as an entertaining and relevant read when so many people are experiencing financial and emotional traumas.' *News of The World*

'Citing examples from both civilian and celebrity life . . . it proves there can be a silver lining in even the most dark, desperate clouds . . . this inspirational chronicle of optimism might just change the way you deal with life's challenges.' *The Daily Record*

'. . . offers life-affirming stories guaranteed to make us change the way we look at adversity.' *Publishers Weekly*

'. . . packed with anecdotes and advice and makes very helpful reading.'
Kate Turkington – CapeTown.co.za

'It is a truly inspirational account, showing as it does, how people with the right attitude to life can overcome some of the most difficult experiences.

In fact, were I in a position to do so, I would make it compulsory reading for all those "Moaning Minnies" out there, who sit waiting for someone or something to turn up and make things better, instead of pulling themselves up by their bootstraps and getting on with life.'

Euroweekly

'The bulk of the book explores the specific strategies that people have used to find the flipside of adversity. The answers will surprise you. Don't miss this one! Now more than ever, when as leaders we have to be "dealers in hope" (to quote Napoleon).' *Gateways Business Consultants*

'This is an inspiring, really energising book. It is just the sort of thing you need when you have watched too many news broadcasts about how the world is going to the dogs.

The book confirms that the flipside is not a chance occurrence. It is an outcome that can be predicted by a person's attitudes and beliefs. What many of the people featured did naturally, others can do by imitation. This is an empowering book. Read it first before you give it to that friend who really needs it.' *The Times, South Africa*

'We are inspired by Adam J Jackson's writings in his book *The Flipside* which is based upon a simple and inspiring idea that every problem or obstacle in our lives however big or small contains an equivalent or greater benefit or opportunity.'
Health budget speech tabled by Limpopo MEC for Health and Social Development, Mrs Miriam Segabutla, 18 June 2009, Limpopo Provincial Government, South Africa

'Whether you're smack in the middle of a crisis or just committed to always seizing all the opportunities in life, *The Flipside* will inspire you . . . and give you the mental agility and resourcefulness to use all the cards you've been dealt, both good and bad, to create more of the life you want.'

www.bottomlinebookclub.com

'They reckon everything happens for a reason and author Adam J Jackson has made it his mission to find the stories to prove that saying . . . you will find fascinating stories here of how others . . . have taken lemons and made lemonade. If nothing else, it's incredibly inspirational.'

The Southland Times

Dear Mr Jackson,
I have just finished reading your excellent book, *The Flipside*, and I just wanted to drop you a line to say thank you so much. I was diagnosed with early stage breast cancer last month and your book has helped me enormously during the first difficult few weeks of coming to terms with the diagnosis.

Thank you so much, I took such inspiration from you and from the case studies in your book. My illness is not life threatening but it has frightened me and made me think about my life. Your book helped me put it into a context and a perspective, thank you.

Anita Thornberry

'Forget lemons and lemonade. Adam Jackson's *The Flipside* shows that there are far greater opportunities in store for all of us if we just give life a second chance. Broken down into easy-to-read segments, *The Flipside* provides small doses of optimism. Reading just one story each morning is guaranteed to get a reader's day started off right.'

Krista Grueninger, Director of Communications, Optimist International

'Have you lost hope or given up as a result of a broken heart or over the despair of a relationship not working out? *The Flipside* may result in you being an inspiration to others who are struggling with what you have been through, it may lead to you making a new discovery, or a new way of problem solving, or how to have peace after such turmoil, who knows?'

Joanne Robinson, © 2009 Donna Intera

'I loved that this book described the specific behaviours of people who find the flipside. It is not just some natural way of being or philosophical choice. It is much more than that. It is focused and determined. I now have some really useful tools to use with clients who have setbacks, disappointments and tragedies that they want to rise above.'

COMENSAnews

For Sam Chapman

CONTENTS

Prologue   xi
Introduction   xv

Part One: Discoveries – Finding the Flipside

1. The Road to Madrid   1
2. Defining Moments   5
3. Crises and Opportunities   15
4. Life Changes: When Bad Things Happen   24
5. The Two Sides of Trauma   38
6. Reasons For Optimism   53

Part Two: Pathways – Steps to the Flipside

7. Finding the Flipside   71
8. Great Expectations: The Strategies of Optimists   73
9. The Entrepreneur's Mindset: Looking For   103
   Hidden Opportunities
10. Reframing Your Life: The Critical Questions   119
11. Lost Dreams and New Directions: Finding   137
    The Future
12. Edison's Legacy: Philosophies to Live By   149

13. The Art of Seeing: Doing the Impossible   161
14. The Paradigm of Possibilities: Hope For the   171
    Future
15. The Three Avenues: The Search For Meaning   185
16. The Relationship Factor: Surrounding Yourself   195
    With the Right People
17. Focusing the Mind: Finding Inner Strength   203
18. Conclusion   213

Part Three: Reflections – Thoughts on the Flipside

Do Things Always Work Out For the Best   221
    on the Flipside?
Where is the Flipside in an Economic Recession?   225
Is Adversity Necessary or Good?   229
Is Optimism Always the Best Option?   230
What is the Alternative to the Flipside?   231

Epilogue   233
Notes and References   237
Acknowledgements   248
Index   250

Flipside: an opposite, reverse, or sharply contrasted side or aspect of something or someone.

Wikipedia

'When the Gods choose to punish us, they merely answer our prayers.'

Oscar Wilde

Adam J Jackson was born in 1962 in Sussex, England. He graduated with a degree in Law from the University of Southampton in 1983 and went on to qualify as a solicitor and practise Law in London. However, after three years, Adam decided to leave Law to pursue a career in natural health sciences.

In 1995 Adam became a monthly columnist for *Nursing Times* and the *Health Guardian*, reporting on the latest developments and research relating to alternative therapies and complementary medicines.

Adam came across the concept of *The Flipside* through his own ill health. At eight years old he was diagnosed with psoriasis and the condition became so severe that he was later hospitalized. However, Adam went on to develop and produce a successful non-steroid treatment for psoriasis known as M-Folia, which is helping people all over the world.

The Flipside is Adam's eighth book. His earlier books, *The Secrets of Abundant Health, Wealth, Love & Happiness* series have been translated into twenty-seven languages. Adam is also a motivational speaker and businessman. He lives with his wife, Karen, children Sophie and Samuel, and their dog in Hertfordshire, UK.

For more information, visit www.adamjjackson.com

PROLOGUE

'All the world is full of suffering. It is also full of over-coming.'

Helen Keller

THE BOY WAS just twelve years old. He sat looking at the ground, picking nervously at his fingers waiting for the doctor to answer. The doctor was a tall, lanky man in his early sixties. There was nothing warm about him. He had slicked-back grey hair, a sharp pointed nose and pursed thin lips. He wore small, round spectacles that made his pale-grey eyes look like small marbles. He picked up his papers, squared the edges and put them down again before removing his spectacles and looking straight at the boy.

'I'm sorry, son,' said the doctor. 'But what you have is not going to go away. If I give you what you're asking for, I'd be doing you a disservice. The sooner you learn to live with this, the better.'

'But if you could just . . .' began the boy.

'Listen to me,' interrupted the doctor. 'It's for the best.'

The boy's eyes began to well. He could feel his chest tighten. Without raising his head, he stood up and left the room.

The condition the boy was suffering from was a skin complaint known as psoriasis. It is characterized by red, flaky lesions of the skin. In many cases it is confined to a patient's elbows and knees and some people suffer with it on their scalp. But the boy had thick, scaly lesions all over his body.

He had first noticed it one morning when clusters of red spots appeared on the sides of his abdomen. That was only two months earlier, but over the ensuing weeks the spots had become bigger and spread over his entire body.

The boy had gone to the school doctor asking not for a cure; he had already been told by his family doctor that there was no cure. What the boy had asked the school doctor for, pleaded for, was an off-games slip so that he wouldn't have to attend the swimming class.

As he walked along the corridor and out of the building, the boy could hold back his tears no longer. Oblivious to everything and everyone, his only thoughts were of how all of the other children would react when he turned up at swimming class looking like a leper. Then the inevitable questions would turn over in his head until he felt nauseous. 'Why me? Why did this have to happen to me? Why is life so unfair?'

Suddenly, he felt a hand on his shoulder. He turned to find his form tutor Mr Greenstein standing beside him. Mr Greenstein was a small figure of a man, hardly a few inches taller than the boy. He wore a plain grey suit with a white shirt and navy-blue tie. He was a gentle man, softly spoken, who was well liked by the children in his class.

'What's wrong?' Mr Greenstein asked.

'Nothing,' sighed the boy as he wiped his eyes.

'Come and take a seat. Just for a minute,' insisted Mr Greenstein.

Mr Greenstein and the boy sat down on a bench under a large oak tree away from the school buildings.

'Now, tell me what's upsetting you? Perhaps I can help.'

'No one can help,' murmured the boy.

'Well, let's at least try,' said Mr Greenstein.

The boy rolled up his sleeve to reveal large red, scaly patches of skin and explained his situation. When he had finished explaining, Mr Greenstein put his hand on the boy's shoulder.

'Who takes your swimming class?'

'Mr Cunningham.'

'You know, if you like, you and I could go and speak to Mr Cunningham and I'm sure we could persuade him to excuse you from the class.'

'Really?'

'Absolutely.' 'But before we do, let me tell you something. When I was seven years old my father died and I developed a stutter. Like your skin problem, it happened very quickly, almost overnight. It became so bad that, like you, I didn't want to go to school. I was frightened that the other children would make fun of me. I argued and argued about it with my mother, but in the end I knew that I had to go to school. And I'm glad I did. Because if I hadn't, I wouldn't have had an education. I wouldn't have become a teacher and I wouldn't be here sitting with you now.'

Mr Greenstein looked the boy squarely in the eye. 'Every difficulty that we face in life has a flipside.'

'What's a flipside?' mumbled the boy.

'Every problem or obstacle contains an opportunity as big, and sometimes bigger, than the problem itself. The flipside is that opportunity.'

The boy pulled up his sleeve. 'What possible flipside could there be in this? What opportunity could there possibly be in having to look like a leper in front of all the other kids?'

'Well, let's think about it for a minute . . .' answered Mr Greenstein. 'Let's see if we can find the flipside.'

INTRODUCTION

'Each problem has hidden within it an opportunity so powerful that it literally dwarfs the problem. The greatest success stories were created by people who recognized a problem and turned it into an opportunity.'

Joseph Sugarman

THE FIRST TIME I met someone who had found the flipside was on a cold winter evening in February 1981. In fact, that night I met not one but two remarkable people, both of whom spoke about the key events that had changed their lives. While I don't remember their names, the events of that evening have stayed with me. It was an evening I would never forget.

I had just watched the student drama society at Southampton University perform an outstanding production of a play called *Whose Life Is It Anyway?*. The play tells the story of a man who wakes up in hospital following a serious car accident to discover that he is a quadriplegic. He has no feeling and no control over any part of his body below his neck.

The story is utterly compelling. The man's life prior to the accident revolved around his work as an artist. Discovering that he is paralysed and unwilling to face the prospect of a life in which he has no control of anything, the man pleads with the hospital authorities to help him die. When they refuse, he initiates a legal battle for the right to end his life.

It is a brilliantly scripted drama that explores the emotional journey of a man whose bright, witty and vibrant mind has become trapped in a useless body. It also highlights the legal and moral issues surrounding euthanasia. In the ensuing legal battle, it becomes apparent that the man starts to feel differently about his life. He starts to build relationships with the people around him and the challenge of the court case gives meaning to his daily life. I won't tell you how the play ends. Suffice to say that, if you get an opportunity to see it (or the film version starring Richard Dreyfuss), I'm sure that you'll find it a very thought-provoking and memorable evening.

As an undergraduate reading Law, I had been especially interested to see the play because at that time we were covering the legal and ethical issues around the subject of euthanasia in our degree course. One of the core issues that arose from the play was whether a person could be considered mentally stable or emotionally capable of making a rational decision immediately after they have suffered such a drastic physical and emotional trauma. If not, what period of time would need to pass, or what test would they need to take before they could be considered capable of making a rational decision?

The evening I saw the play back in 1981 was particularly memorable because the play was followed by an open discussion about the issues raised in the storyline. The play's director was joined on stage by a Law professor, a Psychology professor and two other men, both of whom were sitting in wheelchairs.

The Law professor spoke about the issues that need to be addressed when considering the legalization of euthanasia. Suicide is not a criminal offence in the UK, and therefore one could argue that helping someone who wants to die but who is physically incapable of committing suicide should also not be a criminal offence. If a loved one was suffering and asked you to help end their suffering by handing them a bottle of tablets, would you hand it to them? Should you, by doing so, be guilty of murder or manslaughter?

If an able-bodied person is permitted to take a bottle of tablets to end his or her life, should a person who is paralysed be denied the same right, just because he or she can't physically pick up the bottle?

How far should the Law go in criminalizing the act of helping someone who wants to end their own life? It seems straightforward enough; most people wouldn't hesitate to end the suffering of an animal, so why would we not extend the same compassion to humans? The more one reflects upon the issues, the more one discovers that it is anything but straightforward. One of the key questions that we kept coming back to was how long after such a major trauma could a person who wants to commit suicide be said to be of sound mind and capable of making a rational decision.

The psychologist took up the discussion and explained that any trauma will affect a person's cognitive and behavioural patterns. It is known as post-traumatic stress disorder and usually develops within the first three months following a traumatic event. However, it can take up to a year before symptoms become apparent and these can include depression, suicidal tendencies, nightmares, anger rages and flashbacks.

For an individual who has suffered one of the worst physical and emotional traumas of losing control over virtually their entire body with all the consequences that flow from that, there is no way of knowing how capable or not they are of making a rational decision. All that is certain, the psychologist argued, is that they are incapable of making a decision of such finality within the first three months following the trauma.

At this point, the two men in the wheelchairs spoke to the audience. Their comments had a deep and lasting impression on me, so much so that I can remember it over twenty-five years later. The two men explained that in the immediate weeks following their accidents, they had indeed wanted to die. But, in the months that followed, their lives and their attitudes began to change. They were faced with new challenges every day; challenges that were hardly challenges at all prior to their accidents, challenges like getting washed and dressed in the morning, but challenges nonetheless. Their accidents had forced them to re-evaluate their lives, their hopes, their dreams and their aspirations. It was this, they both said, that brought about something they had not expected. The two men, in their own ways, had found the will to live.

The thing that I found most astonishing was that both men went on to say that their lives had become far richer and more fulfilled following their accidents than they had ever been before their accidents. They claimed that they were much happier now than they had been, and they both went so far as to say that their accidents had been the 'best things to have happened to them'. I found their comments shocking. How could anyone claim that an incident that left them paralysed and confined to a wheelchair for the rest of their life was the best thing to have happened to them?

A $105 SOCIAL SECURITY CHEQUE
AND A CHICKEN RECIPE

Harland Sanders was sixty-five years old when, through no fault of his own, he lost the business that he had spent the best part of his adult life building. At a time when many men his age were either retired or looking forward to retiring, Harland was facing financial ruin. He found himself having to live on nothing but a $105 social security cheque. But this experience proved to be one of the best things to have happened to Harland because the loss of his business would become the catalyst for something incredible. Harland would go on to find the flipside.

That Harland was able to find the flipside was no accident. He was no stranger to difficult times. Born on 9 September 1890 in Indiana, USA, Harland's childhood was anything but easy. Before Harland had reached his sixth birthday, his father died and Harland's mother had no choice but to go out to work.

Instead of attending school, Harland was given the responsibility of taking care of his three-year-old brother and baby sister. This meant that Harland had to cook and clean for his siblings. By all accounts, he excelled in both. According to his mother, by the time he was seven years old, Harland was a master at preparing numerous regional dishes.

At age 10, Harland got his first paid job working on a nearby farm for $2 a month. When he was twelve, his mother remarried and he left his home near Henryville, Indiana, for a job on a farm in Greenwood. He held a series of jobs over the next few years, first as a 15-year-old streetcar conductor in New Albany, and then as a 16-year-old private, soldiering for six months in Cuba.

During the years that followed, Harland worked as a railroad fireman, studied Law by correspondence, practised in Justice of the Peace courts, sold insurance, operated an Ohio

River steamboat ferry, sold tyres, and finally ended up operating a service station in Corbin, Kentucky.

When he was 40, Harland tried a new initiative by offering meals to hungry travellers who stopped at his service station. He didn't have a restaurant at that time, but served his customers simple, local recipes on his own dining table in the living quarters of his service station.

It wasn't long before Harland realized that there was a real opportunity to expand his garage business and he took the decision to open a restaurant in premises across the street that seated 142 people. In a short time, Harland's reputation for serving delicious home-cooked food grew. His restaurant was listed in Good Food Guides for the area and Harland even received honours from the State Governor Ruby Laffoon in 1935 in recognition of his contribution to the state's cuisine.

But life changes, and in the mid-1950s a new interstate highway was planned to bypass the town of Corbin, diverting the traffic and, with it, the bulk of Harland's customers. Harland was sixty-five years of age. A few months earlier, he had a successful business and could have expected to be able to retire quite comfortably whenever he chose. Yet now he was facing financial ruin. His garage and restaurant were auctioned off and this was how, after paying the last of his debtors, Harland was reduced to living on his $105 social security cheques.

However, within a few years, Harland would look back on the catastrophe that befell him when the new state highway caused him to lose his business and see it not as a disaster, but as the opportunity through which he found celebrity and success the likes of which he could never have dreamed of and would, in all probability, never have attained, had his garage and restaurant survived.

Having lost his business and livelihood through no fault of his own, it would have been easy for Harland to have given up. Who could have blamed him, particularly at his time of life, if he had become bitter and resentful? Fortunately for Harland, in those days the practice of attributing blame and seeking compensation from the state didn't come as easily as they do today.

Instead of complaining or finding someone to blame, Harland set out to look for the flipside and found it in the unlikeliest of places – a chicken recipe!

Harland knew that his chicken recipe was special and had been loved by his customers. So, armed with only his secret recipe – a coveted blend of eleven herbs and spices – he travelled across the country visiting one restaurant after another in the hope that some restaurateurs would be so impressed that they would be willing to pay to use his recipe. Harland cooked batches of chicken for the restaurant owners and their employees. If their reaction was favourable, he entered into a 'handshake' agreement on a deal that stipulated a payment to him of a nickel for each chicken the restaurant sold.

The rest, as they say, is history. By 1964, Harland, who was known as 'the Colonel', had opened 600 franchised outlets for his chicken in the United States and Canada. That year, he sold his interest in the US company for $2 million to a group of investors. But the Colonel remained the public face and spokesman for the company. In 1976 an independent survey ranked the Colonel as the world's second most recognizable celebrity.

Today Colonel Sanders' KFC (originally Kentucky Fried Chicken) outlets are found in more than 82 countries around the world and serve up over two billion dinners every year.

Until he was fatally stricken with leukaemia in 1980 at the age of 90, the Colonel travelled over 250,000 miles a year visiting the KFC empire he founded. And it all began with a sixty-five-year-old gentleman who had lost everything but refused to be beaten by circumstances. With nothing more than a $105 social security cheque and a chicken recipe he had found the flipside.

SMILING FROM CRACKED TEETH

When Simon Purchall had a biking accident that left him with a mouth full of cracked teeth, it could have ruined him financially. He had been cycling home from work, and as he turned a corner, he skidded and was thrown off his bicycle. He landed face down and smashed his jaw on the kerb of the pavement. Initially, he thought that only a few teeth had chipped, but four teeth then became infected. After a thorough examination, Simon's dentist discovered that four of Simon's teeth had been badly cracked and would need to be replaced. The total cost to repair the chipped teeth and replace the cracked teeth with implants would be in excess of £20,000.

Initially, it seemed that Simon had little option but to borrow the money and have the work done. However, Simon's wife Veronika, who was a qualified dental nurse from Hungary, suggested that they look at having the work done in Budapest.

'Like most people, I had a few reservations about going to an ex-communist country for dental work, but it was amazing,' Simon said. 'The level of service and expertise was fantastic. I decided to have all the treatment done there and saved about £16,000.'

When he returned to the UK, Simon found the flipside to his accident. It dawned on him and Veronika that there could be a business opportunity helping other people save money, promoting and marketing the specialist dental treatments offered in Hungary.

The fact that Veronika was Hungarian and a qualified

dental nurse made the decision to start the business that much easier and within a matter of months, their company 'SmileSavers' was launched.

Today, SmileSavers is a hugely successful business which has enabled Simon to free himself from his previous work as an IT consultant. Both he and Veronika work in their own business, building a future together.

Whether it was down to fate or just the randomness of life that Simon suffered his biking accident is immaterial to him and to our search for the flipside. The injury itself would have been sufficient to send many lesser people into a state of depression and that is without the financial implications of having to find £20,000 to repair the damaged teeth. But what is significant about this story is that Simon Purchall's accident proved to be a huge opportunity; it was the catalyst that would change his life. Simon managed to grasp that opportunity and turn the incident round to his advantage. He now looks back on the whole affair of his accident with a smile; a smile with a set of straight teeth, knowing that without that accident he wouldn't be enjoying the lifestyle he enjoys today. Simon Purchall had found the flipside.

THE SEARCH FOR THE FLIPSIDE

Was it just a matter of luck that the two disabled men who were confined to their wheelchairs were able to find something in their disabilities that brought their lives greater meaning and happiness? Was it the hand of fate that led to Harland Sanders being able to create a worldwide success that would never have been achieved had he not lost everything first? And was it simply just good fortune that Simon Purchall was able to build a successful dental business following his bike accident?

Or could there be something else involved? Could there

be a common thread that runs through these stories and many others like them? Something which has enabled ordinary people to literally 'flip' a seemingly adverse event or circumstance and find opportunities that would otherwise have remained hidden.

The Flipside is an attempt to answer these questions with the help of a simple yet controversial and life-changing philosophy. At its core is a belief that every problem or obstacle, however big or small, that life places in our path, contains an equivalent or greater benefit or opportunity. That benefit or opportunity is known as the 'flipside'.

To find the secrets of the flipside I am going to take you to South Africa to meet the man with no feet who holds world records in 100m, 200m and 400m track running events and has become a worldwide sporting phenomenon. We will visit Spain to learn from one of the most promising footballers of his generation who lost his career and his boyhood dreams in a tragic car accident, but went on to achieve other dreams, bigger dreams, that led to worldwide fame and fortune.

I will introduce you to a blind magician who will explain why the disease that took away 90 per cent of his eyesight when he was just nine years old was a 'gift'. We will hear from a man who lost his job but, in doing so, went on to change the face of entertainment in America, and we will meet a man who survived Auschwitz and transformed the world of psychology.

We will go back in time to witness past tragedies and personal disasters that were turned into life-affirming events. I will introduce you to many remarkable people and together we will learn from them and from the problems and obstacles that they faced. At times, it will not be easy; we will bear witness to considerable suffering and trauma. We will discover tragedies beyond our own experiences, but by the end of the journey, we may understand something that for many is, and has been, the single most important secret to achieving lasting success and happiness in life.

Welcome to the flipside . . .

Adam J Jackson
Javea, Spain – November 2008

PART ONE

DISCOVERIES – FINDING THE FLIPSIDE

'A year ago my life had collapsed around me. I worked myself into exhaustion. My father died and my relationships were in turmoil. Little did I know at the time, out of my greatest despair was to come the greatest gift.'

Rhonda Byrne – *The Secret*

CHAPTER 1

THE ROAD TO MADRID

ONE MAN'S JOURNEY TO THE FLIPSIDE

'When one door closes, another opens. But we often look so regretfully upon the closed door that we don't see the one that has opened for us.'

Helen Keller

ON THE EVENING of 22 September 1963, four young men set off in a car to travel from Majadahonda to Madrid in Spain. The four were all good friends enjoying the night out, but it was to be a journey they would never forget.

Julio was one of the four men in the car that night. His dream was to become a professional football player and play for the team he had loved as a boy, Real Madrid. He had nurtured his dream and pursued it from his earliest years, and that dream was just beginning to be realized. He had immense talent and emerged as something of a prodigy. Real Madrid had signed Julio as a goalkeeper and he was widely tipped to be the future number one goalkeeper for the

Spanish national team. Life couldn't have been better for Julio, his star was on the rise, until the evening he stepped into the car with his friends. As fate would have it, his dream would end that night.

At around 2.00 a.m., the car Julio and his friends were travelling in was involved in a serious accident. Julio awoke in Madrid's Eloy Gonzalo Hospital to discover that he was semi-paralysed. The doctors informed him that he would need to be confined to a bed for eighteen months in order to give his spinal injuries a chance to heal. Even then, the prognosis wasn't good. They thought it would be unlikely that Julio would ever walk again. But there was one thing that was not in doubt; his football career was over.

At night, during those eighteen months in hospital, Julio would listen to the radio and write poems – sad, reflective, romantic verses that questioned man's fate and the meaning of life. On reading the poems that Julio had written, one of the young male nurses who was taking care of him, a man called Eladio Magdaleno, gave Julio a guitar and suggested he turn his poems into songs.

Singing began as a distraction for Julio; a way of forgetting happier days spent as an athlete. But, as time went on, the singing became more of a passion than a distraction. He scribbled numbers on the guitar to learn the basic chords. Every week, more and more would appear, and within a short time he was creating melodies for his poems.

When the eighteen months had passed and Julio had recovered from his injuries, he decided to return to Murcia University to resume his studies. Later, he travelled to England to improve his English, first in Ramsgate, Kent and then at Bell's Language School in Cambridge. Occasionally at weekends he would sing in the Airport Pub covering songs that were popular at that time from the likes of Tom Jones, Engelbert Humperdinck and The Beatles.

When Julio returned home to Spain, he looked for a singer

to perform his songs. He took his first song to a recording studio in Madrid and asked if they could recommend a singer. The manager, looking at Julio and listening to him perform the song, was confused. Why would a man like Julio need someone to sing his songs? Julio was a strikingly handsome man with jet-black hair, large brown eyes, a smooth, tanned complexion and a smile that could make most women go weak at the knees. He also had a distinctive singing voice that was pitch-perfect. 'Why don't you perform it yourself?' the manager asked. Julio answered, 'Because I'm not a singer!'

But, in the end, Julio took the manager's advice and entered one of his songs in a Spanish music contest. On 17 July 1968, a little over five years after the accident that so nearly destroyed his life, he won first prize at the Fiesta de Benidorm with the song 'La Vida Sigue Igual' (Life Goes on the Same) and soon after, he was offered a contract with Columbia Records.

Chances are, you will have heard Julio singing. You may even own one of his albums. For the man who had lost his boyhood dreams in that tragic car accident went on to become the biggest selling recording artist in the history of Latin American music and a household name the world over. The man who had lost his dreams, found the flipside through a new, bigger dream than the one that was taken from him. His name is Julio Iglesias.

NEGATIVE EXPERIENCES, POSITIVE OUTCOMES

'Every problem has a gift for you in its hands.'

Richard Bach

The flipside is the other side of a problem or obstacle, the side that contains an opportunity that can change our lives for the better. While it may sound like something that is rarely seen other than in a Hollywood movie or a novel, there is now a growing body of scientific evidence demonstrating that the flipside is a very real phenomenon, the secrets of which can literally transform people's lives.

Julio Iglesias's story, while remarkable, is certainly not unique. People of different backgrounds and races and from all walks of life have suffered setbacks and faced seemingly insurmountable problems and obstacles and gone on to transform them into something positive. Often those problems and obstacles are, at the same time, events that trigger change and move us in new directions. In addition, it is not uncommon for people to look back and, with the benefit of hindsight, come to see their experiences in a different light. Some come away feeling that they have actually benefited in one way or another; they are certain that their lives have been enriched rather than injured.

Trauma and adversity of all kinds have literally been flipped into positive outcomes, and often the flipside turns out to be something so powerful and meaningful that it completely overshadows the negative experience. More significantly, in recent years, scientists working in clinics, hospitals and universities all over the world have begun to explore the nature of the flipside and unlock its secrets. Evidence presented from eminent psychologists, behaviourists and economists clearly demonstrates that, more often than not, the greatest problems, obstacles and adversities we face in life are, at the same time, our greatest opportunities.

CHAPTER 2

DEFINING MOMENTS

WHY THE LOWEST POINTS IN OUR LIVES SHAPE
OUR FUTURE HAPPINESS AND SUCCESS

'My good fortune was that I finally came to a point in
my life when I felt like I had hit rock bottom.'
Anthony Robbins – Personal Power Seminar

PETER JONES IS one of a very small, elite group of successful, high-profile entrepreneurs who have attained celebrity status both in the UK and North America. His business empire is said to be worth over £750 million and he has an impressive CV that includes a portfolio with interests in telecommunications, consumer products, incentives and gifts, entertainment, publishing, property and, more recently, television. Following his success in the *Dragons' Den*, he went on to become a judge on the hit TV series *American Inventor*, a programme produced by his own television production company.

If anyone knows anything about what it takes to succeed

in business, it is Peter Jones. Yet when he looks back on his career, he will tell you that the single most significant event that changed his life and was most responsible for his success was not any of his personal achievements. It wasn't the time that he had first been selected to appear on *Dragons' Den*, it wasn't when he set up his first business (a tennis academy, at the age of just 17), and it wasn't the time he received the Emerging Entrepreneur of the Year Award in 2002. According to Jones, the one moment that changed his life was a time early on in his career when he lost his business.

'During my twenties, I ran a thriving computer business which allowed me to own a nice house, a BMW, a Porsche, and plenty of money to spend,' Jones explains on his website. 'However, through a combination of circumstances, personal mistakes and learning the hard way when a few major customers went out of business themselves, I lost the business.'

Losing one's livelihood can be a devastating experience. Yet it can also be a turning point. Looking back, Jones believes that losing his business in his twenties was the crucial factor that changed his life because, he explained, it made him 'more determined to succeed'.

HITTING ROCK ROTTOM TO REACH THE TOP

Anthony Robbins is one of the best-known and most successful personal development 'gurus' in North America. He is an extremely charismatic, inspirational man. His seminars and workshops are sell-out events. Even though the tickets can cost hundreds of dollars, tens of thousands of people all over the world gladly part with the money to attend his events.

Robbins has coached CEOs of global corporations, presidents and political leaders. The *New York Times* reported in December 1994 that he had been invited by President Bill Clinton, along with Marianne Williamson and Dr Steven R.

Covey, to Camp David. Robbins has also helped some of America's top sports teams and athletes to improve their performance including golfer Greg Norman; former world number one tennis star Andre Agassi; the Los Angeles professional Ice Hockey team, the L.A. Kings, and former world heavyweight boxing champion Mike Tyson.

Today, Robbins is a best-selling author and vice chairman of five corporations. Through his books and seminars, Robbins has directly impacted the lives of more than 50 million people from over one hundred countries. Yet, in his seminars, one of the first messages he shares with his audience is that the catalyst for his success was not a specific achievement, it was the time when his life seemed to spin out of control. Only when he had lost everything, he says, and 'hit rock bottom' did his life finally begin to turn around. 'I was totally broke,' he recalls. 'I had wiped out my company. I had wiped out myself emotionally and I weighed about thirty-seven pounds heavier than I do today . . . having basically crashed . . . I began to look for what would be the foundational key to success.'

There is a saying I learned from an American friend: People change, but only when they are sick and tired of being sick and tired. Most of us have to reach the point when we say to ourselves, 'Enough is enough'. Only then are we prepared to take the necessary steps to change our lives. This is supported by the science of Neuro Linguistic Programming (NLP) which suggests that we are all primarily motivated by two forces – pain and pleasure – and, of the two, pain is the stronger motivator. Essentially, we will do more to avoid pain than we will to obtain pleasure. This is the reason Robbins says that he was 'fortunate' to have hit rock bottom. Sometimes we have to feel like we've sunk as low as we can go, before we make the effort to make our way to the top.

Both Peter Jones and Tony Robbins experienced a personal and financial crisis early on in their careers, but both men acknowledge that their crises were largely responsible for their subsequent long-term success. Their assessment of this positive side, the flipside, of the loss and the challenge of a major early crisis as the catalyst that helped propel them to success is not uncommon. Many of the world's most successful businessmen have shared the same or similar experience and credit their long-term success in life to the challenge of a major early crisis or loss.

DISASTER WAS PIVOTAL TO SUCCESS

'We ran out of money. I was three weeks away from getting married, my fiancée had moved to California – jobless – to join me, and the investment market had collapsed in the wake of the telecoms meltdown.' Peter Fiske was only nine months into his first business venture when he faced imminent financial ruin. Today he looks back on the disaster as a defining moment in his career. It was, he says, 'absolutely pivotal to the success of our company'.

Peter Fiske is a Ph.D. scientist and co-founder of RAPT Industries, a technology company in Fremont, California. He is also the author of *Put Your Science to Work* and works with Dr Geoff Davis, commenting on science policy, economics and educational initiatives that affect scientists.

Fiske believes that very few things in business, or even in a scientific career for that matter, are safe and predictable. Things sometimes can and do go wrong. At the same time, he understands that a setback or even what some people would consider a complete disaster is often the catalyst that is needed for positive change. When he looks back on the cashflow disaster that very nearly ruined him, with the benefit of hindsight he believes that the crisis was actually the making of him and his company. 'We needed to run out of cash in order to learn what was really necessary to make our venture succeed,' he says. 'It forced me into a full-frontal assault on potential customers and sponsors.' It was that new strategy that led his company to land a major contract with the US Army later that same year.

'When I tell the graduate students and postdocs who attend my career-development workshops that running out of money was one of the best things that happened to my company, I get some confused looks,' Fiske says. But, he is convinced that detours, setbacks and disasters 'are inevitable parts of the life of a start-up [company]'. 'Our near-death experience forced us to develop the discipline that has allowed us to survive ever since.'

Peter Fiske offers a fascinating insight which is, in fact, shared by leading business people all over the world. Setbacks and disasters, he suggests, are 'inevitable' but they always come with a flipside. This is because contained within obstacles and challenges are opportunities to learn and to grow, and very often the obstacle itself is viewed, with the benefit of hindsight, as having been the stepping stone that laid the foundation for long-term success.

THE POSTAL STRIKE

Sir Richard Branson faced a serious obstacle early on in his career when British postal workers voted to go on strike. Branson is one of the best-known and most successful businessmen in the UK. He has built up a business empire under the Virgin brand name which includes over 200 privately owned companies operating in an array of different industries from entertainment and leisure to travel, from communications technology (including mobile phones, broadband internet access and radio) to publishing, and from cosmetics to clothing. Since its inception in 1970, Virgin has become one of the leading brands in the UK.

Like Peter Jones, Tony Robbins and Peter Fiske, Sir Richard Branson's success can be traced back to one of the most difficult and challenging times early on in his career. In the 1970s new legislation in the UK allowed people to sell records at discounted prices, and Branson was among the first to exploit the situation by setting up a mail order company which he called 'Virgin'. The business proved to be a huge success. Sales rocketed and Branson had the enviable task of having to find more and more workers to keep up with demand. Then disaster struck; postal workers in the UK went on strike. With no realistic alternative mail service at that time, Virgin, along with thousands of other mail order companies across the UK, was facing ruin.

However, history revealed the postal strike to have been something of a blessing in disguise. It certainly marked a major turning point in Virgin's history because it forced Branson to rethink his business strategy and look for alternative revenue streams. As a result, in the following year, he opened a Virgin Records store, the first of what was to become a worldwide chain, and two years later he launched the Virgin record label.

FRIDAY AFTERNOONS

Losing one's job will always be a defining moment in a person's career, and it usually happens on a Friday afternoon. More people get fired on Fridays than on any other day of the week. In an online poll conducted by HRnext.com and its affiliated website BLR.com, human resource professionals said that, in their opinion, Friday was the best day to let a worker go. Firing an employee on a Friday afternoon, they said, gives fired workers the entire weekend to 'cool off' and receive support from friends and family. If you're an employee and worried about your job, the best advice might be to steer clear of your boss and the HR director on Fridays.

While losing your job can be devastating at the time, there will always be a flipside. Salomon Brothers was one of the largest investment banks on Wall Street before it was acquired in 1982 by the commodity traders Phibro Corporation. Shortly before the news of the merger was announced, one of the partners in Salomon Brothers was summoned by the company's board and, along with sixty-two of his colleagues, was given notice to terminate his employment. That day proved to be a major turning point in the young banker's career.

His name was Michael Bloomberg. He used his severance pay and sale of his Salomon shares to finance a new business idea that he had been thinking about for some time. Before the internet, financial data on the movement of currencies and stocks and shares was not easily accessible, and Bloomberg's vision was to create a network of computer terminals through which financial institutions could instantly access the data they needed. The system was a runaway success and today, less than thirty years on, Michael Bloomberg reportedly has a personal wealth in excess of $4 billion. His business interests extend into other areas of technology and the media but today he is perhaps best known as one of the most successful mayors of New York City having won two consecutive elections.

Some might argue that it was hardly a personal crisis when Bloomberg was fired because he was still left with a significant amount of capital on which to build his future. But one only has to look at the fate of many lottery winners to realize that it takes a lot more than capital to succeed in anything. It takes vision, commitment, dedication and a willingness to take calculated risks. When someone loses their job, the issues with which they are faced are not solely related to money. There can be a perceived social stigma which raises feelings of personal rejection and can affect one's self-esteem. Yet, at the same time, there are many people who, like

Bloomberg, have used the experience of losing their job to re-evaluate their careers and their lives and created an opportunity to make a new and fresh start.

In his book *We Got Fired And It's The Best Thing That Ever Happened To Us* (Ballentine, 2004), Harvey Mackay cites case after case of some of the most successful people in a variety of fields, from the car industry to the media and entertainment industries, all of whom owe their success, at least in part, to the time when they lost their job. Bernie Marcus was fired as chief executive officer of Handy Dan Home Improvement Center chain and went on to found his own company The Home Depot, which by the end of 2007 was America's leading retailer of home improvement and construction products and services.

Mark Cuban was a salesperson for Your Business Software, one of the first PC software retailers in Dallas. He was fired less than a year later for not opening the store on time even though, at the time, he was out making a sales call for a large software purchase. After he left, Cuban followed his passion for computing and set up his own company, MicroSolutions, which he sold several years later for $6 million. Today, Cuban is an internet billionaire and the owner of the Dallas Mavericks basketball team.

The list of people who have been fired but gone on to achieve incredible success seems endless. Over a career spanning forty years, the majority of employees will, at some point, be made redundant. For some, it can be financially and emotionally devastating. But for others, losing their job will turn out to be the making of them.

THE SECRET

Rhonda Byrne is an Australian television writer and producer. In 2007 she was listed among *Time* magazine's 'TIME 100:

The People Who Shape Our World', a list of the hundred most influential people in the world for that year. Rhonda was the inspiration and driving force behind a film and book that became a phenomenon. Brilliantly conceived and marketed, *The Secret* explains the universal 'Law of Attraction' to show how we can start to change our lives through the power of thought. 'Without exception,' according to *The Secret*, 'every human being has the ability to transform any weakness or suffering into strength, power, perfect peace, health, and abundance.' The message resonated with millions of people all over the world. Over two million DVDs were sold within its first year and, at the time of writing, the book has sold more than six million copies.

What is most interesting about Rhonda Byrne's success with *The Secret* is that it was inspired at one of the lowest points in her life. Like Tony Robbins, Rhonda Byrne had literally reached rock bottom, and it was only then that she came to a realization that was to inspire her subsequent success. On her DVD Rhonda confides: 'A year ago my life had collapsed around me. I worked myself into exhaustion. My father died and my relationships were in turmoil. Little did I know at the time, out of my greatest despair was to come the greatest gift.'

In an interview on the story behind *The Secret* Rhonda speaks of how she now sees that events in her life were unfolding for a reason: 'They led me to the very point where, on this particular night, what I did was I surrendered. My mind couldn't work out how to resolve all the things in my life. I collapsed in tears.'

It was in her turmoil that Rhonda was given a book by her daughter and that book gave her a glimpse of what is known as the Law of Attraction, the belief that we attract our experiences through our thoughts and beliefs, and this inspired her to research back through history and to then produce *The Secret*.

What is apparent from *The Secret* is also evident from all of the accounts we have heard here. They all echo the same sentiment, the same truth; it is often the lowest points in our lives that define and shape our future happiness and success.

CHAPTER 3

CRISES AND OPPORTUNITIES

WHY A CRISIS IS ALWAYS AN OPPORTUNITY

'When written in Chinese, the word 'crisis' is composed of two characters – one represents danger and the other represents opportunity.'

John F. Kennedy, address, 12 April 1959

THE THREE BOYS, all brothers, were pumped up with excitement and anticipation heading to the local cinema. It was a fresh Saturday morning in the suburbs of Manchester in 1950s' Great Britain. The local cinema was full of children, some with their parents, watching the show. The three boys were not on their way to watch a film. It had all been arranged with the manager. They were going to entertain the audience during the intermission by miming to a record. They were going to be a fun novelty act. But on that morning, as the boys ran to the cinema, they met with a crisis; the record to which the boys were going to mime dropped out of its sleeve and smashed on the pavement.

Without a record to mime to, the boys could have been forgiven for giving up and going home. The cinema manager would have understood. But they chose a different option. As they continued on to the cinema, the brothers agreed between themselves that they would still perform, only this time they would sing for real. The eldest of the three, Barry, played the guitar and together with his two younger brothers, Maurice and Robin, the three boys sang live to the audience. That morning was the first time the boys had ever sung in public, and the audience loved them. They were an instant hit.

The crisis that had so nearly spoiled their day proved to be the catalyst that changed all three of the boys' lives. It marked the beginning of one of the most successful male pop bands, song writers and recording artists, of all time. Those three boys were the brothers Gibb, better known as 'The Bee Gees'.

It was many years later, as they walked along Keppel Road in Manchester while filming a documentary of their lives, that Robin stopped at the point where that record had dropped and shattered. Turning to the camera, he mused, 'Had we not smashed the record that day, we wouldn't have started singing together.' That broken record, or more accurately, how they responded to it, launched careers that would span over five decades.

ORANGES AND MARMALADE

Crises are like triggers that propel us into situations we wouldn't have known and force us to take decisions that we wouldn't have taken. Though we often don't see it at the time, crises always come with a flipside. There is always an opportunity waiting to be found.

Without the crisis that James Keiller of Dundee found

himself facing in the late 1700s, so the story goes, the world might never have enjoyed the delights of orange peel in jelly that we know today as marmalade. In Portuguese, the root of the word marmalade is *marmelo*, meaning 'quince', which was the fruit of choice used to make preserves and jellies at that time. Oranges were used only to eat as fresh fruit or to be juiced, but that was about to change.

A Spanish ship with a cargo of Seville oranges docked in Dundee harbour to shelter from a storm. The ship's captain was offering his cargo of oranges at a knockdown price and Keiller thought he had got the bargain of the century. However, he soon discovered that the oranges were soft, most of them had begun to go rotten and turn bitter. Keiller knew that they would be impossible to sell and he was forced to acknowledge that he was facing an unprecedented financial loss.

In a state of dejection and shock, Keiller took the oranges home and confessed what had happened to his wife. It is uncertain what happened next, whether it was James or his wife Janet who had the idea that saved them by turning their crisis into an instant profit. It was an idea that would create a whole new industry and change the Keillers' lives for ever. All we know, if the story is to be believed, is that Janet Keiller used the oranges instead of the normal quinces to make a fruit preserve. The new orange-flavoured jelly proved extremely popular and the Keiller family went into business producing what we refer to today as marmalade.

The Keiller story of the origins of marmalade may or may not be true – some historians claim the story was fabricated. But regardless of its authenticity, the story contains a valuable message. Crises, as the Chinese sages knew from ancient times, always come with opportunities.

COMING UP ROSES

Sarah Benjamin is another person who has built a successful business on the back of a crisis. After graduating with a science degree, Sarah returned to her hometown of Swan Hill, in Victoria, Australia, to find that there was not much call for scientists. 'I found it quite difficult to get a job,' she says. 'There wasn't any way to use my science degree and I was being told that I was overqualified for the jobs that were available.'

With no prospects in the area, Sarah approached her mother with an idea: growing roses to supply to florists in the region. Sarah's mother, Jan Slater, liked the idea and the two women set up the business together in 2004. However, within the first year, they were facing a crisis that threatened to ruin the business almost before it had started. They couldn't have got off to a worse start. The very first crop of roses was diseased, all the blooms wilting at the head. They were completely unsaleable.

The problem was traced back to a virus in the water, but by that time it was too late to salvage the roses. It was an unmitigated disaster, but at the same time it turned out to be the seed of the future success of their business. The crisis forced Sarah Benjamin to review her business plan, and in doing so, uncover a hidden opportunity that would completely transform her business into the huge international success that it is today.

Sarah realized that if her rose business was going to survive in the long term, she was going to have to search for additional avenues of income. Surfing the internet, she stumbled across something that she believed was an incredible opportunity. She had discovered the dried rose petal industry. The advantages of selling dried rose petals over standard cut flowers were obvious; the rose petals had a much longer shelf life, they were light and cheap to transport. It was also a new and exciting niche market that had been largely untapped in Australia. Dried rose petals, Sarah had discovered, were becoming popular as decoration for wedding ceremonies, parties and functions. 'In the USA and the UK it was really booming,' she says, 'and no one was really doing it in Australia.'

Not everyone agreed with Sarah's idea. A few people told her that she was absolutely crazy. They said, 'You'll be out of business within twelve months. Who on earth would want to buy rose petals?' But Sarah and her mother persisted, researched the market and the industry, and proved their doubters wrong. Today, Simply Rose Petals grows and supplies hand-picked speciality dried petals for wedding decorations, spa retreats and wedding confetti, and the company is exporting all over the world. It is a thriving business that developed from an idea born out of a crisis.

SLIPPED DISCS AND CHOCOHOLICS

Simon and Helen Pattinson live with their two young daughters, Poppy and Daisy, in a quiet village near Chichester on the edge of Pagham Nature Reserve. They live what many would consider to be a very comfortable life and run their own business which is very successful by any standards. The company employs in the region of a hundred people and last year turned over more than £5 million. Yet the lifestyle they enjoy today, their home and family life, and their business, were all triggered by two crises.

Eight years ago, Simon and Helen were both disillusioned with life working as lawyers in the City of London. They didn't know what they wanted to do, but they knew they didn't want the life of a City lawyer. 'We were in sort of a "catch-22" situation,' Simon explains. 'We didn't know what we wanted to do with our lives, but we knew that we wouldn't ever get the "eureka" moment without freeing ourselves from what we were doing.' In the end they decided the only thing to do was to hand in their notice, sell their home in Putney, London, and go travelling. So, with nothing more than what they could carry in their backpacks, they set off to travel the world in search of inspiration and new direction in life.

Even though they were turning their backs on lucrative careers to which they had devoted years of training, their friends and family were incredibly supportive. 'Helen's father had pictured her as a future Law lord,' jokes Simon, 'but if people thought we were mad, they didn't let it show.' The two had become exhausted from the long days and late nights and the constant strain of commuting. 'We felt worn out and wanted a change,' continues Simon. 'The main aim of travelling was to find a business idea or something that might inspire us.' They didn't know what the future held for them, but they hoped that by backpacking around the world, they might find some answers.

Their first stop was South America. Patagonia in Argentina is famed for its mountain range and ski resorts and it was in a small mountain resort called Bariloche that Helen and Simon got their first taste of South American chocolate. 'It was amazing,' Simon says. 'There were chocolate shops literally everywhere we looked.' Although they didn't know it at the time, that town would spark an idea for a future business.

Simon and Helen then travelled north through Chile, to Brazil and ended up on a cocoa plantation in Venezuela. They spent two weeks mesmerized by the cocoa trees and the breathtaking scenery before disaster struck. While putting on his backpack, Simon's back went into spasm. The pain was debilitating and it transpired that he had suffered a slipped disc. The pain was so severe that he and Helen had no choice but to be repatriated home to the UK. Their plans to travel the world were over. It was a bitter disappointment and, to make matters worse, they had no home to go back to, and no income.

They resorted to staying with Simon's parents while he had surgery and recuperated. However, as they reminisce about that time, they both now see that the catastrophe was actually a blessing in disguise. 'Looking back,' remembers Simon, 'it was fortuitous because it gave us the time we needed to work out what we wanted to do. We read through the journals that we had written during our time abroad and one thing kept coming up again and again – chocolate.

'Up until then we had no firm idea of what we were going to do,' he says. 'We thought we might be forced to go back to work in Law or possibly something even worse. My back problem gave us the time we needed to think about our future and create a business plan.

'If we had carried on travelling,' Simon muses, 'we might have become travel bums and never returned to the UK.' Instead, they found something that really excited them. It was an opportunity to try something different and build their own business. Simon's back injury marked the beginning of a new and exciting adventure into the chocolate industry.

Their story didn't end there. While Simon recuperated and spent time working on a business plan, Helen took temporary shop jobs to get experience of retailing. The two then scraped together the money needed to open their first chocolate shop in Brighton, Sussex. However, five weeks before they were due to open, they were hit by another, much larger crisis. This time it was commercial. Their main supplier had gone into liquidation. 'It was a complete shock,' says Simon. 'We were fitting out our shop with less than five weeks to go to the official opening. Then the manufacturers suddenly stopped answering the phone. Initially we didn't think much of it, but then a week went by and we started to get very concerned. Helen drove down to their offices and it was only then that we discovered the business had gone into liquidation.

'The company were making over 50 per cent of our

products,' Simon continues. 'They held all of our designs, moulds, labels, the lot.' Helen and Simon had two options; they could give up on their dream or they could risk everything and manufacture the chocolate themselves. 'We had no experience or knowledge of chocolate manufacture *at all*,' Simon points out. It was a huge crisis by any standards but, by the same token, it proved to be a huge opportunity.

They spent the next few weeks researching exactly how to make the chocolate the way they wanted it, then they ordered equipment, and with the help of family and friends (and a very kind member of staff from one of their suppliers) they began making their own chocolate. 'It was an incredibly scary time,' says Helen. 'We spent weeks in a tiny converted outbuilding on a farm. We had chocolate all over us and up the walls most of the time, but gradually we managed to keep it in the machine and perfect a few recipes.'

Forced into manufacturing the chocolate themselves meant that Simon and Helen had a limited range, but it was *their* range and it meant that they would have far more control over their business. Since they opened their shop 'Montezumas' (named after an Aztec emperor) in the fashionable Lanes area of Brighton in 2000, their business has grown into a chain of seven outlets across the south-east of England.

Theirs is yet another business success forged by two very dedicated people through a series of crises. Losing their main supplier just weeks before their launch proved to be the making of the business. Prior to that point, neither Simon nor Helen had even remotely considered manufacturing their own chocolate. But, by becoming a manufacturer, it gave them credibility and opened up a whole new side to the business, a wholesale arm which, as it turned out, became the main spine of the business. 'Without the wholesale business,' Simon insists, 'we probably wouldn't have a business today.'

Both Simon and Helen see themselves as 'optimists'. 'We

both look at things as opportunities rather than problems,' he says. What we are seeing, time and again, is that there is often a flipside to crises we face in life. A crisis is a message telling us that there is an opportunity waiting to be found, and sometimes it will be the opportunity of a lifetime.

CHAPTER 4

LIFE CHANGES: WHEN BAD THINGS HAPPEN

WHY BAD THINGS ARE NOT ALWAYS BAD AND WHY CHANGE IS A CHALLENGE TO MAKE THINGS BETTER

'Change has a considerable psychological impact on the human mind. To the fearful it is threatening because it means that things may get worse. To the hopeful it is encouraging because things may get better. To the confident it is inspiring because the challenge exists to make things better.'

King Whitney Jr.

THE MOMENT SOMETHING happens in our lives that we think of as 'bad', we tend to look upwards and curse. Whether we have suffered financial loss, experienced a business or career disappointment, been involved in an accident or even been diagnosed with a serious health problem, the common response is, 'Why me? What did I do to deserve this?' However, what we don't realize at the time, but often come to appreciate much later, is that it is precisely those setbacks and challenges, or more accurately, our response to them, that determines our future happiness and success.

How do you know whether any particular experience in your life is 'good' or 'bad'? For some people, anything that brings pleasure is good and anything that causes pain is bad. But what would we think of, say, candy floss, which brings pleasure (to people who enjoy eating brightly coloured strands of sugar), but will also cause tooth decay and thereby bring pain? Or would the pain caused by a dentist drilling out decay in a tooth be considered 'bad' when ultimately the removal of the decay and the refilling of the tooth protects us from even greater pain in the future?

Other people think of something as 'good' if it propels us towards our hopes and desires, and conversely, they say that anything that moves us in the opposite direction, away from our hopes and dreams, is 'bad'. But, when we look at people like Julio Iglesias we see that an event that was perceived as bad because it put an end to his childhood aspirations of becoming a professional footballer, actually turned out to be very good because it enabled him to pursue a different and, in many ways, bigger dream.

Recognizing what are good or bad events in our lives is not as easy as we might think. Many people believe that, at the extremes, it is clear-cut. For example, most people would agree that hitting the jackpot and winning millions in the national lottery would be good, whereas ending up paralysed in a freak diving accident or losing your legs in a plane crash would be bad. But how do we really know whether something that happens to us is good or bad?

THE LOTTERY WINNERS

On the evening of 22 May 1999, police officers were called to a house in the fashionable Kingwood area of Houston, Texas.

When they arrived, the officers found the owner, a man by the name of Billy Bob Harrell, shot dead in an upstairs bedroom. According to the investigators, Harrell had taken his own life. He had locked himself in his bedroom, stripped himself naked, pressed a shotgun barrel against his chest and pulled the trigger.

Shortly before his death, Harrell had confided to a financial adviser about the event that had occurred just twenty months previously which he said had ruined his life. 'It was the worst thing that ever happened to me,' he had lamented. Yet this episode was not an incurable illness or loss of a loved one. He hadn't been involved in an accident and he hadn't lost his job. He and his family were all alive and well. So what was the terrible event that had ruined his life?

The chance of this particular event happening to Billy Bob Harrell was about 1 in 40 million. There was a greater probability of being hit and killed by a bolt of lightning while out walking the dog, if he had walked a dog. But as fate would have it, the event in question happened one evening as he sat at home reading the newspaper. He read and reread the sequence of numbers on the page. Suddenly, it dawned on him. He had the only winning ticket to the Texas State Lotto. He had won the jackpot! Ridiculous as it may seem to most people, the event that Harrell later attributed to ruining his life and which led to his suicide was winning $31 million!

When one takes a look at the biographies of many lottery winners, one discovers that Billy Bob's experience is by no means unique. Estimates suggest that, in the USA, over one-third of all lottery winners end up bankrupt.

William 'Bud' Post won $16.2 million in the Pennsylvania lottery in 1988 and ended up penniless, living on social security. When interviewed, Post said, 'I wish it never happened'. Winning the lottery, as far as he was concerned, had been a 'nightmare'.

Post's nightmare started when a former girlfriend successfully sued him for a share of his winnings. Later, there were reports that his brother had been arrested for hiring a hit man to kill him, in the hope of inheriting a share of William's winnings. Other siblings allegedly pestered him (although not with such grievous intent) until he agreed to invest in a car business and a restaurant in Sarasota, Florida. These two ventures only served to cause further strain on his relationships with his siblings and, of course, lost him more of his money.

Not long afterwards, Post was sent to prison for firing a gun over the head of a debt collector, and within a year, he was not just penniless – he was $1 million in debt. Post admitted he was both careless and foolish in trying to please everyone in his family. Eventually he filed for bankruptcy. According to reports, he lives quietly on $450 a month and food stamps. 'I'm tired, I'm over sixty-five years old, and I just had a serious operation for a heart aneurysm. Lotteries don't mean [anything] to me,' he says.

In the UK there are similar stories. In 1996 John McGuinness was the envy of every person who had ever purchased a lottery ticket in Scotland when he scooped over £10 million, a record-beating sum won by a Scot. At that time, McGuinness had just separated from his first wife and he had been sleeping on the floor in his parents' home in Lanarkshire. After winning the jackpot, he splashed out on, among other things, a Spanish villa, a Porsche, a Bentley and expensive holidays. However, by July 2007 McGuinness was declared bankrupt with debts totalling over £2 million.

In relating these stories, I am not suggesting in any way that all lottery winners end up wretched or dead. Many live up to our expectations and go on to live very happy lives. According to Camelot Group PLC who conducted a five-year study, 55 per cent of lottery winners are happier (at least in the first five years) after winning.

Perhaps we could all learn something from lottery winners

in Norway. Researchers from the Institute of Psychology at the University of Oslo sent a postal questionnaire to 261 lottery winners of prizes of NKR1 million or more in the years 1987–91, and found that the average winner was a middle-aged man of modest education from a small community. Most winners in Norway were cautious and did not go on spending sprees. They had also requested anonymity and tried to keep their windfall a secret. Whatever the reasons, the results of the survey indicated that the quality of life for most of the lottery winners following their newfound wealth was stable or improved.

What these stories suggest is that a sudden increase in wealth, even substantial wealth running into millions of pounds or dollars, is not a guarantee to happiness. According to Dr Edward Diener, Professor of Psychology at the University of Illinois, once our basic needs are met, more money has little impact on our feelings of happiness. Through his research, Professor Diener discovered that happiness was only marginally influenced by money, education, IQ or age. The most significant characteristic shared by the 10 per cent of students with the highest levels of happiness and the lowest levels of depression was a strong social network. It turns out that, more than any other single factor, it is our connections to friends and family and a commitment to spend quality time with them that improves our happiness. This is why Dr Diener advises that 'it is important to work on social skills, close interpersonal ties and social support in order to be happy.' Winning the lottery can have the exact opposite effect, as winners can feel isolated from their friends and family.

However, the main point is this: many people dream of winning the lottery and believe that it will be a passport to guaranteed happiness. But that dream can quite easily become a nightmare. It could turn out to be the best thing – or the worst thing – that could happen to you.

A NEW MEANING TO LIFE

Just as winning the lottery is not always a guarantee to 'happy ever after', a tragic accident that leaves a person paralysed is not necessarily a life sentence of misery. There is no better example of this than Joni Eareckson Tada.

Joni was born in Baltimore, Maryland, in 1950. She was the youngest of four sisters, Linda, Jay and Kathy. Her name is pronounced 'Johnny', as she was named after her father, John. Joni inherited her father's athletic and creative abilities, giving father and daughter a special bond. Her childhood, she says, was an extremely happy one. She grew into a young adult surrounded by love, happiness and security in her parents' home. All of her family shared a great love for the outdoors, enjoying various outdoor activities such as camping trips, horseback riding, hiking, tennis and swimming.

It was on a hot summer's day in July 1967, just after graduating from high school, that Joni's life changed for ever. Joni was to meet her sister Kathy and some friends at the beach on Chesapeake Bay for a swim. When she arrived, Joni dived in quickly, and immediately knew that something was wrong. Though she felt no real pain, she later explained that a tightness seemed to engulf her. Her initial thought was that she was caught in a fishing net and she tried to break free and get to the surface. Panic seized her when she realized that she couldn't move; she found herself lying face down on the bottom of the bay. Realizing that she was running out of air, she resigned herself to the fact that she was going to drown.

Joni's sister Kathy called for her. When Joni didn't surface, Kathy ran into the water and pulled her up. To Kathy's shock, Joni could not support herself and tumbled back into the water. Kathy managed to pull her out of the water and Joni gasped for air. Joni was puzzled as to why her arms were still tied to her chest. Then, to her horror, Joni realized that her arms were not tied, but were draped lifelessly across her sister's back. Kathy yelled for someone to call an ambulance and Joni was rushed to the hospital.

It didn't take long for the doctors to diagnose that Joni had broken her neck. There was a fracture between the fourth and fifth cervical vertebrae which left her paralysed from the shoulders down.

'Lying in my hospital bed,' wrote Joni, 'I tried desperately to make sense of the horrible turn of events. I begged friends to assist me in suicide. Slit my wrists, dump pills down my throat, anything to end my misery!'

But Joni survived and has gone on to find the flipside and live a full and happy life. 'I have discovered many good things that have come from my disability,' she says. More significantly, over the years, Joni has helped and touched the lives of thousands of people all over the world.

Initially, Joni learned to compensate for her handicaps. Being naturally creative, she learned to draw and paint holding her utensils with her teeth. She developed a talent and was creating work that, by any measure, was a great success. She began selling her artwork and gained for herself a degree of independence.

Joni also became a sought-after conference speaker, author and actress, portraying herself in the World Wide Pictures production of *Joni*, her life story, in 1978. She has written several books including *Holiness in Hidden Places*, her autobiography *Joni*, and a number of children's titles. But her most satisfying and far-reaching work became her advocacy on behalf of the disabled community.

In 1979, Joni moved to California to begin a ministry to the disabled community around the globe. She called it Joni and Friends Ministries (JAF Ministries), which she says became her vision of fulfilling the words of Jesus in Luke 14:13: '. . . call to the poor, the maimed, the lame, the blind. And you shall be blessed.'

Joni understood only too well the loneliness and alienation

that many people with disabilities face, and it wasn't long before her ministry was immersed with calls for both physical and spiritual help for the disabled. Through JAF Ministries, Joni records a five-minute radio programme called *Joni and Friends*, which is heard daily all over the world. Her role as an advocate for the disabled led to a presidential appointment to the National Council on Disability. Joni has also begun Wheels for the World, a ministry which restores wheelchairs and distributes them in developing nations.

Joni Eareckson Tada is an outstanding example of how one of the worst tragedies someone can experience in life can be transformed into a life-affirming event. Like the two paralysed men contributing to the discussion following the play *Whose Life Is It Anyway?*, Joni looks back on the events of that afternoon in July 1967 without regret or bitterness. She believes that it led her to places she wouldn't have seen and people she wouldn't have met and achievements she wouldn't have accomplished. In doing so, the accident brought new challenges and much greater meaning to her life.

Reflecting on the fates of Billy Bob Harrell and the other lottery winners, compared to people like Joni Eareckson Tada or Julio Iglesias, raises a number of questions about our own lives. The things that happen to us in life do not, by themselves, dictate our future happiness or success. Their stories suggest that there is something more significant and more powerful than any situation in which we may find ourselves today, which will determine the quality of our lives tomorrow. But what is that 'something'?

THE LESSON OF THE TAOIST FARMER

'It is neither good nor bad, but thinking makes it so.'

William Shakespeare

The ancient Chinese philosophy of Taoism provides an insight that can help us to better understand the differences between the stories of Billy Bob Harrell and Joni Eareckson Tada.

Taoism began in the fourth century BC through the teachings of a man called Lao Tzu, author of the *Tao Te Ching*, which has become the classic text of Taoist thought. One of the most used symbols of Taoism is that of water. Water is in many ways a Taoist ideal because at the core of Taoist belief is the notion that life is like the continuous flow of water in a river.

The Taoist accepts that, at times, the river's current may take us to places that we would prefer not to visit and to experiences that we would choose to avoid. But Taoism offers a message of hope; hope in the knowledge that although we are not always able to influence the flow of events, we are always able to maintain control over our thoughts and beliefs, and control over our mindset is infinitely more powerful than anything that can happen to us.

Taoism also teaches us to look at events in our lives without judgement or interpretation. According to Taoism, nothing is, of itself, good or bad. This may seem counter-intuitive, although less so when we reflect upon the lives of Billy Bob Harrell and Joni Eareckson Tada. It is best explained through the parable of the Taoist farmer.

The Taoist farmer lived in a remote village in the furthermost corner of China. He was not a wealthy man, but he was content with his life, and farmed a small plot of land with his son and wife. One day, a wild horse galloped on to his land, jumped the fence and began grazing in the farmer's field. According to the provincial law, the horse now rightfully belonged to the farmer and his family. The farmer's son could hardly contain his excitement, but the farmer put his hand on his son's shoulder and said, 'Don't be quick to judge! Who knows what's good or bad?'

The following day the horse broke out of the field and galloped away. The farmer's son was heartbroken. 'Don't be quick to judge,' said his father. 'Who knows what is good or bad?'

On the third day, the horse returned with four mares. The farmer's son could hardly believe their good fortune. 'We're rich!' he shouted, but again his father said to him, 'Don't be quick to judge. Who knows what is good or bad?'

The following week, while riding one of the horses, the boy fell and broke his leg. The farmer ran to get the doctor; within a short time, both the farmer and the doctor were tending to the boy, who was moaning and complaining about his miserable fate. The farmer wiped his son's forehead with a cool, damp cloth, looked deeply into his eyes, and reassured him once again, 'My son, do not be too quick to judge. Who knows what is good or bad?'

The following week, war broke out in the province, and army recruiters came through the village and conscripted all of the eligible young men – all except for one young man who was unable to fight due to a broken leg!

The story of the Taoist farmer is more than an affable, ancient fable; it offers a simple, yet vital lesson on our journey to the flipside: on the day that something happens, or for that matter weeks, months or even years afterwards, it is impossible to know what significance the event may have on the rest of our life.

A good example of the lesson of the Taoist farmer came at the British Open Golf Championships in July 2008. When Padraig Harrington injured his wrist in the run-up to the Open, he had no idea the injury would be a blessing in disguise. The day before the start of the tournament, Harrington said his wrist had been so sore that he genuinely felt that, in the balance of probabilities, he would not be able to play. The British Open is the oldest of the four major championships in men's golf dating back to 1860. The 2008

Championship was particularly meaningful to Harrington because he was the defending champion and the prospect of not being able to play would have been a huge blow.

However, as it turned out, the wrist injury that nearly stopped Harrington from playing, according to Harrington, was in no small part responsible for him going on to become the first European to successfully defend his title since James Braid in 1906. 'It was a great distraction for me,' Harrington said after winning the title. 'There's no question the injury pushed everything about coming back to defend the title to the side . . . There's an element when you're an Open champion or a major champion of trying to live up to it all the time and that can be a burden. But the injury took a lot of pressure and stress off me. It was a good distraction.'

Harrington went on to explain another flipside to his injury. To safeguard the wrist, he had only been able to play nine holes in practice before the Open began, meaning that he was fresh going into the most demanding week-long tournament of the year. 'The wrist [injury] was a saviour for me really.'

Sometimes the flipside comes quickly and is obvious, as Padraig Harrington discovered. Other times it may take months or years or even a lifetime to find the flipside that lies hidden in a major setback.

REACHING FOR THE SKY

On 14 December 1931, a crowd was gathered at Reading Aero Club watching in awe as a talented young RAF pilot, just twenty-three years of age, demonstrated low-flying aerobatics over the airfield. Suddenly, their awe turned to horror; as the plane came out of a roll, the tip of the left wing touched the ground, and the plane rolled and crashed. An ambulance was on hand to attend to the pilot immediately, but the pilot had suffered severe injuries. Both of his legs had been crushed.

The pilot was rushed to hospital and was fortunate to be seen by one of the most prominent surgeons of the time, Mr Leonard Joyce. The injuries were too severe for even Mr Joyce to repair. The only option available was to amputate the pilot's legs, one below the knee and the other slightly above the knee. In the days following the accident, the pilot made an entry in his logbook: 'Crashed slow-rolling near ground. Bad show.' He didn't know then, but the loss of his legs would, in the years ahead, help him to become a legend as an RAF fighter pilot in the Second World War and this, in turn, would lead to him being knighted. However, even more significantly, the accident that cost him his legs would one day in the future save his life.

Douglas Bader had been an outstanding sportsman. He had played rugby union for Harlequins and, according to some reports, had the potential to play at international level. He was also a very competent cricketer. One would have thought that the loss of his legs would have been enormously difficult to bear, but Bader was focused on two very specific goals – being able to walk again, and to fly. Though in constant pain that required him to take morphine at times, Bader remained determined and worked tirelessly. Within just six months, he achieved his goals. Not only could he walk – unaided – but he was even able to dance and play golf. And, in June 1932, he flew again. Yet, despite his valiant efforts, in April 1933 the powers that be invalided him out of the RAF.

One major flipside to his ordeal came quickly. His time spent in recuperation brought him into contact with a beautiful young nurse, Thelma Edwards, whom he married in October 1933 and remained devoted to until she died many years later.

Six years after Bader had been forced out of the RAF, Europe was plunged into war the likes of which had never been seen. Bader was determined to help in the war effort and pulled whatever strings he could through his old contacts to get re-enlisted. With the need for pilots to help in the war effort, the RAF accepted Bader's application and after a short refresher course on the latest fighter planes, including Spitfires and Hurricanes, he was given an operational posting. He was twenty-nine years old, much older than most of the other pilots, and he wore prosthetic legs, but Bader proved to be one of the best RAF fighter pilots to fight in the Battle of Britain.

By August 1941, Bader had shot down twenty-two German planes. Only four other pilots in the RAF had shot down more enemy aircraft. The remarkable thing, as far as the search for the flipside is concerned, is that Bader's success was not in spite of the fact that he had no legs; it was largely *because* of the fact that he had no legs! One of the observations of aerial combat was that when pilots pulled out of turns at speed the flow of blood could drain from the brain to the extremities causing temporary blackout. But as Bader had no legs, his brain didn't lose nearly as much blood flow. As a result, he could remain conscious that much longer, which gave him a significant advantage over the able-bodied enemy pilots against whom he fought.

However, the real flipside came on 9 August 1941 when his plane collided in midair with a Messerschmidt over Le Touquet in France. As he tried to bale out, Bader became aware that his right prosthetic leg was trapped. The plane careered towards the ground. Any other pilot would have been facing certain death, but it was because Bader had no legs that he survived that day. The strap holding the prosthetic limb snapped, and it was only then that Group Captain Sir Douglas Bader was able to extricate himself from the doomed plane just in time.

One could argue that the positive outcome from a negative event is nothing more than the result of the randomness of life. On the balance of probability, there will always be some people who end up benefiting in one way or another from a personal tragedy or crisis, just as some people will end up disadvantaged and miserable following a personal achievement or success. However, following literally decades of research, scientists and psychologists have begun to discover that the secret to finding the flipside does not, in fact, lie in the event itself; it lies in our response to the event. Every setback in life, every trauma, has two sides, but it takes a special type of person to find the flipside.

CHAPTER 5

THE TWO SIDES
OF TRAUMA

WHY TRAUMA IS NOT ALWAYS DESTRUCTIVE AND CAN OFTEN LEAD TO PROFOUND AND POSITIVE CHANGES

'If you think about all of the heroes and heroines in cultures across the world . . . all of them, in one sense or another, faced some sort of dragon. The transformation from that encounter has been celebrated from antiquity.'

Professor Matthew J Friedman

THE TERM *'TRAUMA'* comes from the Greek meaning 'wound' or 'injury'. However, when we refer to a traumatic experience, we usually think of a deep psychological wound. It is an event that leaves a deep imprint on our body and on our psyche. It can literally smash our core beliefs about life and its meaning, and in doing so it can overwhelm us to the point of despair and depression. It can destroy us, spiritually and mentally, as we struggle to come to terms with the loss and suffering that it often brings.

It is said that only two things are certain in life – death and taxes – but traumas will also touch us, in different times and in different places. At some point in our lives, most of us will face trauma of one kind or another, and usually it will come suddenly and with no warning. However, trauma is not necessarily destructive. It has another side, a side that can change our lives profoundly and for the better.

THE FORK IN THE ROAD

'You reach a fork in the road where you make a decision. You're either going to be a victim and live a life certainly not to its fullest, or you're going to choose this huge opportunity for growth.'

Ute Lawrence

The King's Highway 401 in Canada extends for 815 kilometres and runs across Southern Ontario, joining Windsor to Montreal in Quebec. It is one of the widest and busiest highways in the world, and carries more traffic than any other road in the whole of North America. The westernmost section of road between Windsor and London is noted as being the busiest stretch of road for trucks in North America; it also has the distinction of being one of the deadliest roads in the world. In fact, there have been so many accidents on that stretch of the highway that it has become known as 'Carnage Alley'.

The main cause of the accidents on Carnage Alley is generally attributed to the poor design of that section of the highway. It has narrow lanes and 'soft shoulders' (rather than 'hard shoulders'), which means that the innermost lane is even narrower than the standard lanes. As a result, motorists caught in the inside lane have nowhere to go to avoid collisions. The third problem is even more hazardous; the highway has a very narrow grass midline and, therefore, there is very little to protect drivers from cross-directional collisions. This was always one place where accidents really were waiting to happen.

The worst of all the accidents on that stretch of the 401 happened on 3 September 1999, Labor Day Weekend. The 401 was filled with holiday traffic when a heavy curtain of fog draped over the region. With such bad visibility and the inherent danger of that stretch of road, what happened next may have been inevitable. It became the scene of the most horrific pile-up ever in Canadian history. Eighty-seven vehicles were involved, forty-five people were injured and eight people died.

Ute Lawrence and her husband, Stan Fisher, were in one of the cars in the pile-up that day. In one way they were fortunate, neither of them suffering more than a few cuts and scrapes. However, although not physically injured, they were both left deeply traumatized by what happened that day. During the pile-up, a fourteen-year-old girl became pinned against the Lawrences' car by a van. The girl was crushed against the passenger door and Mr and Mrs Lawrence watched in horror, helpless as the girl burned to death.

Ute Lawrence had been a journalist and a publisher, but her life changed forever the day of the accident. When she went back to work the following Tuesday, she became aware that something about herself was not the same. 'I used to get up full of excitement about the day,' she says. 'All of a sudden you have an event like this, and it destroys everything – your belief system, your self-esteem . . . I used to be a decisive business person; two days later that person was no longer there.' It wasn't long before she found herself unable to work, alternating between states of numbness and near hysteria. It was two months later that she finally sought help and consulted a doctor who referred her to the trauma centre at the local hospital.

According to the US National Center for Post-traumatic Stress Disorder, up to 60 per cent of the population experience some kind of trauma during their lives. Current figures indicate that about 8 per cent of the US population suffer from post-traumatic stress disorder (PTSD) and over five million people receive treatment for PTSD every year in the US. In the UK and Canada, the proportionate figures are very similar. According to the Canadian Mental Health Association and the online information service Patient UK, as much as 10 per cent of the Canadian and UK populations suffer from PTSD at some point in their lives. However, from these figures, it is interesting to note that, of the people who experience a severe trauma, only a relatively small minority end up suffering from PTSD. The vast majority of people don't suffer severe or lasting adverse reactions to traumas.

Ute Lawrence started experiencing symptoms of PTSD within days. She was profoundly affected by what she had witnessed. 'I used to be a very aggressive and decisive person,' she said, 'and that person, two days later, was no longer there.' She was unable to 'conduct anything on a day-to-day basis, from keeping a kitchen clean to running my business.' Ute consulted her doctor and ended up trying pretty much all of the available treatments as well as taking a variety of self-help courses and seminars. Recovery took years, but the process set her on a new career path – providing support for PTSD victims and raising awareness about what is a staggeringly prevalent mental health disorder. She woke up one day and experienced something of an epiphany; she and her husband would found the first PTSD self-help organization in Canada.

In 2006 the Post-traumatic Stress Disorder Association was formed to provide advice, help and support to people across Canada who were suffering from PTSD. Through the association and its work, Ute Lawrence and her husband had found a flipside to their trauma. Their experience inspired them to a mission not just to help people come to terms with a traumatic experience, but to help and inspire them to find something positive in their experience, something that could become a catalyst for personal growth.

When interviewed in the *Globe & Mail* newspaper in August 2008, Ute Lawrence said that when people reach a fork in the road, they have to decide whether they are going to be a victim and live a less-than-full life, or choose to find the 'huge opportunity for growth' which is always there waiting. This is the flipside. In her parting comment, she reminds people that, when faced with any form of traumatic event, even one as horrific as the one she witnessed, there is always a flipside: 'You've had a horrifying experience, and the more difficult it is to get over it, the bigger the opportunity to grow into a more compassionate, giving person.'

POST TRAUMATIC GROWTH

'The positive psychology of growing through traumas is a much more fascinating topic for study than post-traumatic stress disorder, because such knowledge can help increase individual resilience and reduce mental illness.'

Paul T. P. Wong

That severe trauma or loss can be a precursor to positive change and a better life is not as incomprehensible as it might first seem. There is much to support the belief that anything that does not kill us, makes us stronger. For example, when we survive an infection, particularly a viral infection, we acquire a certain amount of immunity. We also benefit from the knowledge that the infection can be beaten. Similarly, if we have the misfortune to break a bone, but the fortune to have it reset properly in its correct position, the healing will lead to a much stronger fusion. The bone will regrow stronger than it had been before it was broken. In much the same way, psychologists have discovered that a psychological trauma, if responded to in the right way, often creates a stronger character and leads to what they refer to as 'personal growth'.

In April 2004 the *Psychiatric Times* published an article that raised some eyebrows in the world of clinical psychology. The authors, Dr Tedeschi and Dr Calhoun, Professors of Psychology at the University of North Carolina, had devoted over twenty years of their careers researching the impact of severe physical and emotional traumas on people's lives. Their findings brought surprising conclusions that challenged the accepted wisdom about the nature of traumas – both physical and psychological – and how they affect our lives. According to the authors, traumas do not always lead to negative outcomes. In fact, their work proved quite the contrary; more often than not, even the severest physical and psychological traumas were found to result in positive outcomes for the people involved. The scientists had discovered that trauma has a flipside.

Since the First World War, many psychologists had assumed that severe trauma would inevitably lead to physical and emotional disorders, and the various schools of psychology devoted their resources and research to finding ways to diagnose and treat post-traumatic stress disorder. However, according to Dr Tedeschi and Dr Calhoun, many people who experience traumatic events do not suffer any lasting psychological damage. In fact, their findings suggest that many people who experience severe trauma will, in the aftermath, look back on the trauma as a life-enhancing experience, and enjoy some degree of personal or spiritual growth as a result. The doctors' findings confirmed something that philosophers and theologians have spoken of for centuries – human suffering can bring with it possibilities for greater good.

In their research, Dr Tedeschi and Dr Calhoun were primarily interested in traumas of a seismic nature rather than ordinary or everyday stressful events. They focused on experiences that could be likened to personal 'earthquakes', experiences that would create upheaval in the trauma survivor's major assumptions and beliefs about the world, their place in it and how they make sense of their daily lives. These experiences would often be unexpected, uncontrollable and potentially (or actually) irreversible, such as a bereavement, receiving a diagnosis of a chronic or life-threatening illness, being injured in a car accident, losing limbs and even being subjected to sexual assault or abuse.

The doctors discovered that some people who experience these kinds of traumas of 'earthquake' proportions were actually less likely to suffer long-term negative or adverse effects (PSTD) than they were to look back on their experiences as positive, defining moments in their lives that led to greater positive outcomes. Through their work, Tedeschi and Calhoun had identified a totally new psychological phenomenon, which they called 'post-traumatic growth'.

To understand exactly how trauma can be beneficial and lead to a feeling of 'personal growth', one needs to look to trauma survivors; people who have experienced severe trauma and come through it feeling that their lives have been enriched as a result. While traumas can happen anywhere and at any time, there is one place where virtually everyone is subjected to severe traumas, and that is on the battlefield.

THE TRAUMAS OF WAR

'Finally my prayers took a new turn to something like "Okay, God, if this is the way it's going to be, for however long, then . . . God help me to emerge from this a better man in every way that I can . . . Help me to make it count for something positive.'

Captain Gerald Coffee, US Navy

In February 1966 Captain Gerald L. Coffee of the United States Navy was piloting an aircraft on a reconnaissance mission over North Vietnam. Captain Coffee's plane was the last to be launched on what was the last mission of the day. Neither he nor his crewman made it back that day. The aircraft was hit by enemy fire which severed the hydraulic lines. Without the hydraulics, Captain Coffee was unable to steer. The control stick froze in his hand as the plane careered towards the sea at over 680 miles per hour.

'I was knocked unconscious immediately, and for all practical purposes had I never regained consciousness, I would have died then,' Captain Coffee recalled. When he did regain consciousness, he found that he was floating a quarter of a mile off the coast. He would discover later that he had broken his arm and dislocated his elbow and shoulder. During the battle that ensued, his crewman was shot dead, but Captain Coffee was captured and taken to Wallo Prison in the capital city, Hanoi.

'I looked around and couldn't believe where I found myself,' he said. 'I was in a tiny cell about the size of a single bed. There was a concrete slab about eighteen inches wide jutting out from the wall which was to be my bed. At the foot of the slab was a set of ankle stocks, wooden on the bottom with a heavy iron bar that came down across the top with a large padlock.'

'There was one window, very high in the cell, with a double row of iron bars,' he recalled, but all he could see from it was the prison's eighteen-foot wall. There was literally nothing in the room save for one small can in the corner. This was where Captain Coffee spent his days in prison. He had to survive the severest deprivation, interrogation and torture day after day until, one day, over seven years later, he was finally released. Yet, despite everything he endured as a POW, when asked, Captain Gerald Coffee was adamant that he wouldn't trade those experiences. After the war, Captain Coffee wrote a book, *Beyond Survival*, considered by many to be one of the best books written on the Vietnam War POW experience. As news of his story spread, Captain Coffee became a sought-after motivational speaker and today is widely acknowledged as one of the top ten speakers in the USA. His presentations are not detailed accounts of his experiences in a Vietnamese POW camp, but he often draws from his experiences to inspire his audiences with a message of hope, faith and the invincibility of the human spirit. 'At some time or another we all get shot down. We are all POWs, prisoners of woe,' he says. He challenges his audiences to 'be tough', 'bounce back' and 'learn not just to survive, but to go beyond survival: finding the purpose in your adversity'.

Captain Coffee talks about leadership when under stress, managing change through uncertainty, working within a team, the value of loyalty and the power of communication. 'The most important lessons that I learned which contributed to my survival and that of my contemporaries during all those years,' he said, 'have served me so well since I have been at home and will continue to serve me well in the future.'

Matthew J Friedman, Professor of Psychiatry at Dartmouth Medical School and Director of the National Center for Post-traumatic Stress Disorder, said that studies of combatants even as far back as the Second World War showed that return-ing soldiers often found that something in their experiences had changed them in a profound, even spiritual way. 'Yes, I've suffered,' soldiers would report, 'but I wouldn't have given up this experience for anything in the world . . . The things I experienced have made me a better man today.' Many soldiers believe that, even after being badly and permanently injured or confined in a POW camp for years, their experiences had changed them. They had come through their trials feeling stronger and more resilient than they had ever been.

These accounts are not meant to imply that war is a good thing. Drs Calhoun and Tedeschi stress the fact that they regard all 'life crises, loss and trauma as undesirable'. Any growth that results from a trauma emerges from the struggle with coping and overcoming, rather than from the trauma itself. What they have demonstrated, however, is that even after enduring the traumas of war, it is still possible to find a flipside.

THE CENTRAL PARK JOGGER

'Life holds a potential meaning under any conditions, even the most miserable ones.'

Dr Viktor Frankl

The sun had set over Central Park. It was around nine o'clock in the evening of 19 April 1989. A loosely organized gang of thirty-two youths was running amok in the park. Five of the youths later confessed to random, motiveless assaults. In a half-hour of senseless violence over a quarter-mile stretch of the park, they assaulted cyclists and pedestrians and, in two separate incidents, reportedly 'pummelled two men into unconsciousness, with a metal pipe, stones, punches, and kicks to the head'.

A few hours later, the body of a twenty-eight-year-old

woman was found by two men walking through the park. The woman had been jogging and was found comatose, having been severely beaten and raped. Her skull was fractured from a violent blow to the head, she had lost over 75 per cent of her blood and by the time she was found, was suffering from severe hypothermia. The doctors at Metropolitan Hospital did not offer an optimistic prognosis. They initially thought that she wouldn't survive her injuries or, at best, would remain in a coma. But, against the doctors' predictions, the woman who became known as the Central Park Jogger survived.

Due to the social stigma associated with being the victim of a sexual crime, and the trauma that victims of these crimes must endure, the identity of the Central Park Jogger was not revealed by the majority of the American media. However, in 2003 Trisha Meili revealed her own identity in an effort to help other victims of similar crimes and she told her story in a book, *I Am the Central Park Jogger*.

Born and raised in Paramus, New Jersey, and Pittsburgh, Trisha was a Phi Beta Kappa economics major at Wellesley College and a double graduate degree recipient (MBA and MA) at Yale University. After graduation, she went on to work as an associate at the Wall Street investment bank Salomon Brothers, until her life as she knew it was ended violently on that horrific night in Central Park.

Trisha's book is an uplifting account not of her attack, but of her journey of healing and of the new life she built for herself. She had to rebuild her entire life, relearning how to do even the simplest thing. Rolling over, being able to tell the time, buttoning her blouse, tying shoelaces or identifying simple objects – things we all learn to do as infants, Trisha had to relearn. She did it all, and in the process completely transformed herself. She was the same person, but she was changed, in some ways stronger than she had ever been.

Trisha is no longer an investment banker. Instead, she gives her time to help organizations that helped her in her recovery including the Sexual Assault and Violence Intervention Program (SAVI) at Mount Sinai Hospital; Gaylord Hospital, where she did much of her rehabilitation, and the Achilles Track Club that helped her run the New York City Marathon in 1995.

Recently, Trisha received the Leadership Award from the National Center for Victims of Crime, the National Courage Award from the Courage Center, the Pacesetter Award from New York Hospital Queens, the Spirit of Achievement Award from Albert Einstein College of Medicine, the Courage Award from Boston's Magic 106.7 Exceptional Women Program and she was an Olympic Torchbearer in New York City.

Today, Trisha is in demand as a public speaker and travels across North America to address businesses, universities, brain injury associations, sexual assault centres and hospitals about her journey of recovery and healing. With her book and her lectures, she offers insights on how to manage unpredictable change in life, whether personal, professional, economic or even spiritual. Her story has encouraged and inspired people all over the world to overcome life's obstacles – regardless of what they might be – and get back on the road to life. She is a living example of what is possible on the flipside of trauma. She did not just survive, even though that was miraculous in itself; she managed to find the flipside of a horrendous experience. She was able to find something positive from it that would change her life for the better and inspire others to do the same.

GROWTH THROUGH TRAUMA

No one would suggest that trauma is good or necessary for us to achieve personal growth. Trauma by its very nature involves suffering, and in an ideal world we would all learn to grow within ourselves without having to suffer. But when it does happen, there is still hope for the future. Leading psychologists have demonstrated that all trauma brings with it unique opportunities that can lead to profound changes.

Post-traumatic growth is a fascinating and relatively new field of study. Throughout history philosophers and theologians have spoken of human suffering bringing possibilities for greater good. Studying people who have grown or directly benefited in one way or another as a result of having been subjected to a physical or psychological trauma, Professors Calhoun and Tedeschi were able to establish that trauma has two sides – the side we see of loss and suffering, and the side of growth and new possibilities.

Through their research the doctors discovered that people who go through major traumas, including life-threatening illnesses, severe accidents, criminal attacks and even natural disasters, often experience one or more of five kinds of positive changes in their lives:

1. A feeling of personal strength

   Survivors of traumas often become more confident and self-reliant. The knowledge that they have survived the trauma gives people a feeling of optimism and a self-confidence that they can beat anything that may be thrown at them in the future. It is evident that big traumas can completely alter our beliefs about ourselves and what we are capable of achieving.

2. Closer relationships

   Traumas tend to bring survivors closer together with their families, friends and work colleagues. They realize that the quality of life is more about the quality of their relationships than anything else and they put greater effort and greater time into building and developing meaningful personal relationships. They have increased compassion and empathy for others who experience setbacks and trauma (although, interestingly, they often become less sympathetic in relation to other people's complaints about more mundane, everyday worries).

3. **A greater appreciation of life**

   Too often, it is only when we lose something that we really understand its value. But, when people go through traumas, any losses that they sustain can serve to make them appreciate those things that remain. There is often a sense of thankfulness for having survived, together with a deeper appreciation of life than they had ever felt before. Suddenly, the world is filled with wonder and everything that many people take for granted or miss completely, the trauma survivor will cherish.

4. **A new personal philosophy of life and stronger spiritual beliefs**

   The spiritual growth that often results from a traumatic experience is very commonly reported by people who survive traumas. More often than not, the survivor has new and very different priorities in life. They begin to find some purpose or meaning to whatever suffering they have endured, and this in turn gives new meaning in their life. Consequently, they emerge with stronger spiritual or religious beliefs.

5. **New opportunities and life paths**

   Even though traumas can shatter people's lives completely, when they start putting the pieces back together, often they will discover new choices, new opportunities and new dreams to pursue.

The discovery of post-traumatic growth demonstrates that the flipside is not a random outcome. It is something that is real and comes with an assurance of new opportunities and hope for a better future. However, finding the benefit or experiencing growth following a trauma is by no means a guaranteed end result. The key to finding the flipside to any setback or trauma lies not in the nature of an event or a specific type of trauma. The secret to finding a positive outcome lies within the people who experience the traumas and how they respond to it. People who find the flipside are no different in most ways to everyone else, but psychologists have identified some critical differences, so it is to those people that we will now turn.

CHAPTER 6

REASONS FOR OPTIMISM

WHY THERE IS REASON FOR OPTIMISM WHEN FACED
WITH ANY PROBLEM, SETBACK OR ADVERSITY

'An optimist is someone who goes after Moby Dick in
a rowboat and takes the tartar sauce with him.'

Zig Ziglar

THERE IS A group of people who are no more intelligent or
hard-working than everyone else but, at school, they get
better grades. They are no different physically than the rest
of us, yet they suffer from far fewer health problems. They
have no genetic advantages, yet they live, on average, seven
and a half years longer. When they do fall ill, despite being
given the same treatments as other patients, this group of
people recover faster and more comprehensively. These
people are no better skilled or trained, yet in business they
outperform their work colleagues and their competitors by as
much as 88 per cent. They also make more money and
achieve a higher professional status. In virtually every area of

their lives, these people tend to succeed and achieve greater things than everyone else. More significantly, they seem to have a knack of being able to get something positive out of any negative experience. These people don't belong to a particular race, colour or creed. The only thing that sets them apart from the crowd is their attitude and outlook on life. They are optimists.

Psychologists define optimists as people who generally expect good things to happen. Pessimists, on the other hand, generally expect bad things to happen. The difference is solely one of expectation, a confidence in the future, but it is a critical difference which, to a large extent, determines how our lives unfold.

THE LUCKIEST MAN IN THE WORLD

'Do you know anyone who is more unfortunate than me?' This is the first question that Hsieh Kun-Shan asks audiences when he is invited to speak at seminars and conferences. He stands before them, a man with no arms, a deformed left foot, his right leg was amputated below the knee and he is blind in one eye. Most people struggle to think of anyone they know, or anyone they have ever heard of, who could be considered to have been anywhere near as unlucky as Hsieh has been in his life. It is then that he confounds his audiences with his second question: 'But, do you also know anyone who is as lucky as me?'

What could possibly make a man like Hsieh feel like the luckiest man in the world? Why would a man whose life seems like it has been cursed, feel so blessed? To many, it seems incomprehensible. That is why what Hsieh has to say is so important.

Hsieh's story goes back over thirty years to the day when he was still a teenager working in a factory in Taiwan. The last thing he remembers of that day was walking barefoot through the factory, carrying steel rods. 'I was helping at the garment factory,' he explained. 'All of a sudden, the steel rods I was carrying were sucked up by high-voltage wires. Making things worse, for some reason I had taken my shoes off that day, which made my whole body an electric conductor.'

Hsieh was knocked unconscious immediately. He woke up two days later feeling unbearable pain from his badly burnt legs and arms. Doctors had no choice but to amputate some of his limbs to save his life. He lost most of his right arm, his entire left arm and his right leg below the knee. His right eye was severely damaged, and his left foot was deformed by the accident.

With such injuries, it seems remarkable that Hsieh considers himself today to be one of the luckiest men in the world. It is even more remarkable when you consider that, several years later, Hsieh completely lost the sight in his right eye when his sister accidentally hit it with a staple as she was mending his books! But, even with his severe physical limitations, Hsieh considers himself to be very fortunate. Not just because he survived an accident that could so easily have killed him, but because of the life he has built and the person he has become through the challenges that he faced which were forced upon him both by his accident and the resulting injuries.

For the seven years following his accident, Hsieh confined himself to his family's small rented apartment. The only short trips he made outside were to get a haircut. 'But I was not in exile' said Hsieh. 'I was thinking of ways to take care of myself so as to start a second life. My body was confined, but my mind was free.'

Hsieh patiently began to learn to live with his disabilities. He invented a special device that could be chained to what was left of his right arm, to which a spoon could be attached so that Hsieh was able to feed himself. He also designed a long hook which could be attached to the chain to unzip his trousers. He even learned to bathe himself.

It was in his small room that Hsieh decided that he was going to paint for a living. He had enjoyed doodling on textbooks as a child during school lessons and so he began teaching himself to sketch with a pencil in his mouth, finding it therapeutic to focus his mind on the creative process. 'I found peace and contentment in drawing,' said Hsieh, who even taught himself to sharpen pencils with his mouth holding a small knife.

In his early twenties, Hsieh put an end to his self-imposed isolation and joined two other self-taught peers in forming a studio selling oil paintings called One Step Behind. He insisted on moving out of his mother's home, and had an artificial leg attached so he could move around.

However, the most dramatic change in Hsieh's life came the day he met the well-known oil painter Wu Ah-Sun at Wu's art exhibition in Taipei. Wu was impressed by Hsieh's eagerness to learn and agreed to let Hsieh attend the class Wu gave at a university, free of charge. Wu also helped promote Hsieh's work. It was at Wu's class that Hsieh met his future wife, a pretty girl called Lin who worked at a local electronics firm.

To make up for the education he had lost following his accident, Hsieh finished six years of high school studies at the age of thirty. He went on to win many art awards and in 1987 he became a member of the Liechtenstein-based Association of Mouth and Foot Painting Artists of the World, which offers grants to hundreds of artists in over sixty countries. Today Hsieh's medium-sized oil paintings sell for over $5,000 a piece.

In 2002 Hsieh wrote his autobiography which was adapted as a children's book a year later. The book was also made into a thirty-episode TV series, in which he played himself as an adult. Hsieh's life story has now become part of Taiwanese folklore and is included in textbooks for elementary and high-school children. He has achieved something that very few people throughout history could ever hope to achieve, not just in Taiwan, but anywhere in the world: he has become something of a legend in his own lifetime.

Today Hsieh is not just a painter, he is a motivational speaker and lecturer. According to reports, he lives in a second-floor apartment in Banqiao, Taiwan, with his wife Lin Yeh-chen and their two teenage daughters. When Lin described him in an interview as a 'man who beams love, warmth and light with extreme optimism', she was also revealing one of the keys to his success.

THE GREATEST CYCLIST OF THE TOUR DE FRANCE

In the world of professional cycling, there is one man who still stands out above all others. He is a man who, at the time of writing, has won the Tour de France, widely acknowledged to be the most prestigious and gruelling cycling event in the world, a record-breaking seven consecutive times, from 1999 to 2005. Among his many honours are four consecutive Associated Press awards for Male Athlete of the Year, and he also won ESPN's ESPY Award for Best Male Athlete four years in succession. In 2003 he was named the BBC Overseas Sports Personality of the Year. His name is Lance Armstrong.

As you can imagine, Lance Armstrong has become something of an icon in the world of professional road racing. His achievements are unrivalled. But there is something else about his story that is even more remarkable; only a few years before he won his first Tour de France, Armstrong was diagnosed with cancer.

It was on 2 October 1996 that Armstrong was first diagnosed with testicular cancer. It is the most common cancer in men aged between fifteen and thirty-five. According to the

UK's Department of Health's records, 46.2 per cent of people get cancer at some point in their lives. If you are a man and are going to get cancer, then testicular cancer would be one of the better types to get. Provided the tumour has not metastasized (spread to other organs or surrounding tissue), the prognosis is usually good. Over 90 per cent of patients recover. However, when Armstrong's test results came back they revealed that the tumour had already metastasized. The cancer had invaded his brain and lungs. The prognosis was not good.

There were a number of factors that were on Armstrong's side in his battle against cancer. He was relatively young, a supremely fit and strong athlete in peak physical condition, and this put him in good shape to withstand the onslaught of aggressive chemotherapy and surgery. He also had a lot of support from his family and friends. But, there was one crucial factor that helped him triumph, even when confronted with terrifying odds. It was the same factor that helped him go on to win the Tour de France, the world's most demanding road race, not once but seven years in succession: Lance Armstrong has the attitude of a winner. He is focused, single-minded and always believes that he will succeed at anything to which he sets his mind – all the key attributes of an optimist.

HEALTH AND OPTIMISM

When anyone is diagnosed with cancer, in whatever form, the one thing they need more than anything else is optimism. Clinical studies have revealed time after time that patients who expect a positive outcome are far more likely to experience a positive outcome. Scientists have investigated patients undergoing treatment for several different types of cancer and even patients receiving bone marrow transplants. The results were virtually identical in all cases; the optimists among the patients experienced fewer complications and had a much better survival rate.

In one study of young cancer patients, optimists were found to have a much better survival rate after eight months than pessimists. A study of patients who had head and neck cancers came to a similar conclusion. The results revealed that the pessimists among them were far less likely than the others to be alive one year later. The optimists among women who were diagnosed with breast cancer experienced less distress before surgery and reported enjoying a better quality of life twelve months following their treatment compared to pessimists.

Research into other health problems came to very similar conclusions. Patients who undergo coronary heart surgery are far less likely to experience complications or have to be rehospitalized in the six months following their operations if they are optimists, and optimists enjoy a higher quality of life even up to five years after their surgery.

There is something special about optimists that enables them to overcome all manner of health problems more speedily and completely than other people. In 1985 researchers in Holland began a fifteen-year study investigating whether and how optimism was related to cardiovascular disease in middle-aged men. A random selection of men was carefully screened to exclude typical risk factors for cardiovascular disease including a medical history of stroke, diabetes, angina pectoris, heart failure and any familial history. The researchers were left with a total of 545 men whom they tested for optimism and pessimism using a short questionnaire with just four questions. Over the following fifteen years the researchers followed the men's medical history and tested for any changes in the men's dispositional optimism at five-year intervals.

In February 2006 the researchers published their findings. The results revealed that there was a 'strong and consistent association between dispositional optimism and about a fifty per cent lower risk of cardiovascular mortality'. At the same time, hopelessness, which is defined as 'a sense of futility and negative expectations about the future and one's personal goals' and is thus very similar in nature to pessimism, was found to be associated with an increased risk of cardiovascular disease including hypertension and atherosclerosis. Optimism was shown to reduce the risk of death from cardiovascular disease by a massive 50 per cent! In fact, the association between optimism and the risk of cardiovascular disease was found to be so significant that the researchers recommended that a person's level of optimism and pessimism should be added to the list of independent risk markers for cardio-vascular disease in elderly men.

Other research studies have revealed that optimists live between seven and a half and thirteen years longer than pessimists, and are also more likely to recover from a range of serious illnesses than pessimists. This may be because pessimists tend to have higher blood pressure than optimists, and that optimists have stronger immune systems. According to Dr Becca R. Levy, Associate Professor of Epidemiology and Psychology at the Yale School of Public Health, optimists live longer and tend to enjoy 'better functional health' throughout their lives.

Dr Michael F Scheier, Professor and Head of the Department of Psychology at Carnegie-Mellon University, has been involved in research looking at the effects of optimism on patients undergoing coronary bypass operations and cancer. He concluded that 'optimists tend to adjust better to health threats and conditions than pessimists do'.

Many scientists suspect that the reason optimists fare so much better than pessimists in surviving health crises is because our expectations have physiological and biochemical consequences. New research is revealing that our expect-ations are extremely powerful in influencing physical and psychological changes in our body. Scientists have measured the resulting changes in the brain following our thoughts and, in particular, our expectations. From the release of natural painkilling chemicals to alterations in how neurons fire in our brain, their conclusions are startling.

The idea that thoughts or expectations can bring about improvements in our health and wellbeing is nothing new. As far back as 1811, *Hooper's Medical Dictionary* referred to what we know of today as the 'Placebo Effect': 'an epithet given to any medicine adapted more to please than benefit the patient'. But, what Hooper perhaps didn't understand is that the mind of a patient is often critical, some would say more critical, than any treatment that a patient may be given.

Today the placebo effect is a recognized medical phenomenon and is the standard by which all medicines are tested. It is generally acknowledged that if you give patients a bottle of sugar tablets but inform them that the tablets are the latest, proven medicine that will cure their ailment, over one-third of patients (usually somewhere between 30 and 60 per cent) will actually experience an improvement in their symptoms.

Until recently, the benefits of a placebo were thought to be purely psychosomatic, or in the patient's imagination. However, scientists have begun to collate direct evidence which demonstrates beyond doubt that our thoughts can trigger *the same* neurological pathways of healing as any chemical drug. In one such study, at the University of Michigan, scientists injected the jaws of healthy young men with salt water to cause painful pressure, while PET scans measured the impact in their brains. The men were told they were getting a pain reliever, which was actually nothing but a placebo. The patients' brains were scanned during the process and the results showed that as soon as the men were told they were receiving the 'medicine', there was an immediate release of endorphins in their brains – chemicals that act as natural painkillers by blocking the transmission of pain signals between nerve cells – and, as a result, the men felt better.

Another study, conducted by Dr Fabrizio Benedetti of Italy's University of Turin Medical School looked at patients suffering from Parkinson's disease, a degenerative disorder of the central nervous system that often impairs the sufferer's motor skills and speech, as well as other functions. Patients were fitted with a pacemaker-like implant in their brains, which helps block tremors. However, unbeknown to the patients, not all of the implants were activated. The study found that giving patients an expectation of improvement, without any medical intervention, would lead to a real and significant improvement in the patients' conditions.

When the doctors came to analyse the benefits of the treatment, their findings were baffling. The patients had shown improvement, and all reported that they moved much better following the treatment. The brain scans also confirmed the improvement; the electrical activity of individual nerve cells in a movement-controlling part of the brain became calm, exhibiting a staggering 40 per cent decrease in activity which correlated with a reduction in patients' muscle rigidity. However, when the doctors analysed the data, they found that the patients who showed the most significant improvement were those whose implants had not been activated. The conclusion was irresistible; the very expectation of improvement was, by itself, so powerful that it led to biochemical changes in the brain which outperformed the very latest cutting-edge medical technology, a surgical procedure costing thousands of dollars.

One of the most intriguing demonstrations of the power of a placebo was described in a radio interview in 1983 by Norman Cousins, best-selling author of *Anatomy of an Illness*. At that time, Cousins was working at the Brain Research Institute at UCLA. More than one hundred medical students took part in an experiment involving two drugs. One was a super stimulant and the other was a super tranquillizer. The students were told how the tablets would affect them. They were told that the red pill, the super stimulant, would make them feel more alert but that it could also cause nausea and dizziness. The blue pill, the super relaxant, would make them feel more relaxed, but it could also cause drowsiness and inhibit their ability to concentrate.

What made this experiment so interesting was that no placebo was involved. Both sets of drugs were real; the researchers switched the contents of the pills so that the red pills were actually tranquillizers and the blue were stimulants.

The researchers then monitored the students' reactions and found that nearly 60 per cent of them reacted in line with their expectations despite the fact they had been given a drug that should have produced opposing symptoms. It was not just a psychological response, the students showed measurable biochemical and physiological changes. The conclusion, Cousins said, was 'inescapable'; our expectations are, at least in this instance, more powerful than medications.

Today, it is acknowledged that our thoughts and expectations can create powerful physiological and biochemical changes in our bodies. It is not a question of the mind tricking the body into thinking that it's well or not in pain. The thought or expectation activates the healing mechanisms in the body and real healing takes place. The really startling thing is that, according to researchers at Harvard University, the placebo effect works for 60–90 per cent of all diseases, including angina pectoris, bronchial asthma, herpes simplex and duodenal ulcers.

This is something that, I believe, doctors need to be mindful of when dealing with patients. There are too many stories of doctors who have appalling bedside manners. When dealing with patients undergoing treatment for life-threatening illnesses, some doctors don't stop to consider what their words are doing to the patient. A negative, despairing prognosis can literally be as poisonous and health-destroying as any chemical toxin. A negative prognosis can become a self-fulfilling prophecy. Lives may be lost unnecessarily or prematurely and, at the very least, patients' quality of life may be damaged. The gloomy statistics just become compounded to the detriment of future patients. While placebos are by no means a substitute for medical treatments, we do know that encouraging optimism – with positive thoughts and reasons to be hopeful – can only serve to help bring about the best possible outcome for all patients.

The evidence is beyond doubt; the way we view the world and, in particular, our confidence in ourselves and in the future, significantly affects our health and determines how successful we may be in overcoming health challenges. Optimists not only enjoy better health and live longer than pessimists, but they also cope better and recover faster from treatment. Consequently, if ever you or a loved one become sick, however serious the condition may be, maintaining a positive, optimistic outlook will be just as important as any medical intervention. In the words of Norman Cousins, 'Drugs are not always necessary. Belief in recovery always is.'

THE THIRD FACTOR IN HUMAN POTENTIAL

Traditionally, psychologists believed that human potential was driven by two personality traits – ability and motivation. However, in the last thirty years, researchers have uncovered a missing third factor, a characteristic that will predict a person's potential in virtually every area of his or her life. That third factor is optimism. Researchers have discovered that a person's success in life is influenced as much by their level of optimism as anything else. Expectations of failure or success are, for the most part, self-fulfilling prophecies.

The benefits of optimism have been confirmed in literally hundreds of psychological studies undertaken during the past thirty years in a wide variety of industries. One of the leading psychologists working in the field of optimism is Dr Martin Seligman, Professor of Psychology at the University of Pennsylvania, and former president of the American Psychological Association (APA).

In many of the studies, people's level of optimism was measured using the Seligman Attributional Style Questionnaire (SASQ). This takes about twenty minutes to complete and comprises a detailed list of questions that present a number of hypothetical situations and then asks the participant to give an assessment against each question, rating each response on a scale of one to seven. It was designed to identify what Dr Seligman refers to as a person's 'explanatory style', which is essentially how people rationalize the causes of their successes and failures in life. This is because, according to Dr Seligman's findings, optimistic people have a completely different way of viewing success and failure than pessimists. When an optimist experiences failure, he or she views it as a learning experience and a temporary setback. In stark contrast, when a pessimist experiences failure, he or she assumes it is due to their lack of ability and believes that it is a permanent situation; if he or she were to try again, they just 'know' that they would fail again, so what would be the point in trying?

One of the most illuminating studies was conducted with life insurance sales people. Working with the Metropolitan Life Insurance Company, Dr Seligman and his team tested 15,000 applicants for a job in life insurance sales, a very difficult job that necessarily involves frequent rejection to the sales person and typically has a high drop-out rate.

For two years the researchers followed the success of one thousand sales people who had passed the insurance company's entry examinations and they also monitored a further 129 people who had failed the insurance company's exam (and would therefore not normally have been hired) but because they had scored very highly on the SASQ optimism test, they were recruited and their sales noted throughout the trial.

When the results were collated, the researchers discovered, as predicted, that within the group of sales people who had passed the insurance company's test, those who were optimists significantly outsold the pessimists by 31 per cent. However, they then analysed the special group of 129 optimists who had failed the industry test and found that this group of high-level optimists outsold everyone! They beat the pessimists who had passed the insurance company's standard tests by an incredible 57 per cent. Similar research projects in other industries – including telecoms, banking, property, office supplies, car sales to name just a few – have come to the same conclusion. Optimists tend to be far more successful than pessimists in terms of sales; on average, the optimists outsell pessimists by 20 to 40 per cent, and extreme optimists outperform extreme pessimists by as much as 88 per cent!

In addition, the researchers found that extreme pessimists were as much as three times more likely to quit their jobs than extreme optimists. The message was clear: if a company wants to get the most out of its sales team, it needs to ensure that the people it hires are not just competent, but are also optimistic in their expectations.

Through the SASQ, optimism has been shown to be associated with stronger motivation and higher levels of achievement, whether at school, at work or even in sport. We have seen how, in business, a salesperson's level of optimism has been shown to be an accurate marker predicting how successful they will be in making sales. In sport, optimism was shown to accurately predict levels of performance among nationally ranked swimmers. In 1988 Dr Seligman worked with the University of California, Berkeley swimming team and found that optimists outperformed pessimists and responded far better when faced with adversity (defined as how they responded in a race following a sub-standard performance). Seligman cites the story of Matt Biondi whose SASQ score showed a highly optimistic outlook. In the Seoul Olympics in 1988 there was high expectation for Biondi to take seven gold medals and equal Mark Spitz's 1972 Olympic record. However, in his first two events Biondi made one or two slight, but critical, errors and only managed to take the bronze and silver medals. This disappointing start led to media speculation as to how Biondi might perform in his remaining five events. Dr Seligman was confident that he would bounce back, in accordance with his SASQ optimism profile. Sure enough, Biondi won gold medals in all five events.

In education, Dr Seligman found that children between third and seventh grade who were shown to be optimists, fared significantly better than children who were pessimistic. Children who began third grade with a low pessimist score on the SASQ, would show a much higher risk of depression and significantly reduced academic achievement. High SASQ scores, on the other hand, were found to correlate with better sleep and far less anxiety or stress. Optimism scores were able to accurately predict which of the students would attain top grades and which would end up dropping out.

When you begin to appreciate the significance that optimism plays in our lives, it shouldn't come as a surprise to learn that leading corporations and organizations around the world use the SASQ to filter applicants, especially those interested in jobs that involve frequent setbacks and ongoing challenges. This is because it is now widely acknowledged that, more than any other group of people, it is the optimists who hold the key to the flipside.

THE KEY TO THE FLIPSIDE

'Optimism is the one quality more associated with success and happiness than any other.'

Brian Tracey

There is little doubt that optimism is a critical characteristic, some would argue the most critical characteristic, found in people who find the flipside. One reason for this, according to Professor Charles Carver, head of the Psychology Department at the University of Miami (who has been involved in much of the ground-breaking research into optimism), is that optimists 'respond to difficulty or adversity in more adaptive ways than people who hold negative expectations'. Optimists, he says, 'have a greater fighting spirit', they exhibit different coping strategies and different responses when confronted by stressful situations.

This all serves to further confirm that the flipside is not a random, ad hoc occurrence. It is an outcome that can be predicted by a person's attitudes and beliefs. This raises further questions about optimism and what it really means to be optimistic. What causes optimism? Where does it come from? And, most important of all, given that the optimist's life is, in so many ways, better than the pessimist's, we must ask if it is possible to become more optimistic and thereby improve our chances of finding the flipside in our own lives? In Part Two of this book we will look at these questions and explore the strategies that optimists use to find the flipside when faced with problems and setbacks.

PART TWO

PATHWAYS – STEPS TO THE FLIPSIDE

'All we can do is study the lives of people who seem to have found their answers to the questions of what ultimately human life is about as against those who have not.'

Charlotte Bühler

CHAPTER 7

FINDING THE FLIPSIDE

'The greatest discovery of my generation is that a human being can alter his life by altering his attitude.'
William James, 1842–1910

IN PART ONE we have seen evidence of the flipside. We have seen how problems and obstacles, by their very nature, are accompanied by opportunities. Generally, the bigger the problem that confronts us, the bigger the opportunity that resides within it. We have heard how the moments that shape our lives are often the low points, the times when events seem to conspire against us. We have seen that crises can trigger positive change and lead to long-term success. We have also seen that adversity – even severe trauma – can turn out to be a catalyst to greater things and lead us in new, and sometimes unexpected, directions in life.

However, it is also apparent that not everyone who has a problem finds an opportunity. Not everyone who is faced with adversity or suffers a trauma finds the flipside. This is because the key to the flipside is not found in any specific event that happens to us; the key lies within the individual and how he or she responds to the challenges of life.

In Part Two we will explore the specific characteristics and strategies that people have used to successfully find the flipside. Along the way, we will find out how a woman who lost her hair through alopecia used her experience to build a new, more meaningful life and has helped and inspired thousands of women all over the world. We will look at the personal philosophy of the man who changed the world and who *Life* magazine voted as the most important person of the last millennium. We will discover the secret behind some of the most successful entrepreneurs and find out how a man confined to an isolation ward in a hospital and, given less than a fifty-fifty chance of surviving the treatment, managed to create something that launched a global business and, even more importantly, how he discovered the true meaning of success. We will speak to some truly remarkable people whose achievements redefine our paradigms of what is possible, and we will ask what steps they took when they were faced with a crisis that turned it to their advantage. Their answers may surprise you.

CHAPTER 8

GREAT EXPECTATIONS: THE STRATEGIES OF OPTIMISTS

'The optimist is more likely to see adversity as a challenge, transform problems into opportunities, put in the hours to refine skills, persevere in finding solutions to difficult problems, maintain confidence, rebound quickly after setbacks and persist.'

Peter Schulman

AN OLD FRIEND of mine from university days recently told me that, in his life, he prefers to expect the worst. I was somewhat perplexed. 'Why?' Without hesitation he answered, 'Because by expecting the best, I'm only setting myself up for disappointment when things don't work out. If I expect the worst, I won't ever be disappointed and if things turn out well . . . then I'll be pleasantly surprised.' His reasoning is not uncommon and may, at first, seem logical and reasonable. It is the classic reasoning of a pessimist. However, there is a critical flaw in his argument; it doesn't work!

The reason it doesn't work is because our expectations are very often self-fulfilling prophecies. Dan Ariely, Professor of

Behavioural Economics at Duke University, North Carolina, has demonstrated through his research that what we expect will invariably determine what we experience. 'When we think something will be good, it generally will be good,' explains Professor Ariely, 'and when we think it will be bad, it will be bad.'

In his brilliant book *Predictably Irrational*, Professor Ariely describes a variety of studies that he has designed or been involved with that investigated the effect of people's expectations on different aspects of their lives. He has found, for example, that our enjoyment of a meal is influenced by our prior expectations of it. Imagine that you are sitting in a chic Italian restaurant and the menu of the day contains two choices: the first is described simply as 'Vegetable Pasta' and the second is described as 'Home-made organic Tuscan pasta tossed in a rich Devonshire butter sauce with garlic and garden herbs served with fresh, seasonal vegetables'. Which choice would you opt for? According to Professor Ariely's work, most people will go for the more descriptive option (assuming, of course, that they don't have any allergies or specific dislikes to any of the described ingredients). However, what is particularly interesting is that Professor Ariely's studies have shown that people who choose the more descriptive option will also enjoy their meal more than people who choose the less-descriptive option, even though both options are exactly the same meal.

Similarly, if a meal is presented artistically we will enjoy it more than if it is just slopped on the plate. The same goes for drinks. Presumably, this is one of the reasons why Starbucks became so popular. People will pay more for a 'full-bodied blend of aged Indonesian coffees, with a smooth, deep, spicy flavour, lively with herbal undertones' than they will for plain 'Asian Coffee', and they will enjoy the drink that much more too. Serve it in an attractive mug and it's going to be a winner.

Interestingly, Professor Ariely has shown that our expectations can even influence how we respond to a medicine; both the description and packaging of a drug will certainly affect our expectations of it, but there is another key element that seems to play a prominent role – the price. When patients wcrc told that the cost of a new drug (which was a proven, effective analgesic) was $2.50 per dose, virtually all of the patients reacted very positively to the drug. However, when they were given the same medicine but told the cost was just ten cents per dose, only 50 per cent of the patients reported experiencing any pain relief. Incredible as it sounds, even though two tablets contain the exact same ingredients, the more expensive one will be more effective than the cheap brand, purely because somewhere in our subconscious we expect a higher priced medicine to be more effective.

His experiments have led Professor Ariely to conclude that, in virtually every area of our lives, our expectations influence not just our experience, but the actual outcome. 'The mind gets what it expects,' he says. Everything that is important to us – love, health, happiness and our enjoyment of life, all the things we want most from life – are conditioned by our expectations of what the future will bring. This is something that goes to the core of the flipside.

MIND MAPPING A FUTURE

A sterile hospital isolation ward is probably not the most obvious of places one would expect to find the flipside. Even less so when you're facing months of aggressive treatments and have been told that your life is literally hanging in the balance. Yet that is precisely where Mike Jetter, a German computer programmer, came to find the flipside that transformed his life.

It began in the early hours of Christmas Day 1989 in the small German town of Starnberg. Mike was awoken by an excruciating pain in his back that literally took his breath away. His wife Bettina called for help and he was rushed to the nearest hospital. After extensive investigations, the doctors managed to identify that his pain was being caused by an enlarged spleen. Mike's white blood cell count was extremely high, over thirty times its normal level. Something was seriously wrong.

It transpired that Mike had chronic myeloid leukaemia (CML), a condition that affects one or two people per 100,000 and typically requires aggressive treatments including chemotherapy, immune suppressive drugs and stem cell or full bone marrow transplants. Mike had his first transplant in February 1991. He was fortunate that his brother Andi was a perfect match for a bone marrow transplant. For a time, the treatment seemed to have been effective, but in the autumn of 1993, Mike had a relapse and less than six months later he was given what, at the time, was a treatment of last resort, a stem cell transplant.

Mike found himself, for the second time, in a hospital isolation unit, with the prospect of months of treatment and virtually no contact from the outside world. In addition, the outcome of the treatment was far from certain. At best, Mike was given a 50 per cent chance of surviving the following twelve months. For a lot of people, the challenges of that situation coupled with the uncertain prognosis would be enough to set them on a downhill slide. Panic and worry can set in, which we have seen is self-destructive in itself. More than any other time, it is crucial to remain positive and optimistic in a crisis, especially one of the magnitude that Mike had to face.

Meeting Mike Jetter, albeit on a webcam over the internet, one cannot help but take an immediate liking to him. He has large, blue eyes and an engaging smile and it would be difficult to detect any of the struggle and hardships with which he has had to cope over the past nineteen years. There is no trace of resentment or bitterness and when he speaks, Mike exudes an infectious enthusiasm for life. He was never one to pay too much attention to pessimistic survival statistics. 'I think I have always been a positive person,' he says, 'as is my wife Bettina.' At the time he was first diagnosed with CML, there was no internet and so Mike and his wife didn't have access to the information that we enjoy today. 'In one way that was a good thing, because we weren't surrounded with all the negative data. We let the doctors get on with the medical treatments, but we also searched for alternative ways that could help such as nutrition, massage, meditation and things that would help the mind and spirit. We were always looking forward and planning a new life and I think that played an important part in how things worked out.'

Mike knew from his first bout of treatment three years earlier that he would need to find a distraction during the months he was to spend in hospital. 'I had been told that I had a 50 per cent chance of surviving the next twelve months,' he says. 'I also knew from the first course of treatment, there is a big mental problem to overcome.

'I was in a small hospital room and people were coming in and out, wearing surgical clothes with face masks and gloves, and I knew that it was going to go on like this for months. I had to find something to keep my mind focused on, something to distract me from the leukaemia and the treatments, and everything that was going on around me.'

Being a computer programmer, Mike thought that it would be a good idea to work on a new software development project. Anyone who has ever spent time in front of a computer knows how quickly time passes and how easy it is to become totally immersed in whatever you are doing. Writing code is even more absorbing. For a time, the whole world fades into the background. There is just you and the computer screen.

The project Mike decided upon was 'mind-mapping'. Mind-mapping is a technique whereby thoughts are noted in a visual format on a piece of paper. A mind map is a diagram in which words, ideas, tasks or other items are linked around a central theme word or idea. It is used to generate and structure ideas, and it has been shown to be extremely successful as an aid to study, organization, problem-solving and decision-making.

The 'mind mapper' starts with a blank sheet of paper and puts the central idea or theme, which may be expressed as a word or picture, in a circle in the centre of the page. Then a structure is developed by drawing branches from the central theme and adding relevant ideas or points to them. Further branches can be added leading to sub-themes and sub-concepts until the structure is complete and looks something like an irregular spider's web with all items linking back, directly or indirectly, to the central theme. All of the elements of a mind map are, therefore, arranged intuitively according to the importance of the concepts and themes and they are classified into groupings, branches or areas. By presenting ideas in a mind map, it is said to encourage an unorthodox brainstorming approach that can generate ideas more effectively than a more formal, hierarchical organization system of note-taking.

When Mike Jetter was taken back into hospital in 1994, he was well aware of the benefits of mind-mapping, and he had regularly used it in his work. But, as a computer programmer, he was also aware of its limitations. 'People can do these creative presentations with coloured pencils and pens,' he says, 'but when you do it on paper, it's a one-time thing. You can't really develop it. You can't share it.' Mike's idea was to bundle the mind-mapping process into a software package which would enable people to take it to another level. On a computer, ideas could be moved around the page easily and the map could be added to, edited, printed and shared.

Mike worked on his new project for five or six hours a day in his hospital room in between his treatments. 'Initially, it was just a distraction for me,' he recalls. 'It stopped me from thinking about what was happening to me'. However, by the time he was discharged from the hospital, he had built the first fully working version of mind-mapping for computer users. It was a unique software package that he called Mindman (later renamed MindManager).

Today, MindManager is used by over one million users worldwide, including many international corporations, and the company that Mike and Bettina formed, Mindjet, has become a global enterprise with offices in Asia, America and Europe. More significant than the software and the business it generated are the ways in which Mike's battle with leukaemia brought about profound changes both for him and Bettina. 'Before my illness, we were just living,' Mike says. 'But it was not what I would call "conscious living". Now we know why we do things and we are much more thoughtful about how and with whom we spend our time.'

This observation is echoed by every other person I have contacted who found the flipside. Rhonda Byrne, writer and creator of *The Secret*, said, 'I was truly existing day-to-day. Life was just kind of happening to me.' It was only after reaching one of the lowest points in her life and subsequently coming across the ideas that formed the basis of *The Secret* that she noticed a profound change. When interviewed about this, she said that since the time she discovered *The Secret*, 'Life happens through me rather than to me.'

Despite a fourth setback in 2003 when Mike needed another bone marrow transplant, both he and Bettina believe that a lot of positive changes have resulted from his illness. Mike's software proved to be extremely popular. Many users reported that it had changed the way they worked, and it formed the basis of the business that Mike and Bettina set up in Sausalito, just outside San Francisco, in 1998. 'There is no doubt that my illness was a trigger both for the business we created and for personal changes in our lives,' says Mike. 'We wouldn't be living the life we enjoy today; we wouldn't be living in the USA today, without having gone through everything with my illness.

'I believe that things happen for a reason,' he continues. 'I don't believe in coincidences. Sometimes you just have to suffer first, or lose something, before you find your task or purpose in life.'

Mike's illness also brought him and his wife closer together. 'There are a lot of things that you need help with during and after treatments that are very time consuming,' he says. 'Bettina was always there. I really don't think I could've gone through it without her.'

Today, Mike and Bettina live together in Corte Madera, fifteen miles north of San Francisco. They left active day-to-day involvement in their company several years ago. Mike wrote about his journey and the lessons that he learned along the way in his book *The Cancer Code*. There is no doubt that his story, and the insights he has gleaned from his illness, help and inspire other cancer sufferers, and a portion of the proceeds from sales are donated to support patients and their families, medical teams and researchers in the fight against leukaemia.

Looking back on his long illness, Mike and Bettina can now see the flipside. Mike says, 'The battle against cancer transformed our lives, helping us understand the true meaning of success.' He echoes the words of Albert Schweitzer: 'We have learned that success is not the key to happiness. Happiness is the key to success.'

Summing up the past nineteen years, Mike says, 'Sometimes, through suffering you become a different person and find a new, more meaningful life. I think, for me, there were a lot of positive changes that were triggered through my illness. I don't know what the future holds, but both I and Bettina are grateful for what we have and we live purposefully and consciously, in the moment.'

THE PROBLEM WITH STATISTICS

'The average human has one breast and one testicle.'

Des McHale

Ever since studying Applied Mathematics and Statistics, I have always been cautious of presumptions based upon statistical data. It is simply too easy to twist statistics to suit our own assumptions, and it is even easier to be misled by figures. For example, just because 99 per cent of cancer sufferers regularly ate baked beans does not imply that baked beans cause cancer. When we are told that the average salary in the UK is £23,000, it doesn't mean that if you earn less than £23,000, you are less well off than the majority of people working in the UK. If you take a group of ten people, nine of whom earn £15,000 and the tenth person earns £80,000, the average (or mean) salary is £23,000 but nine out of the ten people earn considerably less than the average.

It is often a mistake to base important decisions solely on statistics because statistics are as easy as plasticine to manipulate. Also, and more importantly, statistics can never take into account the nature of the individual. For example, I have heard some parents tell their children that they would be better off not pursuing a career in, say, acting unless they would be happy waiting tables for the rest of their lives. 'Acting is extremely competitive,' they say. 'Only a tiny percentage of people who set out to become actors will even remotely succeed. Think about doing something sensible.' By 'sensible' they mean, of course, a career in which one stands a better chance of getting a job and offers a higher degree of job security for the future. Something like book-keeping or office administration, one would imagine, should fit the bill nicely.

What those parents are really saying is that their children

should make what is one of the most important decisions of their lives, based upon statistics. Aim for the best chance of getting a job, rather than something in which they have a passion or a talent. Admittedly, if a person is completely deluded about their talents like so many of those who audition for TV talent shows, then a good dose of reality would be in order. But, one cannot help but question the wisdom of using statistics to base a decision about how someone should spend their working life. Far better, I believe, to look for something you love, something you are passionate about and will enjoy. How much poorer would the world have been had Thomas Edison stuck to sending telegraph messages all his life just because most aspiring inventors do not earn much money? What would have happened if John Lennon had listened to his mother, Julia, who told him, 'The guitar's all very well, John, but you'll never make a living out of it'?

Statistics can rob people of their dreams, and in medicine, they can rob them of their lives. Expectations influence outcomes, and negative expectations lead to negative outcomes. When we are told that statistically there is a one in ten chance of surviving five years, it means that historically, only one person in ten who contracts the particular illness has survived longer than five years. What these figures do not take into account is the nature of the people who were affected.

LAUGHING AT STATISTICS

'Do not put your faith in what statistics say until you have carefully considered what they do not say.'

William W. Watt

In the mid-1960s, writer and peace advocate Norman Cousins was diagnosed with Marie-Strumpell's disease (otherwise known as ankylosing spondylitis), a chronic, painful, degenerative and inflammatory arthritis that causes inflammation and disintegration of the connective tissues in the spine. The severity of the pain caused Cousins concern and so he confronted his doctor about the illness and his chances of making a full recovery.

'He leveled with me,' Cousins wrote, 'admitting that one of the specialists had told him I had one chance in 500. The specialist had also confessed that he had not personally witnessed a recovery from this comprehensive condition.

'All this gave me a great deal to think about. Up until that time, I had been more or less disposed to let the doctors worry about my condition. But now, I felt a compulsion to get into the act. It seemed clear to me that if I was to be that one in 500, I had better be something more than a passive observer.'

As the doctors had no real hope to offer, Cousins took matters into his own hands. He had been told that his ankylosing spondylitis is often triggered by heavy metal poisoning or a streptococcal infection. Cousins thought hard about the sequence of events that led to his illness. He had been heading a US delegation in Moscow and had been staying at a hotel next to the airport. There was a large construction project going on next to the hotel and every night a procession of diesel trucks would deliver materials and remove waste. As it was summer, Cousins had slept with the window open and, when he thought back, he remembered having woken up every morning feeling somewhat nauseous. On his last day, a large jet swung round on the tarmac and Cousins' room caught a large spew of the exhaust. With this in mind, he reasoned that his illness may have been triggered by exposure to toxic fumes while staying in the hotel.

But one thing bothered him about his theory; Cousins' wife had been with him on that same trip, and she was fine. If the fumes were to blame, why hadn't she been similarly affected? There could only be one of two reasons; either he had a specific allergy to the fumes, or – in Cousins' view the more likely culprit – he had been suffering from adrenal exhaustion and consequently his immune system had been compromised, which meant that his body was less able to combat the toxic fumes. The trip had been extremely frustrating. There had been long hours and an array of other factors that caused Cousins agitation and stress. It all seemed to culminate on the flight home. The plane was filled to capacity and it was a long, tiring journey. As soon as the plane touched down in New York, Cousins started to feel unease deep in his bones. A week later he was hospitalized.

Reviewing the onset of his symptoms, Cousins reasoned with himself: 'If the negative emotions of stress and anxiety produced negative chemical changes in the body, wouldn't it be possible for positive emotions to produce positive chemical changes?' From this, he formulated a systematic pursuit of positive emotions and discussed his plan with his doctor. He would stop all analgesics (because these can stress the adrenal glands), and he replaced them with megadoses of vitamin C (because, according to the medical reports he had read, collagen diseases are associated with a vitamin C deficiency). Most importantly, he would focus his mind on positive emotions – hope, love, faith and laughter. As it is not easy to laugh when racked with pain and suffering from a virtually incurable wasting disease, Cousins tried something unheard of at that time; he ordered videos that might make him laugh.

Among his favourite things to watch were Marx Brothers films and the TV show *Candid Camera*, the original prankster show in which unsuspecting members of the public were set up in comical situations and filmed using hidden cameras. Some of their most memorable pranks involved a talking mailbox, where a voice within a mailbox talked to passers-by on a city street, and a 'Rest Room' sign placed on the door of a small cupboard in an office building. The bewilderment of the people and their subsequent reactions is 'laugh out loud' funny. 'I made the joyous discovery that ten minutes of genuine belly laughter had an anesthetic effect and would give me at least two hours of pain-free sleep,' Cousins wrote. 'When the pain-killing effect of the laughter wore off, we would switch on the motion picture projector again and, not infrequently, it would lead to another pain-free interval.' In addition, blood tests showed that Cousins' condition was improving, little by little, after each laughter episode. This was biochemical proof that the benefits were more than just psychological, and that there is real wisdom in Solomon's proverb, 'A merry heart doeth good like a medicine'.

Buoyed by his progress, Cousins made another giant leap towards his recovery. He discussed his next plan with his doctor, who once again was fully supportive, and proceeded to discharge himself from hospital and book into a hotel room. Aside from saving two-thirds in costs, Cousins said the benefits were 'incalculable'; he got uninterrupted sleep and rest, no longer having to be woken for a bed bath or for meals or for medications or change of sheets or examinations by interns. He received fresh, nutritious food and installed an intravenous drip to receive megadoses of the vitamin C he believed could help him.

Slowly but surely, healing occurred. His plan had enabled him to be completely free of drugs. To his doctor's amazement, Cousins was able to get by without any painkillers or sleeping pills. Blood tests showed that sedimentation levels (a characteristic that indicates the severity of the disease) were dropping significantly almost by the day. Fever had reduced and his pulse had normalized. He knew that his plan was working. Norman Cousins had beaten the odds; he was going to live.

Subsequent research has demonstrated that Norman Cousins had, through his own illness, stumbled upon something that had been completely ignored by mainstream medicine in its quest for patentable, chemical cures. Laughter has been shown to be a very potent healer that improves respiration and breathing, alleviates pain, reduces stress, anxiety and tension, decreases depression, loneliness and anger, and improves mental functioning (alertness, creativity and memory). In fact, the originator of *Candid Camera*, a man by the name of Allen Funt, became so fascinated and impressed by the healing powers of laughter that he later set up the 'Laughter Therapy' programme which is a private, non-profit organization whose chief aim is to bring 'a smile, laughter, and hopefully, some therapeutic benefit to those with serious illnesses'.

Cousins' recovery was, by any standards, quite remarkable and proved to be a significant landmark in his life. His book, *Anatomy of an Illness*, became a huge bestseller all over the world, and inspired subsequent research into the healing effects of laughter. He also wrote a number of other books including *Human Options* and *The Biology of Hope* and later served as Adjunct Professor of Medical Humanities for the School of Medicine at the University of California, where he did research on the biochemistry of human emotions.

Norman Cousins found the flipside through what his doctors saw as a hopeless battle to save his own life. Through his efforts, he helped to highlight the therapeutic effects of positive emotions and the possibilities that this opened up within mainstream medicine. Aside from the discovery of the healing powers of laughter and positive emotions on our health and wellbeing, Cousins also left an important lesson for anyone who finds themselves faced with a pessimistic prognosis, and one that optimists like Mike Jetter instinctively seem to know; that is, although statistical data in the field of medicine might reveal a better understanding of the nature of an illness, we should not allow negative statistics to cloud our expectations of recovery. The one thing that statistics cannot take into account is the circumstances and character of an individual, and success or failure in overcoming any form of adversity is determined more by the individual than any statistic.

Commenting on how the whole experience changed him and of the lessons he had learned from the experience, Norman Cousins wrote: 'I have learned never to under-estimate the capacity of the human mind and body to regenerate – even when the prospects seem most wretched. The life-force may be the least understood force on earth.'

TESTING FOR OPTIMISM

'For myself, I am an optimist – it does not seem to be much use being anything else.'

Winston Churchill, 1874–1965

What makes people like Norman Cousins and Mike Jetter and, for that matter, all the people we encountered in Part One of this book, able to remain so positive in the face of seemingly overwhelming odds? Whatever life throws at them, they have confidence in the future, they expect positive outcomes and, more often than not, they experience positive outcomes. But what makes people optimistic? Is optimism hard-wired into us through our genetic make-up? Is it something that we acquire through our upbringing? More import-antly, in view of how important optimism and positive think-ing is in shaping our lives, and in particular how it can help us overcome problems and find the flipside, even in adversity, we must ask, 'Can we learn to become more optimistic?'

Before we try to answer these questions, it may be inter-esting to test your own levels of optimism and pessimism. Psychology departments in universities all over the world use surprisingly brief and very simple questionnaires to measure optimism. The following questionnaire will give you a better idea of exactly how optimistic or pessimistic you really are.

Before you begin the test, remember that there are no 'right' or 'wrong' answers. Be as honest and accurate as you can when answering every question, and answer according to your own feelings rather than trying to give the answer you think you should give; otherwise it will be a waste of time.

You can mark each question with one of five possible answers, each of which has a numerical value:

Strongly Agree	= 4
Agree	= 3
Neither Disagree nor Agree	= 2
Disagree	= 1
Strongly Disagree	= 0

1. Even when things seem difficult or aren't going my way, I believe that everything tends to work out for the best.
2. I have lots of plans for the future.
3. If ever I get stressed, I generally find it easy to relax and unwind.
4. If something can go wrong, it usually does.
5. I expect more good things than bad things to happen to me.
6. I enjoy spending time with my friends.
7. I am always busy doing things.
8. I normally expect the worst outcome. That way, I am never disappointed.
9. I rarely get upset when something goes wrong.
10. I don't tend to expect good things to happen to me.
11. I don't have much to look forward to in the future.
12. When I wake up in the morning, I am excited about the day ahead.

When you have answered all twelve questions, you should have a figure marked against each question that signifies your answer. Ignore your answers to questions 3, 6, 7 and 9. These have no relevance and were included only to act as distractors and to separate the other questions. Now reverse the figures you gave for questions 4, 8, 10 and 11 (i.e. Strongly Agree would now be '0' and Strongly Disagree would be given a '4'). This is because the questions are negatively phrased. Finally, add up your score, which could be anything between 0 and 32.

WHAT DOES YOUR OPTIMISM SCORE MEAN?

The higher your score is, the more optimistic you would appear to be. It is tempting to assume that out of a possible score of 32, a neutral score would be 16, which would mean that any score higher than 16 would suggest optimism and any score lower than that would lean towards pessimism. But average scores for similar tests have been found to vary according to the type of people being tested. That said, as an interesting guide, it is safe to say that a score higher than 20 shows strong optimism and any score over 28 would indicate extreme optimism, whereas a score lower than 12 would suggest a pessimistic outlook and a score of 6 or less would indicate extreme pessimism.

From what we learned in Part One about the impact of optimism on our lives, you may be pleasantly encouraged if your test score was higher than twenty, or you may be feeling a bit disappointed if your score was on the low side. However, this is only a crude indication of how optimistic you may or may not be today. Tomorrow is another day, and as we shall see, optimism is not necessarily something that is set for life. Like everything else in the world, it can and does change, and the most exciting thing about it is this: you can change it.

WHERE DOES OPTIMISM COME FROM?

Many psychologists used to believe (some still do) that optimism is largely 'dispositional'. It is predetermined, a genetic characteristic or something that we acquire (or not) during infancy. One study that looked at same-sex middle-aged Swedish twins found that genetic factors may account for up to 25 per cent of our feelings of optimism. This still suggests that there are other more dominant influences that shape our feelings of optimism.

Some researchers believe that optimism is largely formed during early childhood. For example, researchers at the Department of Psychology in the University of Helsinki found that our levels of optimism are influenced between the ages of three and six. They also discovered that the person most responsible for influencing how optimistic we become is our mother.

Studies have shown that if a mother perceives her child to have a difficult temperament (i.e. that the child is difficult to control), she will invariably adopt what they call 'hostile' child-rearing attitudes, and those attitudes are thought to influence how optimistic a child will become, even into adulthood.

Following up twenty years after initial surveys of mothers and their children, researchers found that people who were perceived as difficult by their mothers when they were infants, invariably grew up to become pessimists as adults. As a father myself, this concerned me. Why should I not have the same influence over my children as my wife? The answer, I believe, is most probably due to the fact that, traditionally, infants spend a lot more time with their mother than their father. There are other studies that share the blame (or credit) between both parents. Their findings suggest that warmth, acceptance, sensitivity and responsiveness (or lack thereof) from both parents towards their children may be responsible for a child growing up to become an optimist or pessimist. Presumably, the discovery of a father's influence is due to the growing trend in Western societies for both parents to go out to work and share time looking after the children.

However, while it is evident that our past largely determines the person we have become, who we were in the past and who we are in the present does not necessarily predict the person we will become in the future. 'Change is possible,' says Professor Carver, one of the leading optimism researchers, and many prominent psychologists agree. There is a compelling argument to support the view that we can all learn how to be more optimistic.

LEARNED HELPLESSNESS

Martin Seligman is one of the most renowned psychologists in the USA today. In 1998 he was elected President of the American Psychological Association (APA) by the widest margin in its history, and a review of psychology literature found that, throughout the last century, Seligman was the thirteenth most frequently cited psychologist in introductory psychology textbooks. He is currently one of the world's leading authorities on Positive Psychology and Optimism, but the area of study for which Seligman became renowned was the complete opposite; it was a theory he developed which explained how and why people come to believe that they are powerless.

Seligman demonstrated that people can be broken down by repeated experiences to the point of extreme pessimism. So convincing were Seligman's experiments that he was invited to give a presentation of his findings to the CIA and, according to some reports, the CIA referred to Seligman's research models in developing interrogation techniques. Seligman called his theory, 'Learned Helplessness'.

Learned Helplessness is a psychological condition which can affect people and animals. It is a tendency to interpret past experiences in such a way that when a similar situation arises, you believe yourself to be powerless to do anything about it. You 'know' that any effort is futile because past experiences taught you that you were powerless to influence change. Nothing you did in the past made any difference. You are convinced that you are helpless, so you don't even bother trying to help yourself.

Seligman arrived at his theory back in 1967 while observing dogs in laboratory settings. The dogs were separated into three groups; the dogs in group one were simply put in the harnesses for a period of time and later released. The dogs in groups two and three were subjected to electric shocks, the difference being that the dogs in the second group could end the shocks by pressing a lever (which they learned to do), whereas when the dogs in the third group pressed the lever, nothing changed. For them, the shocks were random and inescapable.

Seligman found that the dogs in groups one and two recovered quickly from the experiment, but the dogs in group three exhibited symptoms of clinical depression. In the second part of the experiment, the dogs were once again subjected to electric shocks, but this time they could escape the pain by jumping over a low partition. The dogs in groups one and two jumped over the wall and ended their pain, but most of the dogs in group three wouldn't try anything. They had learned through the first part of the experiment that they were powerless, so they didn't try to escape. They became victims of the scientist's torture, and having previously learned that they were powerless to change anything, they just lay down and whined.

However, in all of Seligman's experiments with dogs in the latter 1960s, not all of the dogs in group three became helpless. Seligman observed that about one-third of the dogs did not give up. Somehow, they had found the strength within themselves to continue to search for ways to end their pain in spite of the fact that they had been powerless to affect it in the previous tests. In later, less distasteful or morally questionable experiments that were conducted with humans, Seligman discovered that about one-third of humans also seem to be able to protect themselves from becoming helpless. They continue to try regardless of repeated failures and setbacks. The remaining two-thirds of the population are vulnerable to failure. Through bitter life experiences, most people will learn to feel powerless. They will believe that they have no control over their lives. This feeling of helplessness, Seligman found, is associated with depression and suicidal tendencies, and it also adversely affects our immune systems. Evidence suggests that those people who become helpless rarely find the flipside to their adversities.

LEARNED OPTIMISM

'In order to change your world, you must believe that life doesn't happen to you; you happen to life. You are not a piece of laundry flapping in the breeze. You have to choose to be the cause rather than the effect. You have to decide to make something happen.'

Daniel R. Castro, *Critical Choices That Change Lives*

The flipside of these findings was the realization that if helplessness is learned, it may be unlearned. If people learned to feel powerless, Seligman reasoned, they could also learn to feel empowered. This led to the much more positive discovery that Seligman called 'Learned Optimism'. According to Seligman, everyone has their own 'explanatory style', which is essentially the way that we interpret the meaning of our life experiences. Pessimists feel victimized by events and powerless to change anything, whereas optimists feel that they can make a difference, they are confident that they can influence their own destiny. They believe they can have an impact on the events around them, and do not see themselves as victims of circumstances. Optimists find ways of reinterpreting negative experiences in a way that helps them to move on, to learn and grow from the experience; pessimists will, if allowed, just like the poor dogs in Seligman's experiments, lie down and whine.

Seligman found that an optimistic explanatory style has a positive impact on our health and guards against feelings of helplessness and depression. This is something other scientists have also discovered as mentioned in Part One. However, Seligman's real contribution was his discovery that optimism is not something stable and fixed. He has shown that while a person's 'explanatory style' may be formed at birth or during infancy, it can change; we can learn to be optimistic.

People who are optimists have a fundamentally different belief system and approach to life than everyone else. They believe with conviction that their lives are not controlled by fate. Optimists take responsibility for their future. This is why they tend to act and respond differently to difficult or adverse situations to other people, and why ultimately they invariably find the flipside when faced with problems or setbacks.

For example, Seligman discovered that optimists cultivate healthy lifestyles and seek diagnoses and explore available treatments when they are unwell, rather than sit back and just follow their doctor's orders. Optimists take steps to avoid dangerous or negative situations and, when something does go wrong, they take whatever action they can to remedy it. Their confidence in the future ensures that they don't give up easily. They keep trying, even when times are difficult. If a problem can't be solved, optimists instinctively reframe the situation to enable them to get the best possible outcome; they make plans for the future and they set themselves personal and career goals.

Optimists tend to act from knowledge. They research situations and accumulate information to help them make the most appropriate decisions, and this forms the basis for whatever action they take. They are active in pursuing their dreams, rather than sitting by as a passive observer allowing life to happen to them, as pessimists are prone to do.

Optimists also tend to seek and maintain strong social networks, which is an issue that arises time and again in people's stories of the flipside. Almost without exception, people credit the people closest to them – their friends and family – with helping them get through the most challenging times of their lives.

Strategies of optimists and pessimists

Expects positive outcomes	Expects negative outcomes
Accepts responsibility for life	Absolves responsibility and seeks blame
Believes in personal power	Believes in fate or God's Will
When faced with problems or difficulties, looks for solutions	When faced with problems or difficulties, complains
Focuses on the future	Dwells on the past
Develops abilities	Grieves about lack of ability
Pursues specific goals and dreams	Drifts aimlessly through life
Looks for opportunities in problems	Only sees difficulties and problems
Has strong, supportive social networks	Social network contains people who compound negativity
Persists after failure	Quits after first signs of failure

Professor Charles Carver believes that 'Cognitive Behavioural Therapy' (CBT) is one way through which people can be helped to become more optimistic. CBT is an umbrella term for a number of psychotherapies that attempt to guide a person to change their thought processes and beliefs and thereby, it is argued, help to change the way that they feel about themselves. It is not an overnight process but, in many cases, it does work. But outside CBT, there are several other ways through which optimism can be acquired.

THE SCIENCE OF MODELLING

Identifying some of the strategies optimists use is absolutely crucial if we are to learn how to become more optimistic ourselves, and to find the flipside in our own lives. If we can understand their beliefs and learn their behaviours, or as Neuro Linguistic Programming (NLP) practitioners say, 'model them', then we should start to experience the same results.

Modelling is a technique that is commonly used in NLP. It is a system designed to replicate the results achieved by other people, in any area of life. Essentially it is a form of accelerated learning that is achieved by adopting someone else's behaviours and mimicking their beliefs. Obviously, allowance has to be made for any physical or physiological differences; a man who is two feet smaller than Michael Jordan would not be able to replicate Jordan's play on a basketball court. Similarly, a woman who suffers from diabetes wouldn't be able to expect the same improvement in her health by copying the exercise and dietary regimes of a woman with a healthy pancreas. But, subject to known physical and physiological differences, copying other people's beliefs and actions should produce the same or similar results that they achieve in their lives.

NLP guru and bestselling author Tony Robbins has proved the efficacy of modelling in a number of different settings. In one interview with CNN he cited a situation where he challenged the US Army to give him any training programme, and he would cut the training time in half and, at the same time, increase the competency of soldiers who went through the programme.

The US Army accepted the challenge and gave Robbins the task of improving their pistol shooting training course. The Army had developed its own four-day programme and, according to its own records, 70 per cent of soldiers passed the final competency test. If Robbins could cut the training time to two days and increase the competency levels of the soldiers above 70 per cent, he would be paid. Anything less and he would get nothing.

Robbins knew nothing whatsoever about pistol shooting. In fact, prior to this challenge he had never picked up a gun. But his lack of knowledge and experience were irrelevant. He would learn all that he needed to know by interviewing the best pistol shooters in the Army. 'I got the best shooters in the world, and I had them come and fire, and I'd stop them at each step,' he explained. 'What are you doing in your mind? What are you doing physically? And I saw what they did in common. They didn't even realize what they were doing.' Then Robbins compared their behaviours with soldiers who were poor shots. 'The differences were obvious,' he said. 'Success leaves clues.'

Robbins then developed a pistol shooting course which was based upon the critical beliefs and behaviours of the best pistol shooters rather than standard textbook instruction. His course took just one day to complete and, for the first time in the history of pistol shooting training in the Army, every soldier who went through the programme passed the competency test. It was a massive improvement from the Army's original course.

Modelling can be used for anything we need to learn and is one of the key components of NLP. It has been successfully used to help people achieve better results in sport, in business and in personal relationships. By modelling people who are extreme optimists, the naturally pessimistic person can quickly learn to become more optimistic themselves and achieve much the same results in their lives. If we identify optimists' thought processes and behaviours, elicit their strategies and notice how they respond in times of difficulty, we can gain an insight into exactly what it is that enables people to find the flipside.

Suzanne Segerstrom, is an Associate Professor in the Psychology Department at the University of Kentucky and a highly respected researcher in this field. She also believes that optimism is a highly malleable characteristic. In a ten-year study, Segerstrom demonstrated that optimism is influenced by changes in our resources as well as our experiences. She also contends that these changes can, and do, occur through adulthood. For example, in one study focusing on women, it was found that as problems at work and with their spouses increased, the women's optimism decreased.

Furthermore, Dr Segerstrom states that there is evidence demonstrating that our states of optimism can change 'over fairly short periods of time – weeks to months'. She also confirms that change in a person's optimism is closely related to change in their mental and physical health. 'Optimists are both psychologically and physiologically healthier,' she says. Clearly, there are very good reasons for trying to consciously work towards becoming more optimistic.

In her book *Breaking Murphy's Law*, Dr Segerstrom provides alternative suggestions to encourage optimism other than through CBT. She contends that if we focus on our actions, literally follow in the footsteps of optimistic people by acting optimistically and positively, our thoughts and beliefs will follow. This supports the NLP technique of modelling.

For example, according to NLP theory, people who feel depressed adopt a specific physiology and posture. Their back slumps, their shoulders drop, their head looks down, their breathing becomes shallow and they talk in a tired, monotone voice. Conversely, sitting or standing upright, with head held high, shoulders back and breathing deeply makes it very difficult to feel depressed. The physiology and posture of the body influences our thoughts and emotions.

What NLP practitioners and Dr Segerstrom are saying is that when we act 'as if' we are optimistic, for example, by looking for benefits and opportunities, and persisting even after repeated failure, we will tend to experience the same results as optimists and then we will start to feel optimistic.

FEEDING THE OPTIMIST WITHIN

A Native American Indian once described his inner struggle. He said that he felt as if there were two dogs inside him, one a pessimist and the other an optimist. 'The pessimist is always fighting the optimist,' he said. When asked which dog wins, he thought for a moment and then replied, 'The one I decide to feed.' Peter Schulman, Research Manager at the University of Pennsylvia's Department of Psychology, understands more than most the challenges of staying optimistic. 'Even the diehard optimist will occasionally have pessimistic beliefs when exposed to extreme or prolonged stress,' he says. It seems we all have a pessimist and an optimist inside us, and which one comes through on any given day will be the one we decide to feed.

Twenty healthy men and women whose average age is thirty-three are watching the opening scene in the film *Saving Private Ryan*. It is an intense, very stressful twenty-four minutes following a group of soldiers on the morning of the 6 June 1944 in what became known as the Normandy

Landings. In the largest invasion made on a single day ever witnessed in any war, 130,000 allied troops stormed the Normandy beaches in the face of hostile enemy artillery. The opening scene of the film is notable for the way in which it involves the audience in its realism. The way it depicts the graphic horrors of war is compelling, but at times, very difficult to watch. What the audience is unaware of is that while they are watching, biochemical and hormonal changes are taking place in all of them. Even those members of the audience who had seen the film before are affected. Average blood flow through their veins and arteries is restricted by as much as 35 per cent.

Forty-eight hours later the same audience is shown a fifteen-minute segment of *Kingpin*, a light-hearted comedy film. This time blood flow was improved by 22 per cent, endorphins are released and the aerobic activity caused by laughing is found to be very similar to the benefits experienced when doing physical exercise. Further confirmation that Norman Cousins had come across a huge medical breakthrough when he noticed that laughter relieved his pain.

The biochemical changes that take place in the film audiences show how easily our bodies are influenced by what is going on around us. Professor Dan Ariely has shown in his work at Duke University that our thoughts and expectations are even affected by what we read. He found, for example, that by adding specific emotive words to a wordsearch task given to a group of students, he could influence the thoughts and actions of the students. One group of students were given wordsearch tasks that included the words *aggressive*, *rude*, *annoying* and *intrude*, and another group were given a task involving words such as *considerate*, *polite* and *sensitive*. The students were then told to go to another room and report to a clinician. When they arrived, the clinician (who was a confederate of the researchers) was engaged in a conversation with an associate. The students who had been primed with the polite words waited, on average, 9.3 minutes before they finally interrupted the clinician, whereas the students who had been primed with the aggressive words waited just 5.5 minutes before they butted in.

Similar studies showed the same results; words included in a questionnaire that conveyed the concept of being elderly or old actually affected the students' physical demeanour. Students who were given questionnaires that included words associated with the elderly such as *Florida*, *bingo* and *ancient* would amble out of the test room and down the corridor at a walking speed that resembled an elderly, frail person, considerably slower than a control group of students. My favourite of Professor Ariely's experiments in this field, was that related to honesty. Students were asked to write down the ten commandments prior to taking a simple maths test and then given an opportunity to cheat (by self-marking their test). It turned out that just reminding the students of the ten commandments had a demonstrable effect on their behaviour; their behaviour was significantly more honest than that of a control group.

What Professor Ariely brilliantly demonstrates in his experiments is how easily influenced we all are by the things that go on around us. His work shows that often our decisions and actions are completely irrational (in that they are rarely the result of conscious logic and sound reasoning) but, at the same time, they are very predictable. However, what Ariely also teaches is that by understanding how our thoughts and feelings are impacted by the things that we see and hear, we can begin to use these manifestations to our advantage. In much the same way that Norman Cousins boosted his immune system, improved blood flow and controlled his pain by watching funny videos, by being more discerning about what we watch on TV, what we read and who we associate with, we can start to influence our thoughts and feelings. If we can create stress through a film, and affect honesty, politeness and the feeling of strength and power simply through words, then surely we can use the same methods to raise our expectations and learn to become more optimistic.

We have seen that optimism is a vital component in overcoming any difficulty or setback. Optimists win hands down in virtually every aspect of life. But feelings of optimism can be changed, and there are a variety of ways through which we can learn to become more optimistic. CBT, modelling, acting as if we were optimistic and controlling our environment and, in particular, what we feed our minds are just a few examples of ways through which we can escape pessimism and learn to expect and experience a brighter future. This is the first step on the pathway to the flipside.

CHAPTER 9

THE ENTREPRENEUR'S MINDSET: LOOKING FOR HIDDEN OPPORTUNITIES

'The entrepreneur in us sees opportunities everywhere
we look, but many people see only problems.'

Michael Gerber

Oklahoma, USA, 1936: Sylvan Goldman, part owner of the
Humpty Dumpty supermarket chain, is working late in his
office. He stares ahead looking at a chair, his mind focused on
a problem. Like all businesses before and since, Goldman
needs to increase sales. Supermarkets rely on volume, a rapid
turnover of relatively low-priced items, in order to maximize
their profits. This can be achieved only by either increasing
the number of customers that walk through the stores, or by
increasing the number of items sold to each customer.
Goldman was focused on the latter option, which was where
his problem lay.

Goldman knew that his customers would buy more items
from his stores, and he was aware that they wanted to buy the
more expensive, larger and heavier items. But his problem

was this: there is only so much that a customer could physically carry in the wicker shopping baskets that the supermarkets provided. It was a problem shared by his competitors as well, and this was why Goldman stayed behind in his office working late into the evening. It was a problem he was determined to solve because he understood something that others didn't: this was an incredible opportunity.

Goldman had been faced with problems before. In 1921 he and his brother lost their wholesale business when oil prices slumped. The two then considered the retailing business and moved to California to learn about new methods for retailing groceries. They recognized that the future of the grocery business held great promise. Goldman noted, 'The wonderful thing about food is that everyone uses it – and uses it only once.' In many ways, it is the perfect business; everyone has to eat, and consumable products require ongoing repeat sales.

The two brothers came back from California enthused and set up a chain of self-service grocery stores. Within a few years they sold out to Safeway, but their success was short-lived. The lion's share of their payout came in the form of shares in Safeway, the value of which was completely wiped out during the Great Depression that hit America in October 1929. Over $10 billion was wiped out on the New York Stock Exchange. A lot of people, including Goldman, lost everything. But, while others sunk into a personal depression or threw themselves out of windows, Sylvan Goldman would not be beaten because he understood that, even in crisis, there would be a flipside.

Being wiped out financially and with their only asset being their expertise, the Goldman brothers went back to work in the grocery business, and by 1936 they had acquired half of the Humpty Dumpty supermarket chain. More significantly, they were on the verge of uncovering an opportunity that would change their lives for ever and cause a revolution in the supermarket industry. But, just as Harland Sanders had to lose everything in order to create the KFC empire, it is far from certain whether Sylvan Goldman would have re-entered the grocery business had he not been financially wiped out during the Great Depression. And had he not been in the grocery business, it is even more unlikely that he would have made the discovery that would become his greatest achievement.

It began to dawn on Goldman as he sat alone in his office late that evening in 1936, pondering over the problem that had been troubling him for some time. What could he do that would enable his customers to buy more than they could carry in a wicker basket? The answer came to him as he sat idly staring at a folding, wooden chair. He ruminated over the possibility – put wheels on the legs, the shopping basket in the seat, change the frame from wood to metal . . . and the concept of the shopping cart was born.

Goldman worked on the idea with a friend, an engineer called Fred Young, and the following year, the two of them created the world's first shopping cart consisting of a metal frame that held two wire baskets. The frames were designed to be folded and the baskets stacked. Essentially, they were folding metal frames with handles and wheels. Customers could place hand-held baskets on the carriers, and take them off again at checkout. As the idea was inspired by a folding chair, Goldman called his carts 'folding basket carriers' and formed the Folding Carrier Basket Company.

Initially, customers didn't want to use the carts. Young men thought that the shopping carts made them look weak, young women felt the carts were unfashionable and older people were worried that the carts made them appear helpless. But Goldman had realized that his biggest problem was also his greatest opportunity. If he could overcome these image concerns, his shopping carts could revolutionize the retail industry.

Changing customers' perceptions of the carts turned out to

be relatively simple. Goldman hired models of all ages and both sexes to push shopping carts around the store, pretending that they were shopping. In addition, he had attractive store greeters at the entrance to every store, encouraging customers to use the shopping carts. These two strategies did the trick. The following year, Goldman and Young obtained a patent for their invention, and by the 1940s the shopping cart was seen in supermarkets across America. In fact, most supermarkets were completely redesigned from the entrance through to the aisles, the checkout counters and exit, so as to accommodate the use of the shopping cart.

Sylvan Goldman changed the face of supermarkets all over the world and in doing so turned both himself and Fred Young into millionaires. His success, like most successes, had come from a hidden opportunity contained within a problem.

A DIFFERENT WAY OF SEEING

'Some men see things as they are and say why – I dream things that never were and say why not.'

George Bernard Shaw

Sylvan Goldman's achievements were the result of a very specific mindset. It is a mindset shared by inventors and entrepreneurs who look upon problems not as obstacles, but as opportunities. All invention and innovation, as we shall see throughout this book, is the result of confronting a problem. This is why inventors and entrepreneurs welcome problems instead of trying to avoid them as people generally do. They become excited rather than frustrated by problems, because they know that every problem, no matter how big or small, contains an opportunity, and the larger the problem that they encounter, the larger the opportunity that lies within it.

Louis' problem was far more serious than Sylvan Goldman's. Louis was blind. The year was 1814 and Louis was just four years old. The previous year an accident in his father's harness and saddle workshop cost him the sight in his left eye, but not long after, sympathetic ophthalmia, a common phenomenon in which both eyes become inflamed following trauma to one, left Louis completely blind in both eyes. Louis was faced with the prospect of having to live in darkness for the rest of his life.

At the age of ten, Louis was sent to study at the Royal Institute for Blind Youth in Paris, France. In the early nineteenth century it was commonly accepted that blind people would never be able to read or write, and so the institute taught the students basic craftsmens' skills and simple trades. The school did teach the children to feel raised letters, a system devised by the school's founder Valentin Haüy, but this was cumbersome and difficult. Louis believed that there had to be a better system and made it his goal to develop one.

Louis was a bright and creative student, and became a talented cellist and organist in his time at the institute, playing the organ for churches all over France. But his main focus was his dream of developing a better system for blind people to read and write. From the age of twelve, he experimented with codes, using a knitting needle to punch holes in paper to represent letters, and by the age of fifteen, he had developed an ingenious system of sightless reading and writing by means of feeling raised dots. Two years later he adapted his method to musical notation. Louis used a pattern of just six raised dots in varying combinations to represent letters, numbers, punctuation marks and mathematical symbols. He showed his method to his classmates who liked it and began using it, in spite of the fact that the governors of the institute had decided to ban it.

By the time he reached seventeen years of age, Louis graduated and became an assistant teacher at the institute and two years later he accepted a full-time teaching position there. Yet he still had to teach his method secretly to the students.

The first book using Louis' system was published in 1827 under the title *Method of Writing Words, Music, and Plain Songs by Means of Dots, for Use by the Blind and Arranged for Them.* After some slight modifications, by 1834 it reached a form that has remained to this day. It is the system which is commonly known by Louis' surname – 'Braille'.

In 1839 Louis Braille published full details of the method he had developed for communication with sighted people, using patterns of dots to approximate the shape of printed symbols. Together with his friend Pierre Foucault, Louis went on to develop a machine to speed up the somewhat cumbersome system.

Louis died of tuberculosis in Paris in 1852 at just forty-three years of age. He never received the accolades that he deserved during his lifetime. Although he was admired and respected by his students, his Braille system was never taught at the institute during his lifetime, and when he died, not a single newspaper in all of Paris contained news of his death, let alone an obituary.

However, six months after his death, the Royal Institute for Blind Youth officially adopted Louis' six-dot method, and by 1868 his raised six-dot system became the worldwide standard, helping the blind read books, clocks, wristwatches, thermometers, sheet music and even elevator buttons.

In 1952, on the centenary of his death, newspapers everywhere printed his story. His portrait appeared on postage stamps, and his home is now a museum. In his honour, the French government moved his remains to the Pantheon in Paris. There Louis Braille was laid to rest with other great French heroes.

Louis devoted his life in selfless service to his pupils, to his friends, but most of all, to the perfection of his raised dot method which has enabled millions of blind people to read and write, and achieve a better life. Today, Braille has been adapted to almost every major national language and is the primary system of written communication for visually impaired people around the world. The name of Braille will always remain associated with one of the greatest and most beneficent devices ever invented, and like all great inventions it began with one person who had a problem.

CORRECTING ERRORS

'A man's errors are his portals of discovery.'

James Joyce

Bette Nesmith Graham had all of the problems one would expect of a single mother in the 1950s. To support herself and her son Michael she worked as a secretary in a bank and had been promoted to Executive Secretary, the highest position available to women in the banking industry at that time. However, Mrs Graham had one major problem – she was not a particularly good typist, and had to spend long hours retyping documents on new pieces of paper.

Mrs Graham wasn't the only secretary who was continually frustrated at having to completely retype documents due to simple typographical mistakes, and it wasn't long before she realized that her biggest problem was, in fact, her greatest opportunity. It came to her one night as she was walking home from work. She noticed billboard painters painting over their mistakes and that was the moment the idea came to her. She reasoned to herself, 'If those artists can paint over their mistakes, why can't typists?'

The benefits were obvious; if there was a way to enable a typist to 'paint' over their typing errors, businesses would be able to make huge savings not only by greatly reducing the amount of wasted paper but also, and more importantly, their secretarial staff would save an enormous amount of time that they were having to spend retyping entire documents due to small typing errors.

Mrs Graham's solution was to mix some water-based tempera paint in her blender, so it would match the colour of the paper she was using. Then, using a small paintbrush, she was able to simply paint over typing errors, leave the paper to dry, and then retype over the paint. She tried out the mixture at work and her boss never noticed. However, there was one small issue with the mixture: it took a long time to dry. She consulted a high school science teacher and a supply company for help in changing the mixture (which she originally called 'Mistake Out') so that it became a quick-drying solution.

It wasn't long before other secretaries noticed and begged Mrs Graham for some of her solution. As it gained popularity, orders poured in, and she used her son and his friends to help her label and fill little green bottles with her solution. However, she was soon to face another problem: she was fired by the bank for using its stationery to promote her 'Liquid Paper'. That problem, like her original one, also contained an opportunity because it meant she could now devote all of her time to marketing and selling her invention.

Business soared and Mrs Graham went on to buy her own small factory, hire staff and install machinery to automate production. In 1975, Bette Nesmith Graham decided to sell the rights to her invention to the Gillette Company. The problem that Mrs Graham had struggled with at work twenty-two years earlier had transformed her life and turned into a cash payout of $25 million.

LOOKING FOR OPPORTUNITIES

'Innovation is the specific tool of entrepreneurs, the means by which they exploit change as an opportunity.'

Peter F. Drucker

The exact same problem that faced Sylvan Goldman in 1936 confronted thousands of other supermarket owners throughout the world at that time. What enabled Goldman to find an opportunity that thousands of others missed? Likewise, virtually every secretary in the Western world in 1946 was frustrated by the same problem that frustrated Bette Nesmith Graham. Yet despite having no obvious advantages, Mrs Graham found an opportunity that no-one else saw. And, of course, Louis Braille was just one of thousands of other blind children having to make their way in a sighted world, and even though he was just a teenager, he developed a system that enabled blind people to read and write.

The problems that we all face, more often than not, are the same problems that other people face or have faced, and the opportunities that are hidden within each problem are there for everyone to find. That Sylvan Goldman, Louis Braille and Bette Graham were able to achieve what they did was due, in no small part, to the fact that they approached their problems with a specific mindset. It is a mindset which is no longer spoken of in some schools where fear of failure and rejection has brought about policies of non-competition. And it is a mindset that is scorned and increasingly ignored by people in the blame-and-compensate culture in which we live. But it is a mindset without which we can never find the flipside. It is the mindset of an entrepreneur.

Ted Turner once quipped, 'My son is now an "entrepreneur". That's what you're called when you don't have a job.' He is right, of course. Most entrepreneurs do not have jobs. More often than not, they create jobs, but they don't have jobs, because the entrepreneur mindset is completely different to an employee mindset. Entrepreneurs like to be in control of their destiny, and they accept responsibility for their future. They are the visionaries and dreamers who, just like inventors, can change the world.

When Martin Varsavsky was about to graduate from Columbia University with an MBA in 1984, he was, unlike many of his peers, still without a job. Looking back, he believes that his fruitless job search was the best thing that ever happened to him and reviewing his CV, it would be hard to disagree. In the twenty years following his graduation, Varsavsky founded seven highly profitable companies, and received various honours and rewards, among them European Telecommunications Entrepreneur of the Year in 1998, ECTA's European Entrepreneur of the Year in 1999, Global Leader for Tomorrow by the World Economic Forum in Davos, 2000, Spanish Entrepreneur of the Year in 2000 and the Pickering Prize from Columbia University in 2004.

Varsavsky is also an entertaining and irreverent speaker. He likes to recall how he received the funding for his first venture. At the same time as one bank was rejecting his application for a job, a different department in the same bank was approving him for a $12 million business loan! 'People [on the hiring committee] didn't know that there was another group at that time who was actually looking at my loan application for my first business,' said Varsavsky. 'And the same people who wouldn't give me a $40,000-a-year job gave me a $12 million loan . . . Fortunately, they never found out because these banks are really big and nobody ever talks to each other!'

Receiving rejections on his job applications never really worried Martin Varsavsky. When asked at each interview, 'Where do you see yourself in five years?' he gave the same reply: 'Well, as your boss!' But the reason that he never feared repeated rejection was that he always had the mindset of an entrepreneur. 'Entrepreneurs, many times, like myself,' he said, 'are people who couldn't get a job. We're misfits . . . We hate jobs,' he said.

The one thing that distinguishes them from everyone else is that entrepreneurs live their lives on the flipside. They look for opportunities in everything. When NBC cancelled a TV series called *Baywatch* after only one season due to the high costs of production and low ratings, David Hasselhoff, one of the show's stars, saw an opportunity. The show revolved around a team of lifeguards who patrol the beaches in Los Angeles, California, and Hasselhoff instinctively felt that the show had huge potential. He revived the show, investing his own money and proceeded to syndicate the first series. The second series proved Hasselhoff's instincts had been right. The show went on to run for a further ten years and, according to the *Guinness Book of Records*, *Baywatch* became the most watched TV show of all time, topping over a billion viewers. David Hasselhoff is commonly known for his acting and, in some European countries, for his music. Other than his success with *Baywatch*, he starred in *Knight Rider*. In a show that ran on NBC from 1982–6, Hasselhoff played a character called Michael Knight, a high-tech modern-day knight fighting crime with the help of a sentient 'talking car' that had artificial intelligence. However, what many people don't often realize is that David Hasselhoff is an extremely successful entrepreneur.

One man more than any other changed the entertainment industry in America in the twentieth century. He has been referred to as 'the most significant figure in graphic arts since Leonardo Da Vinci', and he received more than 950 honours and awards in his lifetime from countries all over the world, including twenty-six Oscars, a record that stands to this day. Yet, his success was the product not so much of his artistic skills (the drawing for which he is most famous was not his creation) but more the product of his entrepreneurial skills, or more specifically, his ability to turn any setback into a new opportunity. His name was Walt Disney.

As you enter the gates of The Magic Kingdom, Disney-land Florida, the first thing you see is a bronze statue of Walt Disney, a friendly man with slicked back hair and a trimmed moustache, holding hands with Mickey Mouse. Certainly it was that lovable mouse that was responsible for launching Disney's successful enterprise in cartoon picture movies. However, Mickey Mouse was actually created by one of Disney's oldest friends and former partners, Ub Iwerks.

That Mickey Mouse was created at all was due to a contractual problem involving Disney, Winkler Pictures and Universal Studios. In 1927 Oswald the Lucky Rabbit, a cartoon character also created by Iwerks, had enjoyed a successful run in theatres. Charles Mintz took control of Winkler Pictures after marrying Margaret Winkler and commissioned a new series for the character Oswald. However, when Disney went to negotiate a higher fee, he discovered that Mintz was unaccommodating. It transpired that, behind Disney's back, Mintz had hired most of Disney's staff. He had learned that it was Universal and not Disney that owned the rights to the Oswald character, and Mintz had Disney over a barrel. He demanded Disney go on his payroll and accept a lower fee or he would get the pictures produced himself.

Disney was furious, but would not be bullied. The setback taught him perhaps the most important lesson of his career; he would always control the rights of all the cartoon characters he commissioned. He decided that the loss of Oswald the Lucky Rabbit was an opportunity to create something new, and asked Iwerks to come up with an alternative cartoon character. After a string of ideas including Clarabelle Cow and Horace Horse as well as frogs, dogs and cats, Iwerks came up with the idea of Mickey Mouse and on 18 November 1928, the first Mickey Mouse animated film, *Steamboat Willie*, was produced. The first few Mickey Mouse adventures were animated almost entirely by Iwerks, but then he and Disney parted company. Iwerks was reportedly unhappy with Disney's harsh work demands and the lack of credit he was being given. However, Disney owned the rights to Mickey Mouse and brought in a team of young, talented artists to help him develop what has become the most well-known cartoon character of all time, recognized by children and adults all over the world.

From Mickey Mouse, Walt Disney changed the entertainment industry in North America and arguably throughout most of the world. Today, the Walt Disney Company has annual revenues in excess of $35 billion, larger than the gross domestic product of many countries. Yet it was all triggered by a setback that Disney turned into an opportunity.

COFFEE BURNS

Clare Newton was one of thousands of commuters heading to work when it happened. She was a forty-two-year-old packaging designer from Hackney, East London, and had just stopped off to purchase a takeway cup of cappuccino. Struggling to carry her bags and the hot drink, she slipped and burned her arm all the way to her elbow. It was an accident that would change her life.

Clare could have considered suing the outlet that sold the cappuccino to her. She certainly wouldn't have been the first to seek compensation after spilling a cup of hot coffee. But instead of feeling sorry for herself or consulting a personal injury lawyer, Clare did something that is common to virtually every person who has achieved lasting happiness and success in life – she looked for the flipside.

After her accident, as she was sitting with an ice pack against her skin, Clare became aware of something that none of the thousands of other people who had ever suffered burns while carrying a hot takeaway coffee had noticed. The accident had presented a huge and very exciting opportunity.

Clare explains that, while she had been nursing her injury, it occurred to her that 'many people buy coffee when they're laden down with bags and risk burning themselves . . . I decided to find a solution.' She began thinking of ways to minimize that risk and set about creating a product that would make it easier and safer for people to carry a hot drink, even when they were carrying other baggage.

Clare came up with a simple, yet brilliant, design called 'Cups Carrier' which allows a user to hold a cup in three different ways: via a handle at the side or the top, or by forming a cradle to support the cup which also acts as a desk stand for it.

'I remember one day I went to a meeting and my clients' jaws dropped open when they saw the cup carrier,' Clare says. 'I was loaded down with my portfolio, briefcase, umbrella and handbag but had the two coffees balanced just on the end of my little finger in the double carrier. They were amazed.'

Clare registered her design which went on to win her the British Female Inventor of the Year award in 2001, an award supported by the British Patent Office. The key to Clare's success lay in her understanding that her accident exposed a need for an easy and safe way to carry hot takeaway coffee while carrying other things on the way to work. By focusing on that need and looking for solutions, Clare was able to find the flipside.

Entrepreneurs cultivate the habit of always looking for opportunities. Whenever there is change, whenever they notice a problem or an obstacle, they get excited rather than frustrated because they know that problems and obstacles expose needs. Entrepreneurs understand that the single most critical factor that will predict the success of any business is the size of the problem it aims to solve or the significance of the need it seeks to fulfil.

For any business to be successful, it needs to be able to offer a solution to a problem and thereby fulfil a need. Thomas Edison, widely acknowledged as one of the greatest inventors in history, based his entire career upon this premise. He explained, 'I never perfected an invention that I did not think about in terms of the service it might give others . . . I find out what the world needs, then I proceed to invent.'

The flipside of any problem or obstacle therefore lies in the need that it exposes. Big problems or obstacles tend to reveal big needs, and they contain big flipsides. This is why entrepreneurs like Sylvan Goldman welcome problems and why inventors like Thomas Edison will actually go out of their way to find problems. A problem, to them, is actually an opportunity in disguise.

THE ENTREPRENEUR WITHIN

Michael Gerber, author of the best-selling book *The E Myth*, believes that there is an entrepreneur, which he defines as a visionary and a creator, in each of us. 'We're all born with that quality,' he says, 'and it defines our lives as we respond to what we see, hear, feel, and experience.' That entrepreneurial spirit within us needs to be nurtured and developed because it determines how we react to life experiences, and ultimately our success and happiness in life.

While we all may have the ability to think and act as an entrepreneur, all too often we don't. One of the reasons might be that at some point in the past we learned to be helpless. Another might be that, in times of difficulty, we simply don't look for opportunities. Of course, this does not refer solely to opportunities to make monetary gain, but to the broader and more significant opportunities such as to learn, to understand, to love, to fulfil one's potential and to make a difference.

More often than not, it takes the mindset of an entrepreneur to find the opportunities that remain hidden to everyone else. To develop that mindset requires that we ask different questions of ourselves, especially in times of difficulty. But, if we can ask the right questions; questions that reframe a problem or setback, the answers will point us in the direction of the flipside.

CHAPTER 10

REFRAMING YOUR LIFE: THE CRITICAL QUESTIONS

'In the final analysis, the questions of why bad things happen to good people transmutes itself into some very different questions, no longer asking why something happened, but asking how we will respond, and what we intend to do now that it has happened.'

Pierre Teilhard de Chardin

WHEN JODI PLISZKA lost all her hair, she was just twenty years old. She is a good-looking, outgoing and vivacious woman today, a little more than twenty years on. However, she admits that when her hair fell out leaving her completely bald, she was absolutely devastated.

Alopecia areata affects nearly one in every sixty women at some point in their lives, and of those almost two-thirds are affected while they are still in their teens. Clumps of hair just fall away from the scalp leaving a smooth, bald patch. It is thought to be the result of a malfunctioning immune system. For some reason, the white blood cells target hair much like a virus and cause it to fall out. Alopecia can come in a number of forms; sometimes only small areas of the hair on the scalp are affected, but in other cases every hair on the body falls away. This is the type of alopecia that Jodi had, and is known as *alopecia universalis*; all her body hair including the eyebrows, eye lashes, even nasal hair, was lost.

As you can imagine, alopecia is a terrible trauma for any woman, young or old, to suffer. The moment of realization when one's hair starts falling out and knowing that it may never grow back, is not something anyone would forget in a hurry. From that moment, life may never be the same. It can feel to the sufferer that their life has been cursed, but like any trauma, it could end up being a blessing.

THE FLIPSIDE OF ALOPECIA

When Jodi Pliszka lost her hair, through *alopecia universalis*, she was twenty years old. Jodi is an attractive lady with a wide, beaming smile and large, sparkling eyes, but she had no aspirations to be a model. Instead, she became a therapist and a volunteer for alopecia support groups as well as cancer societies. 'I found that sharing my experiences in life were always very cathartic,' she said. 'Each time I open up myself . . . I strengthen myself.' However, it was through her daily activities that Jodi found the biggest flipside to her alopecia.

'I am a huge fitness lover,' she said, 'and work out every morning, except Sundays.' She runs, cycles and likes to do short triathlons. She also regularly trains in the martial art Tae Kwon Do, along with her daughter Jessica. Jodi has achieved black belt status and her daughter is currently a blue belt. They enjoy going to the dojo and training together. And, it was while training that Jodi had an idea that would mark a change of life for her as well as for thousands of other people. It was an idea born of a sudden realization that would perhaps only be obvious to someone like Jodi who had to wear a wig.

'I wear my wig while doing Tae Kwon Do,' Jodi says, 'because I like to try and fit in when I am with Jessica.' But, it was while wearing a wig when she trained that Jodi exposed a real problem, and a huge opportunity. 'I got so tired of sweat saturating my wigs and then running into my eyes,' she explains. The more she thought about it, the more she realized that it was a problem that must affect thousands of men and women. So Jodi set out to find a solution and design a product that could help. Initially, she put panty liners under her wigs to catch the perspiration, and although she thought it was a little undignified, it worked. So, Jodi spent the following three years developing a product that would do the same job, but also be more discreet and better suited for people who had to wear wigs.

Jodi called her invention 'Headline It!' and explained that it would help not just alopecia sufferers, but literally anyone who had to wear a wig, hat or baseball cap. In 2006 she entered Headline It! on the TV show *American Inventor*, and beat thousands of other people to reach the final twelve. Her presentation to the panel of judges was more of an impassioned plea than a product pitch because Jodi knew only too well what a difference Headline It! could make not only to alopecia sufferers, but also to cancer patients and anyone who, for whatever reason, had to wear a wig. The publicity from the show gave her a platform for her invention, which has gone from being an idea to a real product that has the potential to make a real difference in so many people's lives all over the world. In addition, Jodi's appearance on *American Inventor* raised the profile of her other work and, perhaps most important of all, it created awareness of the plight of people who suffer from alopecia.

Looking back on her life since the condition struck, she says, 'I lost my hair, and God has taken me on a journey to become a therapist, author, inventor and spokesperson.' She said that she now knows that 'trials create a person's inner being. We have the choice to either be a survivor or a victim . . . I am a survivor.'

In the last paragraph of her book, Jodi Pliszka writes, 'Perhaps losing my hair wasn't the horror I once felt it to be . . . there is no greater gift than in knowing our purpose in life.' This is one of the most significant changes that alopecia brought to Jodi's life, a renewed faith and a feeling of purpose. 'I lived with hair for twenty years,' she says. 'I lived without hair for twenty more. And, I am happy with the distances I've come in my forty years.' The motto that she espouses is a plea to anyone who has lost their hair whether through alopecia, cancer or any other condition; there is life after hair loss!

Jodi's motto underlines an important message. 'There is truly life after all illusions break down,' she says. 'Life after all the fallout of our own misbelief. Life after all the pieces have been shattered, after all the threads have come undone.' It is a message to anyone who has faced any trauma or setback: there is life. After anything that may happen to us and all that we may encounter, there is life.

FATE, KARMA AND GOD

Jodi Pliszka admits that when her hair initially fell out, her anguish and fear bordered on hysteria. 'I cried. I screamed,' she recalls. 'I railed against God . . . then demanded to know "Why me?"' But, as she came to terms with her condition, Jodi found that she was asking different questions, the answers to which led her down new and unexpected paths.

Whenever disaster strikes, the first question we tend to ask is 'Why me?' or 'What did I do to deserve this?' Some people would have you believe that we bring about our own crises. You attracted it in some way (through your thoughts or negative energy), or it is the natural outcome of your karma, the result of something you did or said in the past, or even, according to Hinduism, something that may have happened during a past life. Some are certain that a personal tragedy is divine punishment for our sins, and there are others who believe a trauma is a 'test' from God. If the book of Job is to be believed, God allows tragedies as part of a wager to test our love and devotion to Him.

As with any theological question, there is no rational answer, which is why the final reply given by a priest or rabbi to the difficult questions such as 'Why does God permit evil and suffering?' is: 'We cannot understand why some things happen as they do, because God moves in mysterious ways.' However, whatever our religious beliefs, we cannot escape from the fact that if we expect a world of order, a world of fairness and justice, there will be times when we will be disappointed. Sometimes it appears that we are trapped in a life of chaos, surrounded by random happenings that are unfair and unjust. I believe that there are answers, and those answers are found on the flipside. To find them, we need to ask very different questions.

THE CRITICAL QUESTIONS

In Part One we learned that very little in life is inherently good or bad. Winning the lottery can lead to wretchedness and even death, whereas losing one's business or livelihood can turn out to be the making of a person. What ultimately makes something that happens to us a blessing or a curse is often not the event itself, but how we respond to that event. One thing is certain: we are very unlikely to be able to turn any sort of setback into an opportunity asking futile questions that bring nothing but anguish, like 'Why me?'

The human brain will search and find an answer for any question we ask about any event in our lives. For example, if we ask 'Why did this happen to me?' our brain will start to come up with a variety of possible answers: Because you're clumsy! Because you're stupid! Because you're cursed! Because nothing ever works out for you! Our brains will come up with plenty of possible answers to explain whatever predicament in which we find ourselves. But, what would happen if we trained ourselves to reframe any setbacks by asking different questions? How might our lives change if we got into the habit of asking questions like:

'What is good about this?' or
'What could be good about this?' or
'What can I learn from this that will benefit me as a person?' or
'What can I learn from this that will benefit other people?' or
'What can I do right now to turn this to my advantage?'

BLUE FOCUS

'To solve the problems of today, we must focus on tomorrow.'

Erik Nupponen

A woman sits at a desk. Her eyes are welling up to the point where she can no longer hold back her tears. A man puts his arm around her, to comfort her in her time of grief. One by one, people gather around the woman offering their sympathy and support. For a moment, she is inconsolable. She has just lost £223,000!

To be more accurate, she had actually won £27,000, but in her mind she had lost £223,000. She was on the TV show *Deal Or No Deal* and her plight was witnessed by millions of TV viewers. What had actually happened was that she opened her box at the end of the game to find that she would have won £250,000, but she had chosen to 'deal' earlier in the game and accepted an offer of £27,000!

One would think that if someone is handed a cheque for £27,000, they would be delirious with excitement. But the truth is our emotions are not determined by what happens to us, they are purely the result of what we focus on. One of the characteristics shared by people who have found the flipside is that they have learned how to develop something called 'blue focus'.

Wherever you are sitting, try this simple exercise:

1. Take a good look all around you and try and notice everything that is brown. Really try and memorize everything you see that is brown, whether it be dark or light brown.

2. In a moment, without peeking, close your eyes and try and remember everything you saw . . . that was blue!

Most people are stumped. They are so focused on the brown things that they hardly notice anything that is blue. It is a reflection of what many of us have experienced in our lives, at one time or another. Someone shows us a particular type of car or computer, and then we begin to see it everywhere we go. It was there all the time, but we only noticed it when our mind was focused on it. Similarly, we sometimes allow ourselves to get so focused on the negative things in our lives (the brown) that we don't notice any of the positive things (the blue).

The lady who won £27,000 on *Deal Or No Deal* is a prime example. She was focused on the fact that she had lost an opportunity to win £250,000, instead of the fact that she had won £27,000. People who are able to turn adversity to their advantage, practise 'blue focus'. When faced with difficulties and through times of change, they consciously look for the blue things in their lives. Blue focus means to never look backward, except in so far as one can learn a lesson. It means to always concentrate on looking forward. People with 'blue focus' never dwell on what may have been lost, only on what can be gained. They never think about limitations, only the possibilities. In every experience they are always looking to reframe the situation and actively seek benefits.

THE ART OF REFRAMING

The meaning of any experience in life depends upon our interpretation of it, or as NLP practitioners say, the frame we put around it. Whatever happens to us, we can choose the frame; we can decide to give it a positive meaning. For example, when someone loses a job, they could frame it as a negative reflection of their ability or personality, proof that they failed. They may even convince themselves that they'll never be able to find another job, and if they do, that it will never be as good as the one they lost. Or they could reframe it as an opportunity for them to do something different, something new and exciting. Some might think it an opportunity to start their own business.

Some people seem to have a knack of reframing situations. Comedians, writers, inventors and politicians are just a few of the professions that require people to constantly reframe events. The best comedians, for example, are astute observers of life and are constantly asking themselves 'What's funny about this?' or 'What could be funny about this?' In the early 1970s, during the filming of the TV series *Monty Python's Flying Circus*, John Cleese together with other members of the Monty Python team checked into the Hotel Gleneagles in Torquay. The hotel manager, a man by the name of Donald Sinclair, turned out to be quite a rude, eccentric host. 'He seemed to view us as a colossal inconvenience right from the start,' said Michael Palin. He threw a bus timetable at a guest when the guest dared to ask the time of the next bus; he complained about Terry Gilliam's table manners and tossed Eric Idle's briefcase out of the hotel 'in case it contained a time bomb!' John Cleese made mental notes and used the whole experience to write the hit TV comedy *Fawlty Towers*.

Similarly, *Only Fools And Horses* creator John Sullivan used a lot of real-life incidents in his storylines. One of the funniest scenes was in an episode from the second series called 'A Touch of Glass' – the chandelier scene. The scene was based upon a story Sullivan's father had told him of the days when he worked as a plumber in the 1930s. Sullivan's father was part of a crew who were fitting a new heating system into a stately home. In order to lay the new pipes, they had to move some chandeliers. While some of the men were standing under one chandelier ready to catch it in a sheet, one of their colleagues was loosening a different chandelier which fell to the ground and smashed into pieces. When Sullivan's father told him the story, it was told as a serious tale because a number of the men he was working with were given the sack that day. But Sullivan immediately saw a comic side and an entire episode was written around that one scene.

When police in Manhattan pulled over a car being driven by a young man with wild afro-styled hair, they were not aware that the man in question was Malcolm Gladwell, best-selling author of *The Tipping Point* and *Blink!*. The police had been on the lookout for a rapist and, the police said, Gladwell fitted the description. They interrogated Gladwell for about twenty minutes before finally agreeing to let him go. It turned out that when they checked the actual description of the rapist, the man they were looking for was taller, broader and about fifteen years younger than Gladwell. 'All we had in common,' said Gladwell, 'was a large head of curly hair.' It was just the kind of thoughtless 'stop and search' occurrence that can create an added strain on police–community relations. However, Gladwell did not get riled. He became thoughtful, wondering how the policemen could have mistaken him for the actual rapist when there were so many obvious discrepancies in the description of the man they were looking for.

He thought about the strange power of first impressions and this led him to research and write the book *Blink!* In the acknowledgements section of the book, the people Gladwell thanks first (albeit tongue-in-cheek) are the policemen who stopped him in his car and wasted half an hour of his day, because it was that incident that triggered his thoughts and ultimately led to him writing his new book. Gladwell acknowledged that had he not been pulled over that day, it is unlikely that the book would ever have been written.

LOOKING FOR BENEFITS

Maeve Binchy is one of the world's best-selling authors whose work includes *Circle Of Friends*, which was made into a Hollywood film. In 2002 Maeve suffered heart failure that required her to be hospitalized for ten days, and she has been on medication ever since. She said in an interview with the *Daily Mail* that, 'Before it happened, if you'd have asked me how life would have been after something like this, I'd have told you it would inevitably have been a wretched, curtailed experience.' But, in actual fact, she said her life since the illness was diagnosed had been the very opposite.

Maeve got involved in learning about her condition, the medical treatments and dietary factors. She cut out salt, became sparing in her use of butter and cut back on alcohol. But she is also a great believer in a positive attitude which, she said, was 'the key'. In fact, far from leading a wretched existence, Maeve believes she's happier now than she has ever been. And, her latest novel, *Heart And Soul*, was inspired by the conversations she listened in on while sitting in hospital waiting rooms. Interestingly, Maeve Binchy is also an optimist. She has a very positive approach to life. 'I have no wish to live a restricted, nervous life,' she said. 'If you woke up each morning and immediately dwelt on your ills, what sort of day could you look forward to?'

The secret of reframing is similar to the entrepreneurs' habit of consciously looking for opportunities, only when you reframe a situation, you are looking for benefits rather than opportunities. The one critical question that positive reframers ask themselves when facing any difficult situation is 'What is good about this?' or 'What could be good about this?' Through these questions, the situation is seen in a different light and, as a result, people will generally experience different outcomes. Looking for benefits in a stressful situation is, as you might expect, a trait common to optimists. Studies have shown that people who actively look for benefits when diagnosed with serious illnesses such as cancer tend to cope better, suffer less emotional distress and experience a superior quality of life. Interestingly, it is not something that necessarily happens after the passage of time. In many cases, people look for benefits in a trauma or illness very early on. Sometimes, it could be critical because the earlier people start looking for benefits, the sooner they find them.

REFRAMING REDUNDANCY

When ITV and Granada received approval for their proposed merger in October 2003, employees of both companies knew that redundancies would follow. One of the staff at Granada, Gemma Stone, was more than a little concerned when she heard the rumours. 'I had one child under two,' she says, 'and I was pregnant with another. I couldn't help but ask myself, "Who is going to employ me now?"'

But Gemma is not a person to be easily beaten. 'I took

stock of the situation,' she says, 'and realized that there was an opportunity in my misfortune.' This was her chance to pursue her dream of running her own events management company. 'When I started the business, my former boss at LWT reminded me of something I'd said in my original job interview,' she remembers. 'When asked what I wanted to be doing in five years' time, I had said that I wanted to be running my own event agency.

'To be honest', Gemma admitted, 'it was something I just said in an interview. I hadn't really thought much about it. But it had obviously stuck with me somewhere in my unconscious mind.'

Gemma set up her own events management company, Rock And Ruby Event Management, in 2004 and successfully pitched to a number of high-profile clients including Tesco, Ikea and Granada. Building a new business from scratch is never simple or easy, but Gemma succeeded. Today, she enjoys the positive aspects of working from home and having the freedom to spend quality time with her family rather than having to adhere to a strict nine-to-five time frame.

When she looks back to the time she lost her job, Gemma is in no doubt that there was a huge flipside. She says now that, 'All-in-all, it was a blessing. The experience I have acquired running the agency would have taken years working for one employer – the vast range of events I have had the pleasure of producing, working with so many people, it has been fabulous.'

With the current economic downturn in the UK, the events management industry has been among the first to be affected, presumably because events are often perceived as a luxury rather than a necessity. But, Gemma remains optimistic about the future. Whatever happens, she always looks for an opportunity and she is confident that she can turn any negative into a positive. In the summer of 2008, to safeguard her business from the predicted recession, she launched a children's party division as a new, alternative revenue stream. This new arm to her business, she said, took off with unprecedented speed.

'I am an optimist,' Gemma says. 'I'm also a "doer". I get frustrated by people who moan about their lot in life but do nothing about it. I truly believe that you create your own destiny and with visual goals, you really can achieve anything you go out there to accomplish.'

Successful people always look to reframe a negative situation. They ask positive, empowering questions that look to the future, and it is those questions that point to the opportunities hidden in the problem. Reframing is a relatively simple process. It is achieved by taking a negative statement like 'Losing my job is a disaster' and flipping it into a positive statement like 'This is a great opportunity for me to review what I really want to do with my life.'

There is a lovely story of a little boy who dreamed of being a baseball player. He went out into his garden with bat and ball to play. 'The final inning,' he shouts aloud but to himself. 'The home team are two runs down but the away team are batting and the bases are loaded. Can the batter hit a home run and win the game?' The boy tosses the ball into the air and swings the bat at it with all his might, but misses. 'Strike one,' he calls, 'the batter has two more tries to win the game.' Once again he tosses the ball, swings and misses. 'Strike two,' shouts the little boy. 'Now, with all eyes on the batter, he will surely hit the home run on his third try.' For the last time, the boy tosses the ball in the air, swings the bat and misses for a third time. The force of his final swing makes him fall to the ground. As he gets up, dusting himself down, the boy picks up the ball and says, 'Man! What an incredible pitcher!'

The 2008 US presidential election was being battled between John McCain, a seventy-two-year-old Republican and Barack Obama, a young, black American representing the

Democrats. Their ages were factors that both camps brought into their campaigns. The Republican camp suggested that Obama was too young and inexperienced. They argued that McCain had the experience and wisdom needed to govern the most powerful nation in the world. The Democrats, on the other hand, put a different frame on the candidates' ages. They pointed to the fact that statistically there was a good chance that McCain would be dead before the end of his term. While Obama was young and relatively inexperienced, he had youth, energy and enthusiasm on his side. The fact that Obama hadn't had a great deal of experience in government, they said, meant that he was ideally suited to bring about much needed change. Which frame was true? They both were. It just depends upon the frame you want to put around them.

THE PAINFUL LESSONS OF A PROFESSOR

The explosion came suddenly and without warning. A blindingly bright white light followed by a surge of flames and then smoke. Dan Ariely was trapped in a room that was fast becoming a furnace. He was just eighteen years old and he was on fire.

With the fire all around him, Dan realized that the only way out was by going through the flames. Someone called from outside the room and the voice guided him to the fire escape. He rushed through the flames to the exit. When he reached the door, his clothes were on fire. He tore off his shoes, T-shirt and trousers and was left standing in charred socks and underwear. Looking down he saw his injuries for the first time; his right hand was completely black, large pieces of skin hung loosely from his left arm and the whole arm had turned white. The stone floor was covered with the ash that was his skin. Then unbearable pain overcame him.

All he could do was lie motionless on the floor, focused on his breathing, waiting for help.

Months after his accident, Dan Ariely stood in front of a full-length mirror for the first time since his accident. His legs were covered in bandages, his back bent forward and his arms, also bandaged, were collapsed by his sides. 'My twisted body looked foreign and detached from what I felt and knew was me,' he says. 'The worst was my face. The whole right side was open flesh, yellow and red from pieces of tissue and skin hanging from it. It looked as if it were made from colourful wax that was in the process of melting. My eyes were pulled severely to the side. The right side of my mouth and nose were charred and distorted, as was my right ear.'

Seventy per cent of his body had suffered third-degree burns in the accident and it would require three very long years of hospitalization and treatment involving intense physical pain and emotional anguish. Ariely describes his treatments and reflects on his accident and how it affected his life in a very moving, personal essay *Painful Lessons*. Every day for three years (with the exception of the days of his operations), Ariely was given the 'bath treatment'. He would be lowered into a purple-coloured disinfectant and, as soon as he was completely soaked, nurses began ripping off the bandages. They would continue ripping away at the bandages one at a time until they were all removed which would usually take them an hour or so. It was, Ariely says, 'daily agony'. When the nurses had finished, they would lift him out of the bath and apply a layer of Siverol ointment and reband-age his body. There would also be physiotherapy and other treatments but, every day during his three years in hospital, at the back of his mind was the dread of the next 'bath treatment'.

In the introduction to his bestselling book *Predictably Irrational*, Dan alludes to the fact that he started to look at life and, in particular, people's behaviours differently after his accident, and this led him down a career path that he may not have chosen before the accident. After he was released from hospital, he pursued a degree in Cognitive Psychology at Tel Aviv University, and went on to receive an MA and a Ph.D. in the same field from the University of North Carolina at Chapel Hill. He then earned a doctorate in Business from Duke University where he is currently the James B. Duke Professor of Behavioural Economics.

Today, Dan is widely acknowledged to be a leading figure in the field of behavioural economics, which studies the human, social, cognitive and emotional factors that influence economic decisions, and how those factors affect market prices, returns on investment and the allocation of resources. However, his main fascination is in observing and measuring how and why we make the decisions that we do in our lives. He has shown that our decisions are often completely irrational, but at the same time they are surprisingly predictable. He has uncovered some fascinating insights about the things that influence us when we make decisions, and how they affect our lives generally.

When I spoke to him, I found Dan Ariely to be a warm, generous man, happy to share his thoughts and experiences. He has some interesting personal and professional insights relating to the idea of the flipside. 'There is no question,' he says, 'that big changes in our lives change us as people. They change what we think about and what we care about.' In his own life, he acknowledges that there were 'fundamental' long-term positive changes in his life that he can trace back to his accident, including 'changes to my personality, the way I view myself, the way I view others, my motivation, my interests and my reaction to physical pain.'

He goes on to explain that the experience gave him 'a more relaxed perspective of life – knowing how horrible life can be makes the small daily problems I encounter seem less important, if not meaningless.' He attributes a large part of his motivation to pursue an academic career to the changes in his view of the world following the accident. It was a 'powerful, painful and prolonged experience', he says, 'but it has also provided one of the most central "threads" to the way I understand myself and others (and it has also sparked many of my research interests)'.

I hesitate to use the term 'burn victim' when referring to Dan Ariely; he certainly doesn't view himself as a 'victim'. He is both philosophical and pragmatic about his experiences. 'Overall,' he says, 'I try to look at my injury as another experience, one of many that compose my life.'

Would he be the same man that he is today, would he have achieved the things he has achieved in his life so far, had the magnesium flare not erupted and caused such horrific burns all those years ago? Of course not. Because as Ariely says, 'it is the big events that change us'. He is not certain whether his life is better than it would have been had he not had his injury. The three years of agonizing pain were just 'too much', he believes. However, he does acknowledge that there were advantages, there were positive changes; there was most definitely a flipside. Today, he has a beautiful wife, and he is at the height of his profession as well as being a bestselling author.

Even after going through excruciating pain every day for three years and having to live with pain and restricted mobility every day, and even after having to cope with the social and emotional strains that are inevitably put on someone who suffers a severe burn injury, Ariely discovered that there a 'few advantages'. 'In retrospect,' he says, 'it is surprising to see how positively my life has turned out. I think it has turned out to be better than others expected and definitely better than I myself expected.'

Whatever setbacks and changes happen, whether we are hit by a health problem, a financial crisis or a serious disability, the testimonies of people like Jodi Pliszka, Gemma Stone and

Dan Ariely reveal a vital aspect of the flipside; when we learn to ask more empowering questions and reframe situations in a positive light, we often discover that things work out better than we might otherwise have anticipated.

CHAPTER 11

LOST DREAMS AND NEW DIRECTIONS: FINDING THE FUTURE

'The future belongs to those who believe in the beauty of their dreams.'

Eleanor Roosevelt

IT WAS BILLED as 'the story of a man who had everything, but found something more'. In the film *Regarding Henry*, Harrison Ford plays Henry Turner, a successful, high-powered lawyer who, after being shot in the head and chest, suffers brain damage. Both his speech and mobility are affected, and the injury causes severe amnesia. With most of his memory gone, Henry has to rebuild his life from scratch, which includes relearning everything from being able to walk and tying his shoelaces to learning to read and write. There is a particularly poignant scene in the film when Henry's physical therapist, played by Bill Nunn, comes to visit Henry at his home in Manhattan. Henry's physical therapy had finished weeks earlier but the therapist, who had become Henry's friend and confidant following his injury, had been told that

Henry was feeling depressed about the life he had lost.

In the scene, Henry gets his friend a beer and the two men sit down in the kitchen and talk. The therapist tells Henry how he used to be a professional football player and describes what happened in the last professional game he ever played. The ball was coming his way for a touchdown when he was tackled on two sides. At that moment he heard and felt his knee 'pop' and he knew there and then that his football career was finished. 'My life was over. I was dead,' he tells Henry. 'But ask me if I mind having bad knees.' Shrugging his head, Henry starts to repeat the question, 'Okay, so do you mind . . .' when the therapist interrupts him. 'No! No, I don't mind, Henry. Not for one second. Check it out. You're walking. You're talking. We're sitting here drinking this pretty fine, expensive beer. And I had something to do with that. So, no. I don't mind having bad knees.'

That one scene summed up the message of the film; even when dreams are lost, there can still be a flipside, and often that flipside will come in the form of new, different and far more significant dreams. Those who thought the central theme of the storyline in *Regarding Henry* was something confined to Jeffrey Jacob 'J.J.' Abrams' script, need only read Trisha Meili's book *I Am The Central Park Jogger* (discussed in Part One) to appreciate that the film's message merely echoes what is possible even in far worse, real-life tragedies.

Julio Iglesias's road to pop stardom following the loss of his dream to become a professional footballer is just one of many examples of how lost dreams can be superseded by new, bigger dreams. In Iglesias's case, nobody could have blamed him if he had become bitter, resentful and depressed after his accident. He could have dwelt on the fact that life had cheated him and taken away his boyhood dreams. But instead, Julio Iglesias chose a different path; he chose to focus forward and embarked upon a specific course of action which ultimately led to his success as a singer/songwriter.

Even though Julio Iglesias's childhood dream was crushed, he was able to find a flipside, and like Harland Sanders, go on to achieve things that he may never have even dreamed possible had he not had his original dream taken away. In fact, many of the greatest achievers in all walks of life are people who had lost their dreams, but who went on to pursue new dreams.

THE MUSIC GOES ON

'You are never too old to set another goal or to dream a new dream.'

C. S. Lewis

By all accounts, Elaine Rinaldi was something of a child prodigy. At the age of seven she was tapping out Chopin melodies on a Japanese Kawai Baby Grand piano in her parents' Westchester living room. Even at that age, Elaine would practise three or four hours a day and so it wasn't surprising to those that knew her when she started winning local and state competitions. Elaine's piano teacher, Dr Rosalina Sackstein, a renowned music professor at the University of Miami, described Elaine as 'one of the most talented students I had', and Dr Sackstein went on to clarify that she only ever worked with 'people that have the talent, the intelligence and the disposition'.

When Elaine was sixteen years of age, she made her professional debut as a concert pianist with the Fort Lauderdale Chamber Symphony. In 1985 she received a Silver Knight award for music. Her immediate family as well as her grandparents, aunts, uncles, cousins and friends were all in the audience. Her father Leo recalled the occasion with pride: 'You think, well there are so many talented kids out there, but she won!'

Elaine went on to attend the Eastern Musical Festival, one of America's most prestigious centres for aspiring young musicians. She later received a full scholarship to attend the Frost School of Music at the University of Miami, where she continued to study with her childhood teacher Dr Sackstein, before earning a master's degree at Mannes College of Music in New York City.

It is fair to say that Elaine Rinaldi had worked hard all of her life and made considerable sacrifices to achieve her dream of being a respected concert pianist. After receiving her masters degree, Elaine finally realized her dream, but the dream didn't last long. Less than twelve months after her graduation, she was hit by a car while out riding her bicycle on the streets of New York. The dream she had nurtured and worked for all of her life was over.

The accident devastated Elaine – physically, mentally and professionally. The damage to her upper body made it impossible for her to continue to play the piano at a professional level. All those hours of practice over the years – many times as much as eight hours a day – going back to childhood, would account for nothing. Or so it seemed at the time.

It took Elaine a year to recover from her injuries, but when she finally got back on a bicycle, she was hit again. This time by a rollerblader. Her lifelong teacher and mentor Dr Sackstein said of Elaine, 'She had all the workings of a concert pianist. All the ability and all of the talent. Unfortunately, things happen.'

But Elaine's story does not end there. She stayed in New York and in the music business, only she found a new calling – orchestral conducting – and it wasn't long before she began to excel. In 1997 Elaine was hired as the resident assistant conductor and chorus master for the Florida Grand Opera, which was home to the Florida Philharmonic. She admitted that she 'would have taken a job anywhere' but this was her hometown and she described it as 'the ultimate coming home'.

In 2000 Elaine went back to New York to work as a freelance conductor for the DiCapo Opera and later the same year she returned to South Florida to work in Key West at the Island Opera Theatre. There she was reunited with many of her old friends from the Florida Philharmonic which, she was sad to discover, had dispersed due to lack of funds.

Some of the musicians suggested that Elaine create a new orchestra. She was the ideal person for the job; not only could she lead the orchestra, but she had the contacts to help make it happen. 'We have excellent musicians in South Florida,' she said, 'and if we put them together, we have an excellent orchestra.'

In 2006, Orchestra Miami was officially formed. The forty-strong orchestra performed at the Miami Dade County Auditorium – the very same place that Elaine was awarded her Silver Knight award. 'It's all coming home for me,' she said.

Elaine Rinaldi had lost her dream only to pursue and achieve another, in many ways, bigger dream. 'For her to command an orchestra is the epitome of my expectations,' said Dr Sackstein. 'Good for her.'

CREATING THE FUTURE

'I look to the future because that's where I'm going to spend the rest of my life.'

George Burns

What begins to emerge from these stories is that there may be some truth in the belief that if we lose a dream, it can always be replaced with a new dream. When dreams are lost, when our life's endeavours are taken away, we can become bitter and resentful, and we can curse and moan about the unfairness of it all; or we can look forward and find another dream. The truth is, very often, if we choose the latter, we will find an even bigger, more meaningful dream. Occasionally it may resurrect old dreams, dreams that we may have given up on long ago, but have been lying dormant within us, waiting to be reclaimed.

Kim Williams was the fourth of eight children in a family that loved music. By his seventh birthday he could play the guitar and when he was ten he was already writing his own songs. As a teenager he played in a number of cover bands and travelled across the American Midwest but eventually he returned to East Tennessee, fell in love, started a family and decided to do the responsible thing and get a real job. After a series of construction jobs, he accepted a position as an industrial electronics technician at a local glass factory. Any ambitions he had to pursue a career in music he managed to set aside and instead devoted his time to raising his family. Life for Kim and his family was routine but comfortable until one day in 1974, an accident at the factory changed the course of his life.

Kim was caught in a horrific fire inside the factory. His burns were so severe that over the following decade, he needed more than two hundred plastic and reconstructive surgeries. A lot of the treatment was undertaken at the Vanderbilt University Medical Center in Nashville and it was there that he came across details of a songwriting class at the University of Tennessee campus. He signed up for the class and found that it resurrected his love of music and songwriting. Even though he had been working towards a degree in psychology, Kim decided that what he really wanted to become was a songwriter.

He spent the next five years travelling back and forth

between East Tennessee and Nashville, learning the craft of writing songs and occasionally pitching his work. Finally, in 1988 Kim was given a contract with Tree International (which became Sony/ATV Music Publishing). Within his first few months, Joe Diffey, a country and western singer, recorded a song Kim had co-written called 'If The Devil Danced in Empty Pockets'. The song became a major hit and launched Kim Williams within the industry as a recognized songwriting talent. Kim had already been working with a young country and western singer called Garth Brooks, and the two struck up a friendship and writing partnership that would last decades. Since then, Kim has enjoyed a long string of hits with some of the leading stars on the country and western scene, the most notable being 'Three Wooden Crosses', which he co-wrote with Doug Johnson and was recorded by Randy Travis in 2003. That song was voted Song of the Year at the 2003 Country Music Awards and received the same award from the Nashville Songwriters Association.

Doug Johnson says Kim Williams is 'the most positive, high energy person' he knows. 'I really wish everyone could have the opportunity to be around him,' Johnson said. 'He is a huge inspiration.' Reflecting back to the time of his accident, Kim Williams believes that it revived his aspirations to become a songwriter. 'I don't know if I'd ever have gotten back into music if I hadn't had that accident,' he said in an interview. 'Maybe it was God saying "I've got to hit him hard enough to get him to go where he needs to be."'

One of the biggest flipsides of a trauma is that it forces us to have goals. A lot of the time, people drift through life with no real idea as to what they really want. Sometimes, as in Simon and Helen Pattinson's story mentioned in Part One, people instinctively know that something is missing and actively start looking for goals. Simon and Helen were young lawyers, commuting every day into the City of London, until they got to the point where they knew they needed to find something that would inspire them. For many people, it takes a setback or trauma before they come to that same realization, and sometimes it is the trauma itself that gives people goals to pursue in life.

Once you have a specific goal, you're more than halfway to achieving it. I first heard Roger Crawford speak in 1996. He speaks slowly and deliberately and with great humour. His audiences hang on to every word, not because Roger is quite severely physically handicapped, but because he has great wisdom to share, and when he spoke, audiences would come away feeling inspired.

Roger was born with a congenital birth defect known as 'ectrodactyly'. He had two fingers on his left hand, and one on his right hand. He has three toes on his right foot and his left leg was amputated. Yet Roger qualified as a tennis coach with the United States Professional Tennis Association. He's got a bachelor's degree in Communications from Loyola-Marymount University in Los Angeles, he was the first severely handicapped person to play in the National Collegiate Athletic Association and he became a sought-after motivational speaker. Probably the most important message that Roger Crawford shared was the importance of having specific personal goals. 'Anyone can do incredible things,' he said, 'but first you've got to give yourself incredible things to do.'

If you were to ask a hundred people if they had goals, or what things they most wanted to achieve in life, over 90 per cent couldn't give you anything specific other than their wish to be happy and healthy. This is what Natalie du Toit, winner of ten gold medals in two Paralympics (who we will meet in a later chapter) refers to as 'the great tragedy of life'. One of her most precious possessions is a piece of prose given to her by her coach, the sentiment of which she lives her life by:

The tragedy of life does not lie in not reaching your goals;
The tragedy of life lies in not having goals to reach for.

Having goals gives our lives purpose and meaning and direction. It is also one reason why people who suffer personal tragedies often come through the tragedy feeling happier and more fulfilled; every day represents new challenges and new goals, and most often the individual will have specific long-term goals too.

Without a goal, we are like a ship bobbing up and down on the open sea. In May 2008 I took a week off to go on a Day Skipper sailing course. It was probably the hardest thing I have ever done. Other than the first afternoon which I spent hanging over the side, it was an incredible experience. With two friends and an instructor, I sailed across the Strait of Gibraltar to North Africa, visiting the Spanish inlet of Ceuta and then on to Morocco before heading back across the Mediterranean Sea through the night to Sotogrande on the Costa del Sol.

One of the most difficult parts of a Day Skipper course is calculating your journey because there are so many factors that have to be taken into account; aside from the various complexities relating to the boat itself, there are the tides, the current, the wind, waypoints (visual markers to check your location), the weather and the forecasts. Yet, before you can look at any of these factors, the very first thing you must have – and without which there is no point in leaving the harbour – is a destination. You have to know where you want to go, or you'll never make it anywhere. Once you know where you want to go, you then plan a route. You check out the weather forecast, the tides, the sea current and the wind. You plot your course noting waypoints along the way that will confirm where you are at any given time and providing everything is okay, you set sail. Once out at sea, if circumstances change – if the wind changes direction, if a storm hits, or if something blocks the route – the skipper, knowing his destination, plots a new course and resets the sails. It takes time and a considerable amount of effort, but that way the skipper can be confident of reaching his destination.

If life is a journey, how many of us have destinations? How many know even in what direction they want to go or what the waypoints are? Most school leavers don't have a clue even as to the type of work they would like to do. And that is the real tragedy of life. Too many people settle for making a living instead of making a life. Sometimes, it takes a crisis, or even a tragedy, before we stop drifting and, as Mike Jetter so aptly said, start living consciously.

CALLING 911

Brian Gettinger credits his helmet with saving his life in a motorcycle accident in September 1993. He was twenty-three at the time and just three weeks from graduating from the Sinclair Police Academy when he crashed his father's motorcycle after misjudging a bend. 'I wasn't supposed to survive the crash,' he said. His body was thrown against a guardrail, crushing his spine, breaking his back in three places along with several ribs. As he lay helpless and severely injured along the side of the road in Ohio, Brian Gettinger's only thought was, 'I'm not going to be a police officer any more.'

Gettinger survived the crash, but only just. His doctors told him that he'd be unable to walk again, but nine days after the accident he wriggled his toes, and after several operations and months of rehabilitation, he stood up on his own two feet. However, he was still left with injuries that would prevent him becoming a police officer. His lower left leg is paralysed and he has no muscle in his left shoulder. But the accident that ended his dream of joining the police would lead to a new career which would, in some ways, be more meaningful and satisfying for him. In 1996 he qualified as a police dispatcher – a person who answers emergency calls. It is a job that gives him the chance to help people when they most need it. One day he may be comforting someone at the scene of an accident until the emergency services arrive. Another day he may be giving directions to someone who is lost. It is a job that gives him tremendous satisfaction. The job, Brian says, is 'absolutely incredible'.

Lieutenant Robin Schmutz at the Toledo call centre said Brian's accident uniquely qualifies him for the job. 'In a way it helps him better understand what is going through the minds of those in an emergency situation,' Schmutz said. Brian had always wanted to be a police officer out on the road, but his mother said her son's main motivation was always helping other people, and she believes that he was meant to be a dispatcher. 'Sometimes God moves in mysterious ways,' she said. 'Maybe that's where he's able to save more lives.'

CONSTRUCTIVE MENTAL POWER

'Real, constructive mental power lies in the creative thought that shapes your destiny, and your hour-by-hour mental conduct produces power for change in your life. Develop a train of thought on which to ride. The nobility of your life as well as your happiness depends upon the direction in which that train of thought is going.'

Laurence J. Peter, 1919–88

Whether Providence intervened the day Brian Gettinger was thrown from his motorcycle, we can never know. Perhaps it was also decreed from above that Julio Iglesias should not be a footballer and that Elaine Rinaldi would be better off not playing the piano. One would have thought that any Higher Being would have better things to worry about than whether a man was going to spend his days as a police officer or dispatcher, or whether a man in Spain should spend his life singing as opposed to kicking a football. These incidents could, of course, just be the random result of people being thrown about in the river of life. But, whatever the cause, the fact remains that Brian Gettinger did find a 'gift' in the accident that took away his dream, just as Julio Iglesias and Elaine Rinaldi found 'gifts' in their lost dreams.

We can learn from people like Julio Iglesias and Elaine Rinaldi and Brian Gettinger, especially when we experience disappointment in our own lives. As people who had lost their life's dreams, they could have cursed Heaven or been resentful of what could have been perceived as incredibly bad luck. They remind us that sometimes all that is required to find the flipside is a willingness to let go of what has been lost, and to look ahead with expectation and conviction that somewhere in our future awaits a new, bigger, better and perhaps more meaningful dream.

Their lives are testimony that, on the flipside, there is no loss without gain. Theirs is a special message:

No dream is lost without the potential of being replaced by a new dream. The new dream cannot be found by dwelling on what might have been, or on what we think should have been. It can only be found by focusing on what is, what we have and what we could be.

CHAPTER 12

EDISON'S LEGACY: PHILOSOPHIES TO LIVE BY

'If we did all the things we are capable of, we would literally astound ourselves.'

Thomas A. Edison

IN 1997 *LIFE* MAGAZINE published a commemorative double issue listing the hundred most important people of the last millennium. Top of the list was a man born in 1847 in the state of Ohio, USA. As a boy, he had received just three months of official schooling. His teacher, the Reverend Engle, had predicted that the boy would never amount to anything because he was 'addled', he was a daydreamer. So his mother removed him from school and tutored him herself from home. At an early age, the boy developed hearing problems which were later attributed to scarlet fever and recurring middle ear infections. The problem worsened as he grew older and, in adulthood, following an accident on a train, he became profoundly deaf. Yet, for all his trials, the boy grew up to become one of the most prolific inventors of all time and, of all the people who have lived on earth in the last thousand years, it is his life that is generally considered to have had the greatest impact on humankind's future. That man was Thomas Alva Edison.

Thomas Edison had 1,093 patents registered in his name in the USA alone. He was credited with a multitude of revolutionary technological inventions including the phonograph, the motion picture camera, storage batteries and, of course, the electric light bulb, his most famous and arguably most significant invention. Edison played a prominent role in moving the industrial revolution from an age of steam to an age of electricity. More than perhaps any other man in recent history, Thomas Edison changed the world.

Although Edison is most renowned for inventing the electric light bulb, historians generally acknowledge that his most remarkable invention was, in fact, the phonograph (otherwise known as a gramophone). Edison designed and built the first device that could both record sound and then play it back. It is difficult today to imagine a world without being able to record sound, and back in 1877 when Edison invented it, he could not have imagined how his invention would affect all areas of our lives, from the way we conduct business – imagine a world with no voicemails? – to entertainment and leisure – where would The Beatles or Rolling Stones be had it not been for vinyl records? And where would any of today's pop stars be without CDs or MP3 downloads?

That Edison's phonograph worked without fault on his first attempt astounded its inventor, perhaps more than anyone else. Edison was only too aware that most inventions need considerable refinement before they reach their potential. What made this particular device so extraordinary was not the technological breakthrough or what it would come to mean to the world, but the fact that the world's first audio recording and playback device had been invented by a man who was profoundly deaf!

Edison developed the phonograph by biting on the sounding horn and 'listening' through the resulting vibrations in his jaw bone. In fact, he claimed that his impaired hearing was actually an advantage because by using his 'biting technique', he could pick up sound qualities that were virtually undetectable to the human ear. The fact that he couldn't hear and therefore had to devise his biting method ultimately enabled him to refine and improve the quality of the recordings far beyond that which could have been achieved through normal hearing. Seen in this light, the resulting achievement verges on the miraculous. But beyond the invention itself, Edison had demonstrated, through his work, a truth that would inspire future generations: sometimes our biggest liabilities are our greatest assets.

In 1988 a man called Ralph Teetor was posthumously inducted into the Automotive Hall of Fame for numerous contributions to the automobile industry. Teetor was an extraordinary man and, like Edison, a prolific inventor. When he was just twelve years old, he and his cousin built their first car from scratch, machining each part by hand and completely rebuilding a discarded car engine. Teetor graduated from the University of Pennsylvania in 1912, proving a point to the members of the faculty who had said that he would not be capable of graduating. He then went on to become president of The Perfect Circle corporation in Hagerstown, Indiana, a very successful manufacturer of piston rings.

Teetor invented a powered lawnmower, a number of lock mechanisms and holders for fishing rods. However, his most enduring invention, certainly the one for which he is most remembered and was posthumously honoured, was cruise control in cars. Ralph Teetor was an extremely talented engineer, and what made his achievements all the more remarkable is the fact that he was blind. At the age of five he lost his sight in a shop accident.

Teetor preferred not to discuss his disability and lived his life with an almost total disregard for it. Yet, what is particularly interesting is that Teetor, like Edison, was able to turn his handicap into an advantage. For example, he designed a technique for balancing steam turbine rotors used in torpedo-boat destroyers. Teetor had never seen a turbine rotor. He wouldn't have recognized one if he had fallen over it in the street. But, in a way, he said, this helped him. Teetor believed that his inability to see a rotor meant that he was unaffected and unencumbered by conventional designs. In the end, it was thanks to Teetor's imagination and his highly developed sense of touch that he was able to solve a problem that other, sighted engineers had been struggling with for years.

The invention of cruise control was reportedly inspired when Teetor became carsick while being driven by his lawyer who apparently couldn't talk and drive at the same time. Whenever he spoke, he would subconsciously lower the speed of the car and then speed up when it was Teetor's turn to speak.

Being unable to see does make people more prone to motion sickness. But it was because Teetor was sensitive to motion sickness that he became conscious of the idea for an automated speed control in cars. His lawyer was driving like someone on the dodgems at a fairground, and Teetor was trying his best not to throw up, but the experience inspired his idea for an automated system to maintain a constant speed while driving.

Teetor tinkered with the idea for ten years before he was satisfied that he had a reliable working model, and only then did he apply for a patent. However, it was to be a further thirteen years before the first car manufacturer, Chrysler, finally introduced Teetor's cruise control in their new cars. Today, virtually every car manufactured in the US has cruise control as standard. It was far and away Ralph Teetor's most successful invention. Yet, it was his disability – his blindness – that enabled him to achieve things that were beyond the capabilities of sighted engineers. Teetor developed an exceptional sense of touch through which he was able to visualize objects and processes, and this was undoubtably a large factor in his phenomenal success in becoming one of the most thoughtful and prolific inventors in his field during the twentieth century. Like Edison, Teetor's biography is a remarkable testament to the flipside.

Both Ralph Teetor and Thomas Edison left legacies to the world that are much greater than the sum of their inventions. Their personal philosophies of life continue to guide and inspire millions of people to pursue their dreams, even in the face of setbacks and failure. Neither man believed in the concept of disability; only that different people have different strengths and different weaknesses. The secret to their success lies in their determination to focus and work on their abilities rather than any disabilities. This attitude, we shall see, is common to virtually all people who have found the flipside.

It is Edison's insights relating to setbacks and failure in life that perhaps stand out most in his personal strategy for success. Edison contended that mistakes are our best friends because we learn from them. When others saw failure, Edison saw only a valuable learning experience. Once, when asked if he was discouraged that so many of his attempts to invent the electric light bulb had failed, he replied 'I have not failed. I've just found 10,000 ways that won't work!' He explained to a mystified reporter, 'If I find 10,000 ways something won't work, I haven't failed. I am not discouraged, because every wrong attempt discarded is just one more step forward.'

Edison believed that mistakes in life are there to move us forward, and big mistakes move us forward that much further. He maintained that mistakes and setbacks in life are inevitable steps on the path to success. There is a much quoted story of a junior executive at IBM having made a mistake that cost the company $10 million. When news reached the company president Tom Watson, the young man responsible was summoned to Watson's office. The man knew that he was about to be fired, but Watson believed that one of the most critical values at IBM was the development of people. Consequently, when the junior executive asked if he was being fired, Watson quickly responded with an emphatic 'No!' Then he added, 'I just spent $10 million educating you – why would I want to fire you now?'

Mistakes often lead to surprise innovations. In 1970 Spencer Silver was employed by 3M research labs with the task of helping develop a super strong adhesive. What he ended up with was glue that was considerably weaker than the one that they had already developed. It would stick pieces of paper together, but it could also be very easily unstuck. It was a complete failure until four years later when he suddenly realized that it might have some use after all.

One of Silver's colleagues was singing in a church choir and the markers he placed in his hymn book kept falling out. Remembering the disastrous glue that Silver had created, he had an idea to coat his book markers with Spencer's glue and was very happy to discover that the markers stayed in place, but they also came off easily without damaging the pages. This discovery was the beginning of a product that is used today in virtually every office around the world – Post-it notes!

Safety glass, the kind that doesn't shatter or splinter on impact, is everywhere these days because it helps prevent serious injury. But when Edouard Benedictus, a French scientist, was working in his lab at the turn of the last century, nobody had heard of safety glass. It took an accident in his laboratory to spark the idea. Benedictus accidentally knocked a glass flask to the floor. He heard it break, but as he looked down he stared in amazement; all of the broken pieces were still clinging together. The glass hadn't shattered or even splintered. When he examined it more closely, he understood why. It turned out that the flask had been full of liquid plastic which had evaporated, leaving a thin plastic coating on the inside of the flask. It was that thin film that had stopped the glass from shattering.

Although the accident had intrigued Benedictus, he was unaware of any practical uses and took his findings no further until he witnessed a car accident. At the turn of the last century cars were just starting to become popular among the rich set in Paris, and the most common form of injury from car accidents at that time was cuts from shattered windscreens. Benedictus suddenly realized that his discovery presented an opportunity. Plastic-coated windscreens would prevent most of the injuries sustained from road traffic accidents.

Unfortunately, Benedictus's idea was rejected by car manufacturers for the very same reason that they rejected numerous other safety innovations over the past century: cost. However, after safety glass was successfully used to prevent soldiers from being injured by shattered lenses in gas masks during the First World War, the car manufacturers changed their minds. Today, Benedictus's safety glass is used wherever shattered glass would be a danger.

It may have taken four years and a church choir singer for Spencer Silver to find the flipside to his disaster, and it took a car accident before Edouard Benedictus realized the opportunity that presented itself when he dropped the glass flask in his laboratory, but like many other scientists, both men learned and profited from one of Thomas Edison's pearls of wisdom: 'Just because something doesn't do what you planned it to do doesn't mean it's useless.'

While Edison believed in always looking at problems from different perspectives, he never looked upon himself as a scientist like Edouard Benedictus. A scientist is someone who carries out an experiment and observes what happens. Edison viewed himself as an inventor. He didn't 'discover' things, he 'invented' solutions, and he went out of his way to look for problems that needed solving. 'I find out what the world needs,' he said, 'then I go ahead and try and invent it . . . None of my inventions came about totally by accident.' Edison searched out problems because he understood that locked inside every problem is an opportunity waiting to be discovered.

There can't be many things as frustrating as standing in a queue that doesn't seem to be moving. We've all been there, standing at the back of the line at a car rental desk in an airport while the person at the desk is chatting away to a friend on the telephone, or queuing at a checkout counter in a supermarket while the store assistant is flirting with a colleague. Imagine though, how you would cope if you had to wait in line for three days!

In 1995 the people in Katmandu experienced a severe shortage of cooking gas. Sanu Kaji Shrestha found himself at the back of a queue with a three-day waiting time in order to get badly needed fuel supplies for his family. He had been forced to take the three days off work and then wait patiently in line for his turn to come. However, unlike the hundreds of other people, Sanu recognized an opportunity. While waiting in the queue, Sanu started to think of ways to bring alternative, sustainable sources of domestic energy to the people of Nepal. The more he thought about it, the more excited he became.

Over the following five years, Sanu researched alternative fuels and in 2001 he left his job at the World Bank to work full-time on his goal. He travelled to America and Europe to learn the latest technologies and in April 2002 he established the Foundation for Sustainable Technologies (FoST), a non-profit independent organization. Since its inception, FoST has provided sustainable technology solutions to over a thousand households in poor rural villages in Nepal and continues to research new technologies. FoST's website acknowledges that 'Nepal is facing serious problems due to wide-spread deforestation, environmental degradation, excessive pollution ... short supply of safe drinking water and lack of proper management of solid waste.' It predicts that this trend will lead to most of the forest areas in Nepal being turned into desert and that this would inevitably be followed by environmental disasters which 'will be very hard for us to face'. But FoST is fighting back on behalf of the people of Nepal, educating and persuading people to manage their natural resources without creating problems for future generations. Sanu Kaji Shrestha has started a movement to save Nepal from self-destruction, and his mission was inspired from the frustration of being stuck at the back of a very long queue.

On 17 August 2008 the *Mail on Sunday* newspaper in the UK ran an article with the headline 'The farmer who turns his tractor fumes into fertilizer'. It sounded like a perfect example of the flipside in action; a problem, and as it turned out a multifaceted problem, both financial and environmental, had revealed a massive opportunity.

The article told the story of Steve Heard, a farmer from Leicestershire in the UK, who had taken the fumes from his diesel tractor which, when released into the air, are considered to be hazardous to humans and the environment, and literally turned them into a mineral-enriched fertilizer to improve the soil on his farm.

With the continuous rise in the cost of chemical fertilizers, Heard had known for some time that he needed to reduce his reliance on them. In 2008 the fertilizer costs for his farm shot to over £250,000 a year. The price of fertilizer is closely linked to oil prices, and oil hit an all-time high in July 2008 at $148 per barrel on the international market. Fortunately, by that time, Heard had been working on a plan.

Heard had decided in 2007 that it was time to look for new ways to fertilize his 2,500 acres of land. As an amateur engineer, he spent six months and over £10,000 on a revolutionary system that uses the fumes from his tractor to enrich the soil. Diesel fumes are rich in minerals and although they are potentially hazardous to humans, they are extremely beneficial for the soil. A similar system had been trialled on one hundred farms in the USA and Canada, but Heard had reinvented it for the British market.

Heard's innovation involved diverting the tractor's fumes to a large box on the side of the tractor where they are cooled before being pumped via twenty-seven pipes deep into the soil. 'We placed an analyser on the back of the tractor,' he said, 'which shows that 98 per cent of its emissions go into the soil.' As a result of this technique, Heard said, the soil is less acidic, plants create their own nitrates, they develop better root systems and rely far less on chemical fertilizers. Overall, Heard believes that the system has reduced his fertilizer costs by one-third, and that it produces better crop conditions leading to higher yields. His patented system, BLISS (Breathing Life Into Soils System), seems to benefit the soil and the environment while offering huge financial savings to farmers. As for Steve Heard, his invention has succeeded in reducing his costs, but it has also given him a new and potentially huge business opportunity that could transform agricultural practices in the United Kingdom.

Trevor Bayliss is a well-known British inventor who first made his name through an invention inspired in response to the HIV/AIDS crisis in Africa. The first recorded case of AIDS in Africa occurred in 1982. By 1989 the disease had become rampant and was spreading across the continent like a forest fire. It was threatening to become one of the worst epidemics of the century. Bayliss was sitting in front of his TV at home in the UK when the problems surrounding the AIDS epidemic were first brought to his attention. 'I was watching the TV. I had my feet up, my pipe in my mouth and the TV controller was out of reach,' he said. 'I was watching this programme about the spread of HIV/AIDS in Africa. I could've been watching *Come Dancing* or something, but by chance I was watching this programme where they were saying that the only way in which they could stop this dreadful disease was by education and information which could be best brought to Africa by radio.' But, there was a big problem – most of Africa had no electricity supply and the only other form of electricity was through batteries, which were expensive and in very short supply.

This got Bayliss thinking. 'I went in a dreamland,' he said, 'where I'm in colonial Africa and I have a monocle, a gin and tonic and a fly swatter, and I'm listening to some raunchy number on my wind-up gramophone with a big horn on the top. And I think, hang on, if you can get all that noise by dragging a rusty nail along a piece of paper like you're using a spring, there's got to be enough power in the spring to drive a small dynamo which, in turn, will drive a radio . . . While the TV was still on, I went into my workshop, which was the graveyard of a thousand domestic appliances, and assembled the thing.'

The wind-up radio was to become Bayliss's most famous invention. The original prototype included a small transistor radio, an electric motor from a toy car and the clockwork mechanism from a music box. Bayliss patented the idea but it wasn't until 1994 when he was invited to show it on BBC TV's *Tomorrow's World* that people began to take notice. Trevor Bayliss had created the first of several wind-up, self-energized electrical items and single-handedly provided a solution to the problem of supplying information and education to people across the African continent.

Like Edison, Sanu Kaji Shrestha, Steve Heard and Trevor Bayliss are not scientists. They live and work in the real world rather than laboratories, and they share an Edisonian approach to problems and obstacles in life, one which is in stark contrast to the attitude of the man in the street. Most of us become frustrated by problems and obstacles when they come our way, but inventors like Thomas Edison become excited by problems because they know that problems contain opportunities. Problems were what drove Edison both in his work and in his life. When he reached the point of dissatisfaction in any area of his life, rather than becoming depressed and angry, Edison would become energized and search for the flipside. 'Restlessness is discontent and discontent is the first necessity of progress,' he said. 'Show me a thoroughly satisfied man and I will show you a failure.'

Thomas Edison may be renowned for his inventions, but his belief that disabilities can be assets, problems are always opportunities and mistakes are nothing more than learning experiences, helped change the world just as much as any of his inventions. His philosophy of life continues to inspire people to innovate and invent, and, when faced with a challenge, to search for the flipside. This was, arguably, his greatest legacy.

CHAPTER 13

THE ART OF SEEING: DOING THE IMPOSSIBLE

'It's kind of fun to do the impossible.'

Walt Disney, 1901–66

WHEN TOLD BY one of his generals that his plan was impossible, Napoleon Bonaparte replied, 'Impossible is a word only to be found in the dictionary of fools!' A cursory glance in the past shows Napoleon knew his dictionaries. At the turn of the twentieth century it was generally considered impossible that man would ever fly, but two brothers, Wilbur and Orville Wright, disagreed, and in 1903 the Wright brothers successfully demonstrated that a man could sit in a machine that was heavier than air and fly. Although the conventional telephone was invented by Alexander Bell and Elisha Gray in 1876, few would have believed then that it would ever be possible to talk to someone on the other side of the world using a wireless handset. And, if you had suggested to someone before 1969 that man would be able to walk on the moon, they would have looked at you as if you were mad. What we learn, looking back in time, is that today's possibilities were yesterday's impossibilities. This inevitably leads to the conclusion that many of today's impossibilities may become tomorrow's possibilities, and often the people who understand this are the ones who find the flipside.

In 1988 while serving in the Israeli army, Radi Kaiof sustained an injury that left him paralysed from the waist down. For twenty years, Radi has been confined to a wheelchair. With irreparable damage to his spinal cord, Radi had been told that he would never walk again. But 'never' is another word included in the dictionary of fools. Today Radi can walk. He can stand up and raise himself out of his chair. He can climb stairs and he can get in and out of cars. Watching Radi do these things, knowing his history, is inspirational. Forget Neil Armstrong's first steps on the moon. That Radi Kaiof is able to walk and get about without a wheelchair is nothing short of miraculous.

The miracle that enables Radi Kaiof to walk again after twenty years of being confined to a wheelchair is actually the result of the flipside of a personal accident that left another man severely paralysed. In 1997 Amit Goffer was CEO of Odin Technologies, which developed medical imaging equipment such as MRI scanning devices. After his accident, Amit was wheelchair bound and it was his confinement that prompted Amit to notice an opportunity. He couldn't help but wonder why, in the technological revolution in which we are living, wheelchairs were the only solution for paraplegics. He saw that nothing other than wheelchairs existed to enable paraplegics to get around, and he kept asking himself 'why?'

That was the start of what became a revolutionary new product called 'ReWalk™', the device that enables Radi Kaiof to live without the confines of his wheelchair.

The ReWalk™ consists of motorized leg supports, body sensors and a backpack containing a computerized control box and rechargeable batteries. The user needs to use crutches to help with balance, and the device is operated using a remote control wristband selecting a setting – stand, sit, walk, climb or descend. Then, by leaning forward, the sensors are activated and the robotic legs respond.

The difference that the ReWalk™ can make in a paraplegic's life is immeasurable. Kate Parkin, director of physical and occupational therapy at NYU Medical Center, said it has the potential to improve a user's health in two ways: 'Physically, the body works differently when upright. You can challenge different muscles and allow full expansion of the lungs,' Parkin said. 'Psychologically, it lets people live at the upright level and make eye contact.'

When I asked Amit why he thought he had been able to see an opportunity after his accident, he answered matter-of-factly and with genuine modesty. 'It is natural for me. I am an entrepreneur and I saw an opportunity.' He then explained that finding an opportunity is a bit like soup. There was no single magic ingredient. It was made up of a variety of different ingredients, not least of which was the fact that he had an incredibly supportive group of people around him including a wonderful family made up of his wife and three grown-up children. Amit does admit, however, to having a positive and optimistic outlook on life and, he says, he is a born entrepreneur. He instinctively looks for opportunities, and always has. Does he think that he would have developed the ReWalk™ had he not had his accident? His answer is a categorical 'No'. 'The accident definitely drew me to the development of the ReWalk™,' he said, and therein lies a pretty impressive flipside.

The ReWalk™ is a remarkable achievement that has the potential to help hundreds of thousands of people all over the world to walk again, and experience a totally different quality of life. Sadly, it is something that cannot help Amit, its creator, because he does not have the full function of his arms. However, with people like Amit in the world, my guess is that the day may not be so far off when a viable solution is found to enable all paralysed people to walk again.

What could be more impossible than a paralysed man being able to walk again? Let me introduce you to a young teenager from Sacramento, California. His story will truly amaze you.

Ben Underwood is a normal, healthy teenager in every respect, or so you would think. He enjoys doing everything you would expect a young teenager to do; he runs around the house play fighting with his brother and his friends, he rides a bike, he skateboards, he rollerblades, plays basketball and he also likes to play on his Nintendo Gameboy. There is little chance that you could tell just by observing him that he hides an incredible secret. It is a secret that, once learned, will smash all preconceived notions of what is or isn't impossible; he has no eyes, the ones you see are false, purely cosmetic. Yet, as incredible as it seems, Ben Underwood has taught himself to see.

Ben lives with his family in the outer suburbs of Sacramento. When he was two years old, his mother, Aquanetta, noticed that the pupils of his eyes started to look fluorescent. Within a matter of days, the pupils had turned white. It transpired that Ben had a rare, malignant tumour that affects only six children in every million; it is called a retinoblastoma. Ben's eye surgeon Dr James Ruben explained that 'If left to its own devices, it would be lethal. It would kill him. The disease would spread locally and he would never be able to survive.' If Ben wasn't given treatment, the cancer would spread along the optic nerve and into his brain.

Ben was immediately put on a course of intense chemotherapy and radiotherapy in an attempt to save his eyes, but after ten months, the tumour had still not been completely eradicated. Ben's mother had to make the hardest decision of her life: continue treatment and risk the tumour spreading into Ben's brain, which would mean certain death, or allow the surgeons to remove Ben's eyes which would save his life, but condemn him to a future living in total darkness. She chose the latter.

When Ben woke up from his operation he heard his mother's voice next to him and told her 'Mom I can't see any more, I can't see any more, Oh, Mom, I can't see.' But Aquanetta reassured him, 'You can see, Ben. You can see with your hands,' and she put his hands against her face. 'You can see with your nose,' and she put her hands up to his nose, and she said, 'You can see me with your ears. Baby, you hear me.' From that moment Aquanetta refused to allow her son to think of himself as blind. 'You don't have your eyes any more,' she told him, 'but you still have your hands, your nose and your ears...you can still see.' Ben's mother was determined that her little boy was going to live as normal a life as possible. At times, she would lock herself away in her bedroom and cry, but when she came out, she would never let Ben know how much she felt sorry for him. 'Because I didn't want him feeling sorry for himself,' she says. 'I just kept giving him confidence, courage, strength. That's all I've ever done.'

A year after Ben lost his eyes, something happened that astounded his mother. They were driving in the car when Ben said, 'Mom, do you see that big building out there?' Aquanetta was stunned. They were passing a big building. She said, '*I* see that building out there. But, do *you* see that building out there?' Ben had achieved something that, up until recently, most scientists believed was impossible; he had taught himself to see without eyes. Just as his mother had reassured him, he was able to see the world around him . . . through sound.

Ben is the only person in the world who can see using nothing but what is known as 'echolocation'. He trained himself to locate objects by making a sharp clicking noise with this tongue and picking up the echoes. Using echolocation he can identify objects; he can see their size and shape and determine precisely where they are. What Ben has achieved has to be seen to be believed. No one in their wildest dreams would have imagined it possible for a person to see without eyes . . . except for one man, a brilliant neuroscientist who has taught numerous blind people to see again without using their eyes.

In 1969 the science journal *Nature* published an article by a scientist who claimed that he had developed a device that enabled people who had been blind from birth to see. Neuroscientist Paul Bach-y-rita had invented a device that involved a large video camera which sent electrical signals to a plate on the back of a chair. The plate contained 400 vibrating stimulators that rested against the blind person's skin. Each stimulator functioned much like a pixel on a TV screen to represent different shades of black and white. It was called 'tactile vision' and the blind people who were trained to use it were able to read, make out faces, see objects and distinguish distance. When they controlled the camera and described what they were seeing, they were able to pick out specific people, they could tell if a person in the room was standing or sitting, whether their hair was down or up in a bun. They could tell if a person was wearing glasses, if their mouth was open and they could even tell if someone was moving their right or left hands.

Bach-y-rita's invention was largely ignored by the scientific community as it seemed too fantastical. Today, with the exponential leaps in computer technology, Bach-y-rita has refined his invention to the point where he uses tiny cameras that are incorporated into glasses that the blind person wears, and these transmit information to a computerized chip that sits on the tongue. (The tongue was found to be a much better medium as it is more sensitive than the back and the saliva makes the conductivity more efficient.)

While most scientists are impressed with Bach-y-rita's invention, there are some who refuse to acknowledge that it can be called 'seeing'. 'If it's not stimulating the retina, it's unlikely to my mind that it's seeing,' one neuroscientist was quoted as saying. However, Bach-y-rita has demonstrated that the visual part of the brain is being stimulated by his device. He argues that we don't actually see with our eyes. The eyes only transmit data to the brain, where the information is processed and it is there that the real 'seeing' is done. 'There is nothing special about the optic nerve,' said Bach-y-rita, 'The brain doesn't care where the information comes from. Do you need visual input to see? Hell, no,' he says. 'If you respond to light and can perceive, then it's sight.'

Bach-y-rita's work goes some way to explaining how Ben Underwood has taught himself to see. He has trained his ears to detect through echoes what objects are around him and where they are. 'I can hear the wall over there,' Ben says pointing, 'the couch, the wall behind me, and the TV and the computer.' His is a remarkable achievement and has pushed the frontiers of medical science. He has shown that the human mind doesn't deal with impossibilities. Ben has been featured on news channels and documentaries around the world. He is a bright, witty, handsome, young boy who displays a wonderful sense of humour and love for life. He has high hopes and dreams. 'I want to be a writer, an inventor of video games,' he says. And, no one who knows him doubts that he will succeed at whatever he sets his mind to.

Few would argue that Ben is destined for greatness. That he has achieved what he has, is in no small part due to the support and confidence and love that he gets from his family and friends, especially his remarkable mother Aquanetta. His story so far demonstrates that there really are very few limits to what can be achieved with the right attitude. Even more, Ben Underwood has become a symbol of hope and inspiration to hundreds of thousands of people who have seen him or heard his story. In defiance of his adversity and by refusing to accept limitations that others outside his family and friends might have imposed upon him, Ben has achieved something that only a handful of people have accomplished throughout history; he has made the impossible, possible. And, in doing so, he found a monumental flipside.

Impossible was a young boy's dream of playing major league baseball. How could a boy who had lost his right arm in an accident on his family's farm become a professional ball player? It was impossible. Except nobody told the boy.

Peter Gray was twelve years old when he slipped and fell off his father's pickup truck's running board. He fell under the truck and two of the wheels ran over his right arm and crushed it. The doctors were left with no option but to amputate the arm at the shoulder. As one would expect, Pete was devastated at the loss of his arm, but he refused to give up on his dream. Over time, he learned to throw and catch with his left hand, and he also batted using his only arm. He learned to field using a baseball glove; in one motion, he would catch the ball in his gloved left hand, tuck the ball under his right stump, shake the glove off his left hand, grab the ball and throw it.

After he graduated from high school, Pete played in the lower minor baseball leagues until, in 1942, he got an opportunity to play with the Memphis Chicks in the Southern League. Within two years, he had stolen sixty-three bases and had a .333 batting average. He was voted the League's Most Valuable Player and before the following season began, a major league baseball team, the St Louis Browns, bought his contract. The following season, Peter Gray achieved his boyhood dream and played major league baseball, the highlight of which was playing for the New York Yankees. The Browns won the series in a straight three wins and Gray played a major role in that victory contributing five hits, two of which led to runs for his teammates.

While he was never included in the Baseball Hall of Fame,

Peter Gray did more than achieve his boyhood dream of playing major league baseball. He became an inspiration to American soldiers returning home from the Second World War, especially those who had lost limbs through the fighting. He was featured in newsreels and often was seen visiting army hospitals and rehabilitation centres reassuring amputees that their lives were still worth living.

Peter Gray's achievements back in the 1940s raises the question: could someone with one arm play major league baseball in today's highly competitive world of sport? The answer is an emphatic 'yes'. Not only is it possible for a one-armed man to play major league baseball but a one-armed man can become a key player on the team – the pitcher.

On 4 September 1993 a young man stepped up to the mound to pitch for the New York Yankees against Cleveland. By the end of the game, the Yankees came out winners by 4–0. Throughout the entire game, not one of the Cleveland players had managed to hit the ball. It was the first time in over a decade that any Yankee pitcher had taken a clean sweep in this way. Not many baseball fans who watched that game will forget the man who pitched for the Yankees that day. His name was Jim Abbott. He only had one arm.

To be precise, Jim Abbott had two arms, but he had been born with only his left hand, so his right arm was only good as acting as a stump on which he could rest his glove while he pitched. I saw Jim Abbott play while visiting my father in Canada, and remember being mesmerized by the way he was able to command centre-stage as pitcher. On one occasion, the ball was hit at him, and in one flowing but extremely fast motion, he caught the ball, removed his glove and fired the ball off to first base to get the batter out. Whenever he pitched, he had to get the catching glove back on to his left hand incredibly quickly, within a second or two of throwing the ball, to make sure that he was ready to catch the ball if it was hit at him. Occasionally, teams who didn't know any better tried to do just that, always to their detriment because Abbott could manoeuvre the glove on and off his left hand with lightning speed and his throw was deadly accurate.

Jim Abbott was one of a handful of major league baseball players who never graduated from the minor leagues. He had been noticed by the scouts from his time as an amateur baseball player. He won the Sullivan Award voted as the Best Amateur Athlete in the USA and he was awarded US Baseball Federation's Golden Spikes award as the best amateur player in the country. In 1988 he led the United States to a 5–3 victory over Japan to win the gold medal in the Olympic baseball tournament. It was the first time the USA had won gold in that event.

For the decade between 1989 and 1998, Abbott played for four different teams in major league baseball, and in that time won awards and honours too numerous to mention. Today, he is a professional motivational speaker, always in demand by organizations that want to instil among their members a belief that, with the right attitude, nothing is impossible. It is this paradigm of possibilities that gives hope for the future and leads to the flipside.

CHAPTER 14

THE PARADIGM OF POSSIBILITIES: HOPE FOR THE FUTURE

'Don't listen to anyone who tells you that you can't do this or that. That's nonsense. Make up your mind, you'll never use crutches or a stick, then have a go at everything. Go to school, join in all the games you can. Go anywhere you want to. But never, never let them persuade you that things are too difficult or impossible.'

Group Captain Sir Douglas Bader CBE

On 13 July 2007 eight of the fastest men in the world lined up in the Stadio Olimpico in Rome to race over 400 metres. They were there to compete for a share of the $1 million prize offered by the IAAF Golden League. It was a formidable line-up that included the 2007 US 400m champion Angelo Taylor, and LaShawn Merritt and Darold Williamson, gold medallists in the 2005 World Outdoor 4x400m relay. But in the outside lane was a man who was about to make history. He stood out from the other runners, not because of his bright yellow vest or the fact that he was wearing sunglasses. What made him stand out, what raised gasps and cheers from the crowd as he prepared himself for the race ahead? The man in lane eight had no feet!

Oscar Pistorius was born on 22 November 1986 in Pretoria, South Africa. He was the younger son of Henke and Sheila Pistorius. Oscar's father recalls the anguish he felt at Oscar's birth. 'I saw it when he was born. Neither the nurses nor doctors saw it. I held him in my arms when his umbilical cord was cut and I told the doctor that there was something different about his feet.' It was a very rare condition, with his lower legs and feet being severely deformed. Bones in both of his lower legs and feet were missing. Oscar had no fibulas. The ankles were present but there were just two toes on each foot, and all of the lateral bones were absent.

After his birth, Oscar's parents were faced with a terrible choice: watch him grow up unable to walk, confined to a wheelchair, or amputate both feet in the hope of a better future and the chance to walk using prosthetics. Henke remembers how troubled he felt at this dilemma. Oscar had very ticklish feet. 'To cut those feet off and throw them in the dustbin was not a nice feeling,' Henke says. 'It's hard.' What if his son grew up resenting the fact that his feet had been amputated? But Henke and Sheila made the decision and opted for the chance that their son might walk one day, albeit with prosthetics. Before Oscar reached his first birthday, both of his feet were amputated.

NO REGRETS

'Would I want my legs back? I'd have to sit down and think about it.'

Oscar Pistorius

'There was never a time when I sat down with my parents and said, "Why don't I have legs?" or "What happened to my legs?" or anything like that,' recalls Oscar. 'My mum and dad always told us that the phrase "I can't" doesn't exist.' He has lived his life by this philosophy and hasn't let his disability stop him from doing anything. Whether it is water-skiing, tennis, ice skating, rollerblading or quad biking, Oscar would always give it a go. Interestingly, while Oscar remembers trying virtually every sport available, athletics was not one of them. 'Athletics was never one of the things I enjoyed,' he says.

At school, Oscar wore standard prosthetic legs yet still excelled in most sports. By all accounts, he became an accomplished water polo and rugby player. However, his dream of playing rugby was brought to an abrupt end when he was injured in a school rugby game. He was receiving a pass from his outside-centre when his opposite wing crashed into him from one side and another opponent landed on his leg from the other side. The damage to Oscar's knee forced him to stop playing the game he loved. However, the knee injury that curtailed his days of playing rugby was the primary catalyst in the extraordinary achievements that would follow.

Dr Gerry Versveld, the surgeon who looked after Oscar from birth, says, 'I was totally bowled over when he told me that he'd been playing rugby.' The fact that Oscar had played the sport while wearing standard, rigid prosthetics made it even more remarkable. But rugby's loss would be athletics' gain. While Oscar was advised to stop playing contact sports, at least until his knee had healed, he was still able to run. Oscar made his way to the athletics track unaware that he was about to turn the world of athletics upside down, and in the process would become an international sporting phenomenon.

BREAKING WORLD RECORDS

'I didn't have the right kit or anything,' Oscar recalls when he first arrived at the athletics track, 'and I broke the paralympic world record for double amputees, right off the bat, in rugby shorts and a T-shirt.' On 5 January 2004, at the age of just seventeen, Oscar ran the 100m race in an open competition at the Pilditch stadium in his hometown of Pretoria after training for only two months. He ran it in 11.51 seconds; the paralympic world record at that time was 12.2.

Eight months later, Oscar became a sensation when he represented South Africa in the Paralympics in Athens, Greece. He took the silver medal in the 100m but won the gold in the 200m final. Despite a disastrous start which, following four false starts, saw Oscar frozen for 1.8 seconds after all of the other competitors were out of their blocks, Oscar came through to win the race, breaking the world record with a time of 21.97 seconds. That made him the first amputee ever to run the 200m in under 22 seconds. Sadly, Oscar's mother Sheila died before he took up athletics, but watching from the stands were his father and, sitting beside him, Dr Gerry Versveld, the surgeon who had amputated Oscar's feet. Both men were reduced to tears.

Before the end of the Paralympics in Athens that year, Oscar had broken four world records, and his athletics career had barely begun. He went on to break 26 world records for his category including the 100m, 200m and 400m events. But Oscar had his sights set on bigger challenges – his goal was to compete at the highest level against able-bodied runners.

THE SECRET OF HIS SUCCESS

As Oscar trained harder and ran faster, he began to be seen as a real challenger to able-bodied runners. His remarkable progress led some people to become suspicious as to whether the winning factor was Oscar's athletic ability or whether he was gaining an unfair advantage from his Cheetahs, the carbon fibre prosthetics that had been specially made for him.

Dr Elio Locatelli, a spokeman for the International Association of Athletics Federations (IAAF), the world governing body, was the first to voice concern. 'I was a little suspicious about his performance in 400m because he was finishing very quickly,' said Dr Locatelli. All 400m runners tire as the race goes on but Oscar got quicker.

In March 2007 the IAAF changed their rules and introduced a ban of all 'technical aids' in athletics. Whether the ban was imposed as a response to Oscar's success on the running track is open to conjecture. Oscar and his team denied that his Cheetah 'blades' could be considered a technical aid, and that Oscar would always be at a disadvantage compared to able-bodied runners as the blades could never be an equivalent or better replacement for human legs.

After rigorous tests, on 10 January 2008 the IAAF found that the blades did give Oscar an advantage and this effectively banned him from running in 'open' competitive races. However, Oscar and his team appealed to the highest authority in athletics, the Court of Arbitration for Sport in Lausanne, and on 16 May 2008, the Court ruled that the original scientific study upon which the IAAF had based their decision had 'gone off the rails' and was fatally flawed. As such, the IAAF had not provided sufficient evidence to prove that Oscar Pistorius's prostheses give him an advantage over able-bodied athletes.

Oscar had won his appeal and became eligible to run in open competition, including the Olympics, although he failed to qualify for the Beijing Games. However, the Court's ruling left one question unanswered: if Oscar's prosthetics were not giving him an advantage, what was the secret of his success?

Ironically, many believe that it was Oscar's disability itself that held the key to his remarkable achievements in the world of athletics. According to Oscar's surgeon and his coach, the tragedy of Oscar being born with deformed feet which had to be amputated before he could walk, was the main reason that he became such an extraordinary athlete.

Dr Versveld has no doubt that Oscar's birth defect uniquely equipped him for speed because he was forced to develop a very natural, fast leg movement just to keep up with the other kids. Oscar's brother, Carl, agrees. 'Oscar's leg movements had to be so much faster to actually get up to the same pace as anyone else, whether it was me or anyone else that he might have been playing with in the garden or racing against on the beach.' Evidently, Oscar's disability meant that, throughout his childhood, he was developing a unique athletic physique without even knowing it.

Oscar's coach Ampie Louw is in no doubt that it is Oscar's unique leg movements that enabled him to become such an exceptional athlete. 'The first time I saw him, I thought "Hey, I can work with this guy." You know why? As a sprint coach I saw his leg speed. Oscar is special,' he says, with firm conviction.

One of Oscar's most important character traits is one that is common to all champions. He doesn't dwell on the past or concern himself with what might have been, and he doesn't look for excuses. He only focuses his mind on what possibilities lie ahead.

'You could use all of what's happened as a reason to fail – people would understand,' Oscar said. 'You've got no legs. Your mother died; such a shame. But I don't want to live my life with people saying, "That's too bad", filling my life with all those negatives.'

It rained in Beijing on 17 September 2008. But the weather didn't deter over 91,000 people from attending the magnificent Bird's Nest stadium to witness the last day of the thirteenth Paralympics. The very last event was the

T44 400m race and the athlete that most eyes were on was Oscar Pistorius. He had already won the gold medal for the 100m and 200m events, but could he win a third in the 400m and retain the title that he had won in Athens four years earlier?

As he crossed the finishing line, Oscar was over ten metres clear of his nearest rival. He had broken his twenty-seventh world record and won his quota of three gold medals, yet after the race, being the champion that he is, Oscar's thoughts were on qualifying for the World Athletics Championships in 2009.

Watching Oscar win the final of the 400 metres, I couldn't help but think of an interview his mother gave on the radio in South Africa in 1999. She said that she hoped her son's story would be 'a message of hope and encouragement to any listeners who had been through traumatic times in their own lives'. But I think the 91,000 people watching her son in the Bird's Nest stadium that night and the millions of people all over the world who were witnessing the event on TV would all agree that watching Oscar Pistorius brought much more than a message of hope and encouragement; he brought inspiration.

MAKING HISTORY

Seville, Spain, 3 May 2008: fifty-one women are lined up ready to swim ten kilometres in open murky waters. It is the start of the World Open Water Swimming Championships. They are about to take part in one of the most gruelling and difficult swimming races in the world. It is not an event for the squeamish. Participants in previous races have been stung by jellyfish and suffered from seasickness. One swimmer in Seville, Cassie Patten from Great Britain, reported afterwards that, during the final lap, remnants of what she could only think from its foul odour and taste as being duck poo got into her mouth. The true sportswoman that she is, Cassie didn't let it slow her down and went on to finish second in the race, just 3.1 seconds behind the winner, Russian Larissa Ilchenko.

However, all the spectators were watching the woman finishing in fourth place, exactly two seconds behind Cassie Patten and five behind the winner. Natalie du Toit is a twenty-four-year-old woman from South Africa. It was only when Natalie climbed out of the water that people could begin to fathom the magnitude of her achievement; her left leg below the knee is missing. She had competed against able-bodied swimmers with no prosthetic aid and, by finishing in the top ten, she had made history. Natalie du Toit had accomplished her childhood dream and qualified to represent her country at the Beijing Olympics later the same year. She was the first amputee in history to qualify to compete in an able-bodied Olympic event.

Natalie du Toit was born on 29 January 1984. As a child, she loved to swim and when she was just six years of age she dreamed of swimming in the Olympics one day. For the next ten years she trained hard to reach her goal and the swimming community in Cape Town could see that they had a potential world beater in Natalie. She set numerous national records in her age groups in both medley events and dominated most of her races. At barely sixteen years of age, she very narrowly missed qualifying for the 2000 Sydney games.

Then in February 2001, as she was riding her scooter back to school after swimming practice, a careless driver crashed into her as he was pulling out on to the road from a parking lot. The impact completely smashed Natalie's left leg. The scene was described as 'gruesome'. Natalie remembers calling out, 'I've lost my leg. I've lost my leg.' Although doctors spent four days trying to save her leg, in the end they had no choice but to amputate the lower limb.

Incredibly, 124 days after the accident and still unable to walk, Natalie was back in a swimming pool. 'Lying in hospital, there was never a doubt in my mind that I would get back to swimming,' Natalie says. 'Swimming was my life, it was my passion.' Looking back, she says that she got back in the water to see what she could do. Little did she know then that she would find the flipside, and that it would help her to realize her childhood dreams and more; she would soon become something of a sporting legend.

In 2002, less than two years after her accident, Natalie qualified for the 800m final at the Commonwealth Games, a huge achievement; it was the first time anybody with an amputated limb had reached the Commonwealth finals or, for that matter, any other able-bodied international swimming event. Although she didn't come close to winning against able-bodied competitors at those games, she did win two gold medals for the multi-disability 50m and 100m freestyle events and she received the 'David Dixon Award for Outstanding Athlete of the Games' ahead of the Australian swimmer Ian Thorpe who won six gold medals and one silver as well as setting a new world record.

In 2003 Natalie competed in the Afro-Asian Games where she won silver and bronze medals for the 800m and 400m freestyle races. In the same year, at the All-Africa Games she won a gold medal for the 800m freestyle. Incredibly, these victories were won swimming against able-bodied competitors. The following year, 2004, Natalie won a total of six medals, five gold and one silver at the Paralympics in Athens.

But, it was in Beijing in the summer of 2008 that Natalie du Toit realized her dream of representing her country in the Olympics. In the 10km open water race, she finished in sixteenth place in a field of twenty-four world-class able-bodied swimmers. It was an outstanding achievement. She was honoured to carry the South African flag in the opening ceremony, which was another record as it was the first time a disabled athlete was given the honour of carrying a flag at an able-bodied Olympics. The same honour was given to her in the subsequent Paralympics where Natalie won a staggering five gold medals.

Today, in addition to her swimming, Natalie du Toit studies sports management and is a motivational speaker. She achieved her childhood dream of competing in the Olympics. It was a huge achievement just to qualify, bearing in mind that she is so disadvantaged physically compared to able-bodied swimmers. Her achievement in qualifying for the Olympics is staggering; it is like someone entering a world kayaking race using only a one-sided paddle. But, now that she has achieved her dream, she is focused on another, looking forward to the 2012 Olympics in London where she hopes not just to qualify, but perhaps do the impossible and win a medal.

Natalie du Toit represents the Olympic ideal; it is not the winning that is important, but the taking part. The victory is not just found in the moment of triumph, but in the struggle to achieve one's goals. Like her fellow countryman Oscar Pistorius, Natalie du Toit has a paradigm of possibility. She demonstrates that even following a tragic setback, with the right mindset, anything is possible; in the face of adversity, we can accomplish great things.

It wasn't just Oscar Pistorius and Natalie du Toit who inspired those who watched the Beijing Paralympics. Every one of the 4,000 competitors reminds us that, even after tragedy, life can be full of possibilities. Each athlete has a personal story of triumph over adversity, and their presence at the Paralympics was, in itself, a tremendous flipside. Their struggle to compete, to be the best that they can be, brought meaning and purpose to their lives. More significantly, it is a flipside that each individual created out of the tragedies and accidents in their past by focusing on the possibilities of the future.

THREE FINGERS, THREE TOES
AND A POSITIVE ATTITUDE

'I would rather have one leg and a positive attitude
than two legs and a negative attitude every single
time.'

Roger W. Crawford II

Roger W. Crawford II was born with a congenital birth defect
known as ectrodactyly. All four of his limbs were affected. He
was born with two fingers on his left hand and one finger on
his right. He had three toes on his right foot, his left leg was
amputated when he was just five years old. Yet today Roger is
a renowned and sought-after motivational speaker, and like
Oscar Pistorius, Roger Crawford II's success can be traced
back to his disability.

'I imagine that you will be surprised to find out that I feel
my handicap has helped me in many, many ways,' he said.
'Isn't it interesting that when we wrestle with our weaknesses,
we uncover our strengths?'

Despite his disabilities, Roger earned certification from
the United States Professional Tennis Association as a
professional tennis coach. He holds a bachelor's degree in
communications from Loyola-Marymount University in Los
Angeles and he became the first severely handicapped person
to play an NCAA Division I college sport.

Roger found the flipside to his disability through his
chosen career as a professional speaker. 'The feeling that I
have,' he said, 'is that through my work I have made a
difference. I love my job and I believe in my job. So to me, I'll
never have to work another day in my life.' His advice to
people who ask is simple, but profound: 'Concentrate on what
you can do instead of worrying about what you cannot do.'
Oscar Pistorius put it this way: 'I have a few disabilities, but I

have millions of abilities. I'm not going to let my disabilities overshadow my abilities.'

THERE ARE SOME BIG ROCKS UP THERE!

In the heat of the Texas summer, a veteran climber is making his way down the Guadalupe Peak in Texas. As he looks ahead, he becomes somewhat perplexed. In front of him is a group of men who are on their way to the top. He looks around at the men incredulously. There is no way they are going to be able to make it to the top of the mountain. The old man does his best to warn them: 'You boys know there're some big rocks up there?' But the men just smile and reply, 'Yeah, we figured there might be.' All of the men in the party were aware that climbing to the top of the mountain would not be easy, but none of them had any doubts that they would make it to the summit.

Guadalupe Peak is the highest mountain in Texas, just ten miles from the New Mexico border. The summit rises to 8,749 feet and is marked by a stainless steel obelisk, erected by American Airlines in 1958 to commemorate the centenary of the Butterfield Overland Mail, a stagecoach route that passed south of the mountain. From the summit there are magnificent 270-degree views. Salt flats stretch into the distance westwards, and the Chihuahuan desert extends south and east, beyond the imposing outline of the El Capitan cliffs. The full circle of the horizon is obscured only to the north by the lower peaks.

The climb is, by all accounts, an incredible experience. It is a 4.25 mile trail that starts from the National Park campground and passes different kinds of terrain and a variety of views along the route. Climbers see the central Pine Springs Canyon, the desert plains to the south, then flatter land within the mountains before finally arriving at the peak itself, which becomes visible only towards the end of the trail. By the time climbers reach the summit, they will have climbed over 3,000 feet.

Most climbers reach the summit in less than five hours, but it took the group of men five long days to climb to the top. However, the important thing was, despite the old man's warning and a lot of other people's misgivings, the men succeeded in reaching the summit. They had achieved what many people had said was impossible. They had climbed the highest mountain in Texas in their wheelchairs!

One of the wheelchair climbers that day was a man called Don Rogers. When Rogers was just twenty-one years of age, he was involved in a motorcycle accident that left him paralysed from the waist down. It was a devastating tragedy, but at the same time it was also the catalyst for change that brought new challenges and gave him new directions for his life.

'The accident left me with decreased motor function and sensory function,' Rogers says. 'I still have pretty good use of my legs, but not enough to walk without braces and crutches, which are a bit cumbersome. I found pretty quickly that the wheelchair was really the best way for me to get around.' And, it was in his wheelchair that Rogers found a new life.

'It's somewhat ironic,' Rogers says, 'because I think the accident created opportunities for me to do some things, kind of more consistent with my attitude on life, that I might not have had otherwise.' One opportunity was playing wheelchair sports. 'After I graduated from high school,' he says, 'I really thought the sports part of my life was over, at least from a highly competitive standpoint.' But, through his involvement in wheelchair sports, Rogers found not just a new world of opportunities; he also found a new career path had been presented to him in the form of recreational therapy.

Rogers took to wheelchair sports just a few weeks after recovering from his accident and found that he had an aptitude for wheelchair track and field events. He went on to become the world record holder for the 100m dash. He enjoyed playing basketball, tennis and even touch football. It was through becoming more and more involved with wheelchair sports that Rogers realized that this was now a real passion in his life, which prompted him to give up his career in engineering drawing and design to work in recreational therapy. 'I soon realized I didn't want to come into an office every day and sit at a computer or drawing board. I turned in my notice and left.'

Today Don Rogers is Associate Professor for Recreational Therapy at Indiana State University and an advocate for the disabled community. He directs the Challenge course at the university, which he designed to help people with disabilities experience outdoor trail-type activities where they have to negotiate trail-like scenarios and overcome various obstacles along the course. He demonstrates that when we approach a goal with a positive attitude, we can achieve things that, previously, we had thought impossible. And that belief is the cornerstone of the flipside; when we come through adversity, we often become aware of our own potential for the first time. Overcoming difficulties can create a paradigm shift, where people come to believe, through their struggle and conquest, that even though they may have suffered loss, life remains full of possibilities.

CHAPTER 15

THE THREE AVENUES: THE SEARCH FOR MEANING

'We must never forget that we may also find meaning in life even when confronted with a hopeless situation, when facing a fate that cannot be changed. For what then matters is to bear witness to the uniquely human potential at its best, which is to transform a personal tragedy into a triumph, to turn one's predicament into a human achievement.'

Viktor Frankl, *Man's Search for Meaning*

THEY CAME FOR him on 25 September 1942. Along with his wife Tilly and his parents, Dr Viktor Frankl was transported to Theresienstadt concentration camp in the north-west region of what is now the Czech Republic. It was to be the beginning of an unimaginable nightmare that would last three years, in which Dr Frankl lost almost everything and everyone that he held dear. With the exception of his one sister who had escaped by emigrating to Australia, all of his family were murdered. Dr Frankl survived one of the darkest, most shameful periods in Europe's history and bore witness to depravation and killing on a scale that had never been seen before. Yet even in those direst of circumstances, enduring extreme hardship and facing the constant threat of death, Dr Frankl was able to find something in his suffering and through his experiences that would not just change his life, but would also go on to help literally hundreds of thousands of others. Dr Frankl did not just survive Nazi persecution, he found a flipside.

The Fortress of Terezin was built in the latter part of the eighteenth century and took its name from the mother of the Austrian emperor Joseph II who commissioned it. During the First World War it was used as a prison, but in 1941 the Gestapo turned the fort into a concentration camp and it became known by the German name of Theresienstadt. The main fortress had been a Czech town before the war and had the capacity to accommodate 7,000 people. After the Nazis had converted it into a concentration camp, at any one time, over 50,000 Jewish men, women and children would be crammed in.

In his book *Man's Search For Meaning*, Viktor Frankl describes the horrific living conditions in Theresienstadt:

> Fifteen hundred captives were cooped up in a shed built to accommodate probably two hundred at most. We were cold and hungry and there was not enough room for everyone to squat on the ground, let alone to lie down. One five-ounce piece of bread was our only food for four days.

All the inmates of Theresienstadt were used as slave labour, and those who were too weak to work were deported to Auschwitz to be gassed. Food was scarce, medicines and tobacco were forbidden and the camp rules even forbade men and women to meet. Anyone caught breaking the rules or not seen to be working hard enough could expect to be beaten or worse. But the thing that they feared most was the constant threat of being transported to one of the Nazi death camps such as Auschwitz or Bergen-Belsen.

The final records show that when the Russian Army liberated Theresienstadt at the end of the war on 9 May 1945, they found a total of just 17,247 survivors. Of the 144,000 Jews who were sent to Theresienstadt, 33,000 died in the camp, mostly from hunger, stress and disease (especially the typhus epidemic which affected the camp inmates at the very end of the war); more than 88,000 people were deported to Auschwitz and other extermination camps, and of the 15,000 or so children who had been living in the children's home inside the camp, only ninety-three survived.

With that background, it is difficult to imagine how it is possible that anyone could find any solace or meaning in the sufferings endured in a Nazi concentration camp. Yet Dr Frankl managed to do just that, and more. His experiences led him to what many psychologists believe was one of the most significant discoveries of the twentieth century in the field of clinical psychology. It was a discovery that has helped people in the darkest periods of their own lives, and has repercussions for anyone facing any form of adversity, trauma or suffering. That discovery was a new approach in psychotherapy that was based upon what Dr Frankl referred to as the Three Avenues to the meaning of life.

THE THREE AVENUES

Viktor Frankl was born on 26 March 1905 to a Jewish family in Vienna. His father was a civil servant, but Viktor developed a passion for medicine and, in particular, psychology. His specialist areas were the treatment of depression and the prevention of suicides. From 1933–7 Viktor Frankl was head of the 'Suicide Pavilion' at the Vienna General

Hospital, which sought to help people who were prone to be suicidal.

It was through his subsequent observations and experiences in the Nazi concentration camps that Dr Frankl kept coming back to one question: How can one say 'yes' to life in spite of tragedy and suffering? The answer to that question was what formed the basis of a completely new field of psychotherapy developed by Dr Frankl which became known as 'logotherapy'. The word *logo* derives from the Greek word for 'meaning'. Logotherapy differs from other schools of psychology in that it is concerned with helping patients or clients find meaning in their experiences, particularly in times of adversity. Dr Frankl had concluded that human beings are not primarily motivated by pleasure or power. He believed that what moves us, above all else, is the will to find meaning in our lives.

Logotherapy teaches that there are three main avenues through which people may find meaning. The First Avenue is the meaning we find through creating something or doing a deed. This could literally be anything we do that we believe has some value or that we consider is worthwhile; from writing a poem, to taking care of another person or a pet, to tending a garden or building a house.

The Second Avenue to meaning in life is found when we experience something or encounter someone. Logotherapy helps people to appreciate that they do not need to win or necessarily to succeed in achieving their goals in order to find meaning in life. The Second Avenue supports the Olympic ideal; it is not the winning that is important, it is the taking part. Dr Frankl taught that the experience itself – the taking part – can be as valuable, or sometimes more valuable, than winning a medal.

For me, one of the best examples of the Second Avenue to meaning in life came from a wonderful story that appeared in the *Chicago Tribune* in May 2008. The women's softball teams of Western Oregon and Central Washington Universities were playing against each other in a vital league game.

The diminutive figure of Sara Tucholsky, just 5ft 2in, stepped up to the plate. Two of her teammates were on bases. Sara swung and missed the pitcher's first throw. She steadied herself for the second throw and with the best swing of her life, she hit the ball out of the park. It was the first time she had hit a home run in competitive softball and it meant that her team would get three runs which would put them in the lead.

Sara was ecstatic, but her excitement was short-lived. As she rounded the first base, she forgot to tag it and, in turning back to touch the base, she twisted her knee and collapsed. All she could do was crawl back to first base. Unless she could make it round all of the bases, the home run would not count. The first-base coach warned that she would be called out if any of her teammates tried to help her. The umpire said that she could call for a 'pinch' runner (someone to run in her place) but that would only count as a single run. The three runs that she had been expecting (the other two from her teammates who had been standing on the bases) would not count.

Then something happened that stunned everybody – the spectators, the players and the referees. The Central Washington player holding first base, Mallory Holtman, asked the umpire if she and her teammates could help Sara Tucholsky. Although it was something that had no precedent, the umpire confirmed that there was no rule against it. So Holtman and one of her teammates, Liz Wallace, put their arms under Sara Tucholsky's legs as she put her arms around their shoulders, and they carried her around the bases, gently lowering her at each of the three other bases so that she could tag each one with her good leg. As they reached the home plate, the crowd were moved to tears and on their feet, cheering.

Mallory Holtman took her softball seriously. She was the career holder of the most number of home runs scored in the Great North-West Athletic Conference league. Helping Sara Tulcholsky to make her three runs that day cost Holtman and her team the game (which they lost 4–2) and, as a consequence, ended their chance of winning the conference league and earning a place in the play-offs. But when interviewed later, Holtman said, 'In the end, it is not about winning or losing so much. It was about this girl. She hit it over the fence and was in pain, and she deserved a home run.'

Although Mallory Holtman and her teammates lost the game that day, they discovered something far more significant than any trophy. They had found the Second Avenue to meaning in life. Perhaps their story will inspire others to do the same. Central Washington coach Gary Frederick said afterwards that it was an 'unbelievable' act of sportsmanship. It was something that everyone involved with that day will remember and talk about for the rest of their lives.

The Third Avenue to meaning in life, Dr Frankl wrote, is the 'most important'. It refers to the meaning of life that can be found even in unavoidable suffering and insurmountable adversity. The Third Avenue offers hope that, even through the direst of personal tragedies, in the face of the inevitable and the incurable, people are still yet able to find a flipside. 'Even the helpless victim of a hopeless situation,' wrote Dr Frankl, 'facing a fate he cannot change, may rise above himself, may grow beyond himself, and by so doing change himself. He may turn a personal tragedy into a triumph.'

In 1978 Dr Frankl received a letter from a young man called Jerry Long who, a year earlier, had broken his neck in a tragic diving accident. Jerry Long was eighteen years old when he wrote to Dr Frankl, but his words sparked a friendship that lasted a lifetime.

In the letter, Long had written: 'I view my life as being abundant with meaning and purpose. The attitude that I adopted that fateful day has become my personal credo for life: I broke my neck, it didn't break me. I am currently enrolled in my first psychology course in college. I believe that my handicap will only enhance my ability to help others. I know that without the suffering, the growth that I have achieved would have been impossible.'

Though just eighteen years old at the time, Long had been moved when he read Dr Frankl's book *Man's Search For Meaning* and he had been determined to give his accident a positive meaning. In the few years following his accident, he learnt to type using a stick held by his mouth and he went on to finish college. Long attended courses at college via a special telephone system that allowed him to hear and participate in class discussions. Through dogged determination and hard work, Jerry Long later obtained a doctorate in Clinical Psychology and went on to receive numerous professional accolades and awards in that field. However, perhaps his greatest accolade came from his friend and mentor Dr Viktor Frankl, who described Jerry Long as 'a living testimony to "the defiant power of the human spirit"', a phrase referred to in Logotherapy to explain the Third Avenue to meaning in life.

The Third Avenue was one of the first steps on the path that led to the discovery of the phenomenon known as post-traumatic growth (PTG). But, while other psychologists were demonstrating that all trauma brought opportunities for growth, through Logotherapy Dr Frankl had provided a prescription to help people achieve that growth. The Third Avenue became the path to the flipside where there was no tangible or obvious benefit to be found in the trauma.

In their work as therapists, practitioners of Logotherapy will, through reflective questions, guide a patient to find meaning in their suffering, and give new meaning to their life. Following on from earlier chapters, the stages of recovery and redemption in Logotherapy will hopefully sound familiar.

In the first instance, Logotherapy practitioners try to help the client to distance themselves from the problem and see it more objectively, as if they were an outsider looking in. Then, they have the client reframe the negative problem by looking at positive possibilities, and helping in a search for new goals and potentials in their future. Finally, it is through the new goals and future potential that the client is able to appreciate new positive meanings in life.

Dr Frankl said that through Logotherapy, 'you dig out, just make people more conscious of something that has been within them all along'. It is something he referred to as 'the wisdom of the heart'. He went on to explain that we all know intuitively what life is all about. We all have a thirst for meaning in our lives, and Logotherapy reminds us of that need and helps people find it even in what appears to be a hopeless situation. Each situation in life confronts us with the question, 'What will this mean for me?', but it is a question that can only be answered by our response to what happened.

GIVING MEANING AND GETTING MADD

It was a beautiful sunny May day in Fair Oaks, California. Thirteen-year-old Cari Lightner was walking with a friend to a local carnival. As she chatted with her friend, Cari was unaware that a car had turned into the residential street and was speeding and swerving erratically. The car accelerated and swerved straight into Cari. The impact literally knocked her out of her shoes and catapulted her over 125 feet. Her friend was frozen with horror. The car's driver passed out, but when he came to, he sped away leaving Cari dying on the road.

It wasn't until Candace Lightner returned home later in the afternoon with the shopping that she found her father and her ex-husband Steve sitting on the front lawn, waiting for her. Her father went up to her and held her in his arms. When she asked what was wrong, Steve said 'We've lost Cari.' Candace wasn't sure what he meant. Then he looked her in the eye and said, 'She's dead. She was hit by a car and she is dead.' Candace collapsed, screaming.

The day after Cari's funeral, the police called to say that they had caught and arrested the driver. Later that day, Candace was driving past the spot where her daughter had been run over and saw police looking over the scene. She immediately got out of the car and asked if they were investigating her daughter's death. 'They said that they were and I told them I was her mother,' Candace says. 'Their response was, "Well then, I guess you know the circumstances."' She didn't know what they were referring to, but managed to prise the information out of them: that the forty-seven-year-old driver of the car that had killed her daughter had been drunk. Candace was horrified to learn that the man had a history of drunk-driving. This would be his fifth conviction in five years, but worst of all, on the day he killed Cari, the driver had been out on bail following another recent drunk-driving incident.

Candace was astonished and incensed by what she learned. She asked how much prison time the man would serve for killing Cari. One of the officers looked at her and his answer was chilling. 'The man wouldn't spend any time behind bars. 'That's the way the system works.'

'I felt so helpless. So lost. So angry,' said Candace. As she thought about what the police had told her, she became more and more irate. Later that day, she decided that she was going to do something about it and stop the senseless tragedies caused by drunk drivers throughout North America. She called her crusade MADD – Mothers Against Drunk Drivers – and its headquarters were Cari's bedroom.

Cari Lightner became the face of the MADD campaign. In October of that year, Cindi Lamb, whose six-month-old baby daughter Laura had been paralysed from the neck down following an accident caused by a drunk driver, joined the campaign. Alcohol is involved in nearly 60 per cent of fatal car crashes.

On 1 October 1980 Candace Lightner and Cindi Lamb created a momentous shift in public awareness at a press conference they gave on Capitol Hill in Washington, DC. Chuck Hurley, who was then working for the National Safety Council, says, 'On that day, public tolerance of drunk driving changed for ever.' Since that day, through its powerful public campaigns and political lobbying, MADD has helped change the law. According to projected statistics reviewed by the US National Highway Safety Administration, MADD has contributed to saving more than 300,000 lives since its inception in 1980.

Nothing can compensate for the loss of a child. There is no flipside in losing a loved one yet, in a sense, those are the times when we need to find a flipside most. This is why many people, like Candace Lightner and Cindi Lamb, respond to tragedy by giving meaning to their loss through supporting or setting up a charity to help other people facing similar circumstances. Candace Lightner and Cindi Lamb created a flipside that gave their loss a meaning and saved the lives of hundreds of thousands of people across North America.

CHAPTER 16

THE RELATIONSHIP FACTOR: SURROUNDING YOURSELF WITH THE RIGHT PEOPLE

'The quality of your life is the quality of your relationships.'

Tony Robbins

IN APRIL 1998 Mark Pollock remembers being 'on the crest of a wave'. Everything was going his way. He was in his fourth and final year at Trinity College, Dublin and he was just weeks away from sitting the final exams in a Business & Economics degree. As captain of the college rowing team, he was looking forward to participating in the summer regattas, and he had a job lined up to start at a City investment bank in September. Life was sweet, until one day while doing circuit training in the gym, he noticed that something was wrong.

It happened without warning. Mark noticed his peripheral vision was becoming blurred. Having had detached retinas as a child, he was aware that it could return but, as he had managed fairly well in the past, he was not overly concerned. When the diagnosis was confirmed, Mark was not prepared for the seriousness of the condition this time around. Within a matter of weeks, surgeons operated to repair Mark's eyes, but when he came round from the operation, he was completely blind. A second operation also failed and Mark was now facing a very uncertain future. 'The shock of going blind was almost unbearable,' he says. 'One moment I was on the crest of a wave with everything going my way, the next I went blind. I thought my life was over.'

Mark remembers that time as being a 'disaster'. 'Suddenly everything that I had worked for had been lost,' he says. He still went to Henley Regatta, but not being able to participate and hearing all of his friends planning to go travelling through the summer and start new careers only made Mark feel worse about his own life. It was the lowest point in his life, yet in hindsight, it was the catalyst that would trigger unexpected changes and lead Mark on a new life path that took him all over the world to places and experiences that he would never have dreamed possible prior to losing his eyesight.

Since becoming blind, Mark's life has been anything but the 'treadmill' he thinks his life might have been in invest-ment banking. He has become an international motivational speaker, an adventure athlete and an author. Mark has made many inspiring presentations throughout Europe, Asia and North America, focusing on core issues such as taking personal responsibility for our actions, facing facts and making success happen.

Mark practices what he preaches and uses his adventures as models in his motivational presentations. In 2002 he won silver and bronze medals in the Commonwealth Rowing Championships and on 10 April 2004, six years to the day since becoming blind, he completed the world's most extreme marathon at the North Pole.

Mark now recognizes that his blindness brought new and

exciting possibilities. 'None of the career advisers I saw at college even outlined a career anything like the one I have now,' he says. 'I'm not sure that they were aware that a career like mine even existed.'

What does Mark consider the most important factors responsible for him becoming the person that he is today? 'There came a point when I realized that there were still possibilities for me to do things with my life, and possibilities of continuing sports, in particular rowing.' Mark has always been what he calls a 'positive realist' and he thinks this unquestionably played a part in his success. In addition, he has always been goal-oriented. 'I find it very natural to focus on goals,' he says, 'and run lots of different projects'. As a result, he is always looking forward to the challenges ahead. But his final comment echoes the sentiments of so many people I interviewed about the flipside. 'The most important thing for me, the thing that made a real difference, was having the right people around me, to help me. It wasn't easy suddenly being reliant on other people. I had to swallow my pride. I needed to learn to be willing to ask for, and receive, help and support from other people. But the support I received made all the difference.'

THE SCIENCE OF HAPPINESS

'Word needs to be spread; it is important to work on social skills, close interpersonal ties and social support in order to be happy.'

Professor Edward Diener

In January 2005 *Time* magazine published an article entitled 'The New Science of Happiness', exploring what it is that makes people feel happy. It is a subject that has intrigued psychologists for decades, but it is only in recent years, with the interest led by Professor Martin Seligman in what has been called 'Positive Psychology', that scientists in this field have begun to turn their attention to those emotions that promote health and well-being in place of the traditional approach of treating mental health problems.

The article referred to a research study conducted in 2002, led by Professor Edward Diener and Professor Seligman, that seemed to contradict commonly held notions of precisely what makes us feel happy. Many people assume that money and material possessions will bring happiness. Professors Diener and Seligman surveyed university students and the results revealed that once our basic needs are met, additional income does very little to raise our feeling of happiness. They found that happiness is not associated with youth, marriage or intelligence, and it is not significantly affected by the weather, although lack of sunlight can cause Seasonal Affective Disorder (SAD), otherwise known as winter depression or winter blues, a mood disorder caused by lack of sunlight. The single most significant factor that contributes to people's happiness is their relationships.

Connecting with other people on a personal level, according to most, if not all, of the scientific studies on the subject, is what makes us feel happiest. Helping others is something that gives life purpose and meaning. This explains how and why people who experience setbacks and adversity often report being happier than they were before the setback or trauma. The traumatic event is often seen as a spark that ignites closer relationships with people in our social circle, especially our friends and family, and it invariably leads to more profound relationships with new people.

Today, most happiness exercises being tested by 'positive psychologists' are focused on helping people feel connected to others. Science has finally begun to understand the wisdom of the Dalai Lama:

We humans are social beings. We come into the world as the result of others' actions. We survive here in dependence on others. Whether we like it or not, there is hardly a moment of our lives when we do not benefit from others' activities. For this reason it is hardly surprising that most of our happiness arises in the context of our relationships with others.

On Friday, 29 February 2008 the Wayne High School Badgers, the school basketball team in Bicknell, Utah, were playing in the state 1A semi-finals. Leading the team was eighteen-year-old Porter Ellett. At first glance, spectators who didn't know him may have wondered why he was there. Why would a college basketball team include a young man who only has one arm?

Porter lost the use of his right arm when he was only four years old following an accident when he fell out of a pickup truck and crushed his arm under the wheels. His arm remained weak and, after over a dozen breaks, he elected to have his arm amputated. 'It just seemed a lot less hassle that way,' he says. What is even more remarkable is the fact that Porter was right-handed and had to learn how to play all sports using what was his weaker left arm.

Despite having only his left arm, Porter Ellett developed into an outstanding athlete. In addition to representing his school on the basketball court, he plays for the school's track, cross country and baseball teams. He is not there to make up the numbers. He scored sixteen of his team's fifty points the night of the state semi-finals. The team coach, Kade Morrell, says Porter is a natural leader. Porter's got 'a winning attitude', the coach says, and 'he's a prime example of how far attitude can take you'.

Once the game starts, spectators are transfixed by Porter's abilities on the basketball court. He is in the starting line-up because he is an exceptional player who played a major role in the team's success in reaching the semi-finals. When asked how he feels at some spectators' reactions the first time they see him walk on to the court, Porter smiled and said, 'It's kinda fun to see people's reactions when they doubt you and they see you walk out on the court and wonder why you're even playing; then you get to go out and prove what you're worth'.

Yet while the spotlight was on Porter Ellett for most of the season, he credits his success to his teammates and friends. 'Without my teammates, my friends, I wouldn't be anything,' he says. 'They are my support. When other people knock me down, they are always there for me.' When Porter Ellett was asked to appear on *Good Morning America* on 3 March 2008, he agreed, but only on the condition that he could bring all of his basketball teammates with him. 'They are the reason I am successful,' he said.

This importance of having a strong network of support from friends and family is something that arises time and again in people's stories of the flipside. Almost without exception, people credit their friends and family with helping them get through challenging times. If nothing else, being surrounded by positive people tends to have a supportive and energizing effect.

Mike Jetter is certain that having the unconditional love and support from his family and friends helped him enormously in getting through the years of aggressive treatment for chronic myeloid leukaemia. 'There is one person, in particular, without whom I wouldn't have been able to get through it all,' he says, 'and that is my wife Bettina.' Then Mike added an interesting insight: 'I don't think it is necessarily the number of people in your life that counts as much as the quality of the relationships that you have.' There seems to be general agreement among people who have found the flipside that, in times of difficulty, it is better to have one or two devoted people by your side than a hundred who are not.

When Amit Goffer found himself paralysed and facing an uncertain future in a wheelchair, and then developed the ReWalk™, a device that helps paraplegics to walk again, it was, he said, largely thanks to a very supportive family – his wife and children – that he was able to overcome his adversity and go on to find the flipside. Mark Pollock agreed: 'Having the right people around me was absolutely key', he said, in overcoming the problems he initially encountered when he lost his eyesight.

In New Zealand, Anna Fitzpatrick said that her family and friends played a 'huge part' in helping her through the challenges that came with having alopecia. 'They have been such a strong support and have let me become my own person. They supported me when I wanted it,' she says, 'and took a step back when I didn't. Trying to find a cure is what all parents want, but when I decided I was tired of all the medications when I was ten years old and said I no longer wanted to try and "fix" my problem, they respected my wishes. That must have been really hard to do when all you want to do is help your ten-year-old get something back that she has lost.'

We discussed earlier how our relationships with friends and family are key influences for our feelings of happiness. This goes some way to explaining why studies have found that lottery winners do not wind up significantly happier than a control group of ordinary people. In fact, it may explain why so many end up miserable. Winning money doesn't necessarily enhance our relationships. In some cases, it destroys them. It also sheds light on why people who lose the use of their limbs in an accident (even though they can often be full of anger and anxiety immediately after the injury) relate happiness as their strongest emotion eight weeks after the accident. Relationships tend to become much stronger and more intimate following an illness or injury. People feel connected rather than isolated and often draw strength and encouragement from each other. This is why developing strong, close relationships improves people's chances of finding the flipside following any setback or personal tragedy. As Rabbi Harold Kushner reflects in his bestselling book *When All You've Ever Wanted Isn't Enough*: 'Sooner or later, the wave will come along and knock down what we have worked so hard to build up. When that happens, only the person who has somebody's hand to hold will be able to laugh.'

CHAPTER 17

FOCUSING THE MIND: FINDING INNER STRENGTH

'In the midst of winter, I finally learned there was in me an invincible summer.'

Albert Camus

THE SCENE IS set in 1964. A little boy, just seven years old, sits in front of a black-and-white television enthralled by the most exciting TV show he has ever seen. The show is called *Maverick* and stars James Garner as the hero, the cowboy gambler who could outplay any cardsharp. The boy dreams that one day, he will grow up and be just like Maverick. He will beat all the gamblers at the card table.

Cut to 2008. In the world of professional cardsharps, no one can touch him. He is not a magician but what he does is the closest thing to real magic that you'll ever see anyone do with a regular pack of playing cards. As an amateur magician myself, I had heard stories about Richard Turner for a number of years. He is the man, they said, who can deal from the second top, bottom and even the middle of a pack of cards, right in front of your eyes without anybody suspecting a thing.

He makes his childhood hero Maverick seem like an amateur. Richard is both admired and revered in the magic community and affectionately referred to as 'The Cheat'.

I finally caught up with The Cheat, aka Richard Turner, in February 2008 at a lecture he gave at Alicante University on the Costa Blanca in Spain. Along with every other person in the audience, I sat in awe as he demonstrated exactly what he could do with a pack of cards. What he does has to be seen to be believed. At one point, he handed a pack of cards to a member of the audience to shuffle and return to him. He then asked another audience member to imagine that they were playing a game of five card poker with four other people. 'I am the dealer,' he said. 'Who do you want me to ensure has the winning hand? Player number one, two, three, four or five?' The man looked perplexed and sceptical, as were we all. 'Number four,' he answered. But how could Richard take a freshly shuffled pack of cards and then deal five hands but make sure that a specific hand nominated by the spectator would win?

Without any hesitation, Richard quickly dealt out five hands, each with five cards and then revealed each hand, one by one. Hands one through to three contained nothing but a few low pairs, hand five had nothing, but as the fourth hand was revealed, to the utter amazement and disbelief of everyone in the audience, it showed a full house!

Everyone in the room was a magician, yet none of them had a clue how Richard had been able to do what he did. No one could believe what they had just seen. I examined the cards myself and could find nothing out of the ordinary, they appeared to be standard Bee playing cards used in casinos all over the world. Before we had time to reflect upon what had just happened, Richard followed it up with more equally remarkable demonstrations. Everyone who has seen Richard in person and witnessed his work agrees that he is without equal in the world of cardsharps. But, what makes Richard's work even more remarkable is the fact that he is blind!

After the lecture, I met up with Richard in person, one to one. He is an unassuming, gentle man, 5ft 8in in height and of medium build. He has blond hair, clear blue eyes and has a trim beard and moustache. He certainly looks the part of a cardsharp in a black suit and crisply ironed shirt and bolo tie. Aside from the tie, which is rarely seen outside North America, there was nothing out of the ordinary in his appearance. But as I talked to him, I soon realized that Richard is far from ordinary.

Richard explained that he began to lose his eyesight when he was just nine years old. It happened quite suddenly; one day, he noticed that he was unable to see the blackboard at school. It wasn't long afterwards that he was diagnosed with a condition known as 'birdshot retinochoroidopathy'. Today the condition is treatable, provided it is diagnosed early enough. But back in the 1960s no treatment was available. It was incurable and, over time, it caused Richard to go blind.

By his mid-teens, Richard's vision was approximately 20/400. That means that Richard needed to be twenty feet away from an object that a person with normal eyesight would be able to see at a distance of 400 feet. It is also generally considered to be twice the threshold of what is defined as 'legal blindness'. In his thirties, Richard could still hold a playing card close to his eyes and be able to tell court cards (the jacks, queens and kings) from the rest of the pack, and he could make out the aces as they appeared as large white blurs. But today his eyesight has reached the point where he can't tell whether a card is face up or down.

Yet Richard has never considered his vision (or lack of it) to be a handicap. In fact, remarkably, he refers to it as a 'gift'! When I asked him to explain, he said that, in hindsight, his blindness may have been the best thing to have happened to him. He mentioned, for example, that his blindness made him develop his sense of touch to a level that enables him to do the things he does. Part of the reason he can work with cards in the way that he does is that he can feel cards by their weight; the court cards have more ink and therefore weigh slightly more than the number cards. Although the difference is minuscule and undetectable to you and me, Richard has developed his sense of touch so he differentiates the court cards from the number cards.

The research and development department of the United States Playing Card Company, the largest manufacturer of playing cards in the world, regularly sends cards for Richard to 'analyse'. The head of the department admitted that he has tried fooling Richard a few times by sending him decks made from old stock mixed with new decks, but Richard always manages to pick up the discrepancies.

Richard Turner is one of those people who excels at anything to which he puts his mind. He has studied martial arts for over thirty-five years and has fought hundreds of full contact fights, some of which can be seen on his DVD. How does a man who is blind fight against a man who can see? Richard Turner's answer is 'carefully!' At the time that Richard did most of his full contact fights, while he couldn't see anything directly in front of him, he still had limited residual peripheral vision. But, Richard taught himself to 'see' with his mind. This may have sounded far-fetched had we not already met Ben Underwood (who also studies Karate) and learned of the work of Paul Bach-y-rita in previous chapters. It is very difficult to detect Richard's blindness watching him train in a dojo (which can also be seen on his DVD).

Like many of the other people who have found the flipside in their lives, Richard always looks for the positive in all of his life experiences. He says that his blindness has, in many ways, been an advantage to him in his work with cards. It stopped him from being distracted by anything that may be going on around him, whether it was television in the home or the things that were going on outside a car or train whenever he was travelling. Consequently he was always able to practise without distraction. Richard's ability to focus his attention without distraction on whatever he does, he says, is largely responsible for him achieving what he has achieved and becoming the person that he has become.

However, the one characteristic that Richard Turner has in abundance is the one that has helped people to find the flipside even through the most severe adversity. It is a combination of self-discipline, mental strength and a determination to succeed. It is a stubborn refusal to give in to anything or anyone, it is the ability to confront any challenge in the knowledge that every event that happens to us in life has the potential to help us grow from within and become the best that we are capable of being.

INNER FOCUS

Richard Turner believes that his blindness contained a gift, not just because it gave him challenges that he would not otherwise have had to conquer, but because not being able to see enabled him to focus more completely on the things he does in his life. This is not to say that he believes it is better to be blind than sighted. Far from it. What it means is that he instinctively learned to look for a flipside, something positive and life affirming, in all of his experiences. Like so many of the people we have met in this book, Richard has learned to reframe what others see as his disability, and focus only on the positive side – the flipside – of his experiences.

On 19 January 2008 KFox news ran a report on a seminar being given that weekend in El Paso, Texas, by a man called Miguel Valdez. Like Richard Turner, Valdez is a fifth-degree black belt and like Richard Turner, Valdez is registered blind. 'I am unable to drive. I'm unable to read without extreme magnification, and I'm unable to see faces,' he said. He runs his own martial arts school in El Paso, but that weekend he was not there to talk about Karate. He was there to address a group of disabled children to remind them that whatever obstacles they may have to face throughout their lives, no matter how big or seemingly insurmountable, if they always looked for the positive side of any experience, they could achieve their dreams.

'My message for these young people,' Vadlez said, 'is not to focus on their limitations, but to focus on what their abilities are, and what their assets are, and the things they're good at.' The seminar was part of a programme called 'Training Tomorrow's Mentors Today', which aimed at empowering people with disabilities. The programme co-ordinator Lucila Lozano said that it was an important message for the children. 'They may be told by key people in their lives that they can't do things,' she said. 'Unless we all see positive people in our lives, then we may not believe we can reach a certain goal.'

FINDING INNER STRENGTH

'When you feel you have met an insurmountable obstacle, I want you to think of me. And then say to yourself "If he can be successful, I can too."'

W. Mitchell

San Francisco, 19 June 1971: twenty-eight-year-old W. Mitchell is on top of the world. That morning he had flown solo in an aeroplane for the first time. The day before he had bought a brand new motorcycle and he was now riding it to work. But life can change in an instant, and it did for W. Mitchell that afternoon. That he would still be alive by the end of that day could be considered a miracle, but the fact that he would find the flipside and through it happiness and success is, to many, a mystery.

As Mitchell approached the junction of 26th Street and South Van Ness on his new bike, a laundry truck pulled out in front of him. The two collided and in the crash that ensued, the bike skidded along the road, crushing Mitchell's elbow and pelvis, and then the petrol cap popped off. The heat of the engine ignited the fuel and, in an instant, Mitchell was engulfed in flames. 'I became a human bonfire,' he says. It was only thanks to an alert man working at a nearby car lot that he survived at all. The man raced over and doused Mitchell with a fire extinguisher. By the time the last of the flames had been extinguished, 65 per cent of his body had been severely burned. Thanks to his helmet, his scalp was largely unscathed and his leather jacket saved his torso from more serious damage. But his face, arms and legs were hideously burned. His hands were black and charred and his legs were red and raw. Mitchell lost consciousness and didn't wake up for two weeks. When he did finally awake, he was in searing agony, facing a very different future.

It took thirteen transfusions, sixteen skin-graft operations and other operations over a period of four months before W. Mitchell was finally able to leave hospital. Once he had been discharged, he remembers having 'a lot of time to figure out how to do stuff'. He had to relearn how to do things for himself. 'I couldn't pick up a fork,' he says, 'take my pants off, go to the bathroom, or dial a phone, without help.' But W. Mitchell is not one to give up. He worked at everything and within six months of the date of his accident, he was flying planes again.

It takes enormous courage and strength to overcome any major trauma, but to overcome two major tragedies requires that much more. Four years after the bike accident, W. Mitchell crashed his plane; he was the only person on board who couldn't walk away from the wreckage. The impact of the crash bruised his spinal cord beyond repair. He was a paraplegic.

Mitchell confesses that he had dark moments. 'I wondered what the hell was happening to me,' he says. 'What had I done to deserve this?' But, ultimately, Mitchell is an extreme optimist and has an 'I can' attitude. He recalls seeing another patient in the hospital gym, a young man who was also paralysed. 'He had been a mountain climber,' says Mitchell, 'a skier, an active outdoors person, and he was convinced his life was over.' Mitchell went over to the man and told him something that gave him reason to think again. 'Before all of this happened to me, there were 10,000 things I could do. Now there are 9,000. I could spend the rest of my life dwelling on the 1,000 that I lost, but I choose to focus on the 9,000 that are left.'

What W. Mitchell went on to achieve after his accidents is, by any standards, astonishing. Following his motorcycle accident, he cofounded Vermont Castings, a $65 million company that manufactures wood burning stoves and employs thousands of people. He later became mayor of the town of Created Butte in Colorado and successfully served two terms. During his time in office, Mitchell used $120,000 of his own money in a campaign to save a nearby mountain from aggressive mining companies. He is a self-made multi-millionaire, a qualified commercial pilot, a media personality and author. Mitchell is an active environmentalist and sits on the board of directors of the National Parks and Conservation Association and American Wildlands. He is an acclaimed public speaker (and currently serves as President of the International Federation of Public Speakers 2008–9), he sky dives and enjoys white water rafting.

W. Mitchell's life is a testimony to how rich life can be on the flipside of extreme adversity. What he enjoys most is inspiring others to see setbacks as new starting points, and to realize that, if he can succeed, so can anyone else. 'I hope to be a touchstone for people, a route to a new way of thinking,' he says on his website. 'Symbols are potent. In America the Liberty bell conjures the concept of freedom in a single image. In India the Taj Mahal shows us, at a glance, the depth and extravagance of human love. In San Francisco, my adopted hometown, the Golden Gate Bridge is a testament to engineering ingenuity that speaks volumes . . . What I want, is to be a symbol for you. With my scarred face, my fingerless paws, my wheelchair – and real, genuine happiness in my heart – I want to be your mental image of the power of the human mind to transcend circumstances.'

Looking back at his life since the accidents, Mitchell believes that there were two main things that got him through it all. One was the love and support from his family and friends, the other was his personal philosophy to life. He is an extreme optimist, focusing on his abilities rather than dwelling on anything he cannot do. He pursued specific goals both in business and in his personal life, and he has made his life meaningful, not just to him, but to everyone he meets. He enjoys helping and inspiring others. In his speeches he stresses one key point to his audiences, summarised in a phrase that he chose as the title for his book: 'It's not what happens to you, it's what you do about it.'

Reflecting on his past, he is in no doubt that he has benefited in many ways from both of his accidents. 'I had the good fortune to learn a few important points along the way – both before and after my injuries – that helped me immeasurably.' Through his experiences, he says, he has a 'great life', and he hopes that his story will remind others that even through extreme adversity, they can have a great life as well. But the most telling comment from Mitchell comes from the value he places on his life's experiences. 'Would I trade what I've learned?' he says. 'Not in the world!'

W. Mitchell overcame two major crises yet he is adamant that what he has achieved, most people can achieve. 'I don't have any special powers,' he says, 'or any magical gift of birth that has allowed me to create my own happiness in the face of tremendous trials. I am no stronger or smarter than the average person. I am a long way from ever being a "saintly" guy . . . All of us are blessed with an inner strength buried inside us somewhere. It's just that most don't get the opportunity to use it as much as I have.'

CHAPTER 18

CONCLUSION

'Avoid problems, and you'll never be the one who overcame them.'

Richard Bach

At THE BEGINNING of *The Flipside*, we set out to discover whether the problems and setbacks that we face in life come with opportunities, and if so, how do we find those opportunities? In the search for the answers, we have heard many stories of problems, obstacles and all manner of adversity that became catalysts for change. From Julio Iglesias and Sir Richard Branson to Oscar Pistorius and Sir Douglas Bader, we have seen financial and personal loss, freak accidents, life-threatening illnesses and human tragedies, transformed into positive and life-enhancing experiences.

It may be tempting to defer the future to Fate or God's Will, and some prefer to believe that life is nothing but a series of random outcomes; they roll the dice, cross their fingers and pray that Lady Luck is on their side. But in analysing the lives of people like Harland Sanders and

Michael Bloomberg, or Walt Disney and Peter Jones, we are led to a very different conclusion as to exactly what it is that drives our destinies.

What has become evident is that, in many instances, the transformation of a problem or setback into an opportunity is not a random occurrence. Although the precise nature of an outcome cannot be foreseen, that the people involved found something within their experiences on which to build a hopeful future was, in many ways, quite predictable. This is because while every problem brings with it an opportunity, it takes a specific type of person with a specific set of beliefs and behaviours to find it.

This is the first key to the flipside. Finding the hidden opportunities in life does not depend upon what happens to us; what matters is how we respond to the challenges that come our way. People like Hsieh Kun-Shan and W. Mitchell demonstrate that, even in the face of extreme tragedy, it is possible to build a new and, in many ways, richer and more meaningful life. That is because they are extreme optimists; they have positive expectations of their future.

Without optimism, even in the face of financial devastation, Harland Sanders might have ended his life wretched and bankrupt, Peter Jones may not have become a Dragon and Tony Robbins may have ended up living on the streets. We know that by becoming optimistic, we dramatically increase the chances of recovering from a life-threatening illness; and leading psychologists from around the world have discovered that whatever we choose to do with our lives, an optimistic outlook will greatly improve our chances of success.

In addition to becoming more optimistic, people who find the flipside tend to have an entrepreneur's mindset; they actively look for opportunities and benefits. They look to the future and focus on their potentials and on future possibilities. Hsieh Kun-Shan explained that this was the secret to his overcoming the harsh challenges following his accident: 'I always think about the bright side,' he said, 'appreciating what is left in me rather than wallowing in regret over what has been taken away.' When we consider the lives of Ben Underwood and Amit Goffer – a boy with no eyes who taught himself to see, and a man who, through his own tragedy and genius, has made it possible for the paralysed to walk – we realize that we can never be sure that anything is impossible. With the right attitude, there will always be unexplored possibilities and potential for the future.

Finding the flipside sometimes requires us to take a step back and look at a problem from different angles and perspectives. To consider, as Edison did throughout his life, what lesson can be learned from any experience and what *need* a situation may expose that will lead us to new discoveries. Had Amit Goffer not been confined to a wheelchair himself, he would not have been drawn to look for alternative solutions for wheelchair users. That he did may enable hundreds of thousands of people to walk again. Had Louis Braille not lost his eyesight, the Braille system of writing and reading for the blind may never have been developed.

Likewise, it was only because the price of chemical fertilizers was becoming exorbitantly expensive that farmer Steve Heard began to look for alternative, more economic and environmentally friendly solutions that could revolutionize farming practices all over the world. And, it was only while waiting in a queue for three long days that Sanu Kaji Shrestha was inspired to change his life and work to save his country from environmental disaster.

The concept of the flipside may, at times, require us to reframe the way we look at life. Many times we have difficulty believing that a loss can lead to gain, or that failure is sometimes a necessary step on the path to success. We cannot conceive that a tragedy, in any form, contains within it the catalyst for a new, meaningful life. Yet, we have seen that loss can lead to gain on the flipside. When Julio Iglesias lost his dream of becoming a professional footballer, he found a new dream and became an international pop star. When Mark Pollock lost his eyesight, he built a new life, full of adventure and excitement that he never dreamed possible, and in doing so he has inspired thousands of people around the world.

Similarly, we have seen that, with the right mindset, failure will hold the key to success. A failed super glue became the 'must-have' office stationery supply known as Post-it notes, and Bette Nesmith Graham, a frustrated typist, through her errors developed a solution that turned her into a multimillionaire. These and other stories demonstrate that if we can focus on the lesson in all failure and disappointment, we will be that much closer to finding a flipside.

In times of personal tragedy, the flipside shows a way forward. People like W. Mitchell, Hsieh Kun-Shan and award-winning songwriter Kim Williams testify that it is possible to not just cope with pain and unspeakable loss, but to go on to transform suffering into something more powerful and life-changing than anyone could have imagined. People like Holocaust survivor Dr Viktor Frankl, trauma survivors like Joni Eareckson Tada and war veterans such as Captain Gerald Coffee, have inspired scientists to investigate how and why some people are able to come through extreme adversity and suffering feeling stronger and more powerful, and certain beyond doubt that they had grown personally or spiritually from their experiences. The resulting studies have demonstrated that any adversity will contain a flipside because there can always be potential for meaning. Dr Viktor Frankl discovered through his experiences as a Holocaust survivor and in his work as a psychiatrist that all suffering, even unavoidable suffering, holds potential for meaning and, in the deepest recesses of our hearts and minds, more than anything else, it is a meaningful life that we all crave.

Stories from the flipside remind us that perhaps the most

important thing in life is the love and support from friends and family. The quality of life is linked to the quality of our relationships. Not only are they the principle cause of our happiness, virtually all people who have found the flipside have acknowledged that their ultimate success was in no small part due to the people around them – their family and friends. Dr James Ruben, the Paediatric Eye Surgeon who cared for Ben Underwood, underlined the importance of the love and support of those closest to us: 'In all my experience, I don't think I've ever seen anyone quite as remarkable as Ben,' he said, 'nor have I seen anyone quite as remarkable as Ben's mom. And, I think that is the secret to a lot of Ben's amazing talents.'

Professor Peter Schulman of the University of Pennsylvania cautions those who think they can face everything alone: 'Even the diehard optimist will occasionally have pessimistic beliefs when exposed to extreme or prolonged stress.' When the time comes to face adversity, it is made all the more possible by the support of the people around us.

Ultimately, the underlying message from the people who have found the flipside is that when things go badly wrong, which they may do from time to time, we need to reframe them and ask questions that will help us find something positive and meaningful. Critical questions that focus on the possibilities ahead of us instead of trapping us in the past. But, mostly, the message from the flipside is that life, much as we would like it to be, does not always conform to our sense of fairness or justice. We can look to the heavens or curse Fate, but until we can accept that fact, we will never be free to let go of past hurts and disappointments and move on and look forward to the future with hope and expectation.

The most enlightening lesson, for me, that comes from the flipside is that, through life's struggles, there often comes an astonishing realization that all of us, as individuals, are more powerful than we might otherwise have known. It is an awareness that life doesn't happen to us, it happens through us. Sooner or later, we learn that the future is not determined so much by what happens to us; who we are and what we become will be decided predominantly by how we respond to challenges that confront us.

This is the most important lesson of the flipside; it is a reaffirmation of the potential within all of us, not just to cope with the challenge of change, but to find something within it that will help us create a better future.

PART THREE

REFLECTIONS – THOUGHTS ON THE FLIPSIDE

'Isn't it amazing how adversity introduces us to ourselves! If we learn a valuable lesson in the face of adversity, the sting will eventually go away and we will emerge a smarter, more resourceful person.'

W. Mitchell

DO THINGS ALWAYS WORK OUT FOR THE BEST ON THE FLIPSIDE?

'There are no mistakes, no coincidences, all events are blessings given to us to learn from.'

Dr. Elisabeth Kübler-Ross

WHILE RESEARCHING THIS book, I was a little surprised to discover that almost everybody who I spoke to had a story, or knew of someone who had a story, relating to the idea of the flipside. From people who had lost their jobs, to people who had been diagnosed with a chronic illness or suffered a personal tragedy, virtually everyone agreed that, in hindsight, there had been a flipside. Most were eager to share their experiences of how their problems or setbacks became to be seen as catalysts that changed their lives for the better, and it was through those discussions that a number of questions and issues were raised that are worth further reflection and clarification in this final part of the book.

When I first began researching *The Flipside*, I came across a posting on a blog that troubled me. The blogger was a man who had been diagnosed with multiple sclerosis (MS) and he wrote, 'I really major-league resent people who try to suggest that MS brings something positive in your life like it makes you a better person or makes you stop and sniff the roses or something equally trite.' Of course, he was right. Or so I thought. What possible flipside could there be for someone who has been diagnosed with a chronic, degenerative illness? Are there not some things in life that are so tragic, so devastating, that it would be, as that man wrote on his blog, 'complete and utter blithering nonsense' to suggest that there could be a flipside? How could an illness like MS bring anything positive into someone's life?

I continued reading the blog and was amazed to find that

further down the page, the same man had acknowledged that MS 'may have brought some positive things' into his life. 'When I take my thirty-minute walk in the cool of the evenings,' he said, 'she [his ten-year-old daughter] gets to come along with me, and we talk as we walk, something that we seldom used to do.' However, taking everything into account, he said that such positives are 'insignificant compared to the negative things'.

The promise of the flipside is not that life will be the same following a setback or trauma because, of course, it won't. It is also impossible to say whether life will necessarily be better. But what it does promise is that life will change, and in that change, there will be new opportunities and new challenges that, if accepted, can offer meaning and hope for the future. I then came across an interesting research study which examined optimism and 'benefit-finding' among patients who had MS. Researchers surveyed 127 MS patients for optimism and conscious 'benefit-finding' and then monitored their progress over a period of a year. When the data was collated, the results led to some fascinating conclusions. The researchers had found that patients who consciously looked for benefits in their illness, experienced significantly less depression, and those who were optimists fared even better. The report concluded that having a positive, optimistic outlook and consciously looking for benefits can make a significant difference in the quality of life of an MS sufferer.

Six months after reading the blog, I came across a story that confirmed the findings of the researchers and gave further insight into the power of the flipside, even for someone who had been diagnosed with a chronic, degenerative disease like MS.

Nancy Davis lives with her husband and their five children in Los Angeles. She runs her own successful jewellery business and, in her spare time, she skis, plays tennis, she exercises, travels and she has a black belt in Karate. Yet at the age of thirty-three, Nancy was dealt a devastating blow. She was told that she had MS.

'When I was first diagnosed in 1991, multiple sclerosis was a mystery disease with no known cause and no known cure,' Nancy says. There were no drugs on the market at that time to help stop the progression of MS and she is critical of the doctors who were unable to give her the information that she believes a newly diagnosed MS patient needs. They didn't give Nancy any constructive advice or tell her how the disease might affect her family or her life, and they certainly didn't give her any plan to follow that might slow the progression of the condition or keep her healthy.

It became clear from what happened next, that there is an answer to the MS sufferer's blog. There can be a flipside even after being diagnosed with a chronic, degenerative illness like MS. But the flipside is not found in the disease, it is found in the individual's response to the disease. Nancy Davis did not waste much time or energy mulling over what she had lost. Instead, she immediately started educating herself about MS. This is a trait common to optimists and to people who ultimately find the flipside. Unlike fatalists who believe that they are powerless and that their future is already predetermined, optimists believe that they have power to influence their future. Rather than lie down and accept their situation, they do whatever they can, with whatever they have, to make changes.

The more she read, the more Nancy was determined to be involved in helping find a solution. In 1993 she founded the Nancy Davis Foundation for Multiple Sclerosis, which has a mission to raise funds for the most cutting-edge, aggressive and hopeful research in finding a cure for MS. In the same year, Nancy organized a fund-raising event she called 'RACE to Erase MS'. It was held as part of a ski weekend in Aspen, Colorado, and raised over $1.3 million for her foundation. Since then, 'RACE to Erase MS' has become an annual event and grown into a spectacular gala benefit and has raised tens of millions of dollars to fund the much-needed research.

One of the things that Nancy discovered was that many researchers were duplicating research and rarely communicating with their colleagues or sharing their findings. So Nancy decided to set up what she called 'The Center Without Walls', a body that funds research in a network of the top seven MS institutions that have established and innovative research programmes. Thanks to Nancy's initiative, all centres collaborate, sharing their findings and never duplicate any research. This enables them to work much faster in achieving their shared goal of finding a cure for MS.

According to reports, MS affects between 250,000 and 350,000 people in the USA and just under 100,000 people in the UK. Over 75 per cent of sufferers are women, and most are diagnosed between the ages of twenty and forty. It is a terrible disease which slowly eats away at the nervous system. Incredibly, in the sixteen years since Nancy's foundation was created, it has helped initiate profound changes in the treatment of MS. Fifteen years ago there were no medications available to help stop the progression of MS, but today there are six drugs approved by the US Food and Drug Administration (FDA), with others in the pipeline. 'While there's no cure for MS yet,' says Nancy, 'we have broken so much new ground in a very short space of time, and we will not stop until we cross the finish line and find a cure for MS.'

In addition to her work supporting research, Nancy has also written an inspiring book, *Lean On Me*, which aims to help people who are newly diagnosed with MS and any other degenerative disease for that matter. The book's subtitle 'Ten Powerful Steps to Moving Beyond Your Diagnosis and Taking Your Life Back' underlines the passion and ambition of the author. 'At some point in your life, you or someone you love will be diagnosed with a life-threatening disease,' Nancy writes. 'I get calls from some of the most brilliant, well-educated people who absolutely fall to pieces when they get diagnosed. They don't know which end is up, how to get a second opinion, or how to sort through insurance or medical coverage.' The book, she says, 'is about becoming CEO of your health'.

In addition to all of these achievements, Nancy Davis also launched a life-saving medical ID program which involves participants carrying their own unique medical ID card which is supported through a round-the-clock, user-friendly service. It is the first of its kind as it is linked to a central database that holds users' medical records that, in the event of emergency, can be accessed at any time, from anywhere in the world.

Nancy Davis doesn't claim to have beaten MS yet, but she is making giant strides. Through her illness, she has touched the lives of thousands of people and played a significant part in the progress of research into finding a cure for MS and, in doing so, she proved that even when facing a chronic, incurable illness, it is still possible to find the flipside.

WHERE IS THE FLIPSIDE IN AN ECONOMIC RECESSION?

'Be courageous. I have seen many depressions in business. Always America has emerged from these stronger and more prosperous. Be brave as your fathers before you. Have faith! Go forward!'

Thomas A. Edison

As I write the final pages of this book, the world is on the verge of economic recession. Many consider that it could be the worst recession since the Great Depression of the 1930s. According to the media and economic forecasters, we are heading for very difficult times; global banks have gone bankrupt, businesses are going into liquidation, people are losing their jobs and their livelihoods and many are losing their homes. This all leads to the obvious question: where is the flipside?

I hope that the point has been well made in the preceding chapters that all change brings opportunity, and a recession is no different. The secret to finding the flipside in times of an economic downturn is developing an entrepreneur's mindset and consciously looking for those opportunities.

Some businesses do exceptionally well during a recession. For example, tough economic times can seem like Christmas to liquidation lawyers and bailiffs, and where the property sales market loses, the rental market usually gains. Businesses that focus on the changing needs of consumers will also do very well. Cut-price discount stores such as Lidl, Aldi and One Pound shops experience a sharp increase in business during a recession as consumers look for the cheapest, best value products. According to newspaper reports, at a time when M&S (a high-end, luxury retailer) was showing a 44 per cent drop in profits, Lidl was showing a 22 per cent increase and Aldi a 10 per cent increase.

Companies providing outsourcing services also seem to profit from a falling economy. Barnaby Lashbrooke, managing director of TimeEtc Limited, a company that offers a range of office support including secretarial and administrative services, enjoyed a 400 per cent increase in business in the first seven months of 2008. The company has grown from six to eleven employees and during a period when many companies are laying off staff, TimeEtc is continuing to recruit, such is the demand for its services. Lashbrooke believes the company is prospering for a number of reasons:

'Firstly, we're helping small business owners to get up and running in a much more cost effective way than they would have been able to without such a service. We enable them to tap into the skills of a fantastic person but buy just the share they need, rather than employing them full time. They get the benefit of working with a whole team of people for far less than the cost of employing someone, and they don't have the overheads or worry of office space too.

'On the other hand, we're also helping bigger or more established businesses that have perhaps lost an employee recently and are looking to downsize the role rather than rerecruit. By making the role more efficient, and using the technology we have to schedule tasks, we can normally fit the role into a much smaller time period, and produce a massive saving as a result.'

A relatively new business concept of car hire by the hour has also seen a boom in business. People are able to hire a car in the UK for as little as £5 an hour, which is cheaper than a taxi and, for those who only need to use a car occasionally, the scheme offers huge savings on car ownership. WhizzGo is a company with a network of low-emission cars located in dedicated parking bays in towns and cities across the UK and hires them out by the hour. According to reports, in the last year they have seen their business increase by over 30 per cent.

Businesses that supply seeds for people to grow their own fruits, vegetables and herbs also have experienced a growth in business as consumers look to save on paying retail prices. Similarly, sales of home brew kits which enable people to make their own beer and wine at home have increased sharply over the past six months.

During a recession, most people need to either reduce their overheads or increase their income. Any businesses that can offer ways of saving money on essential products and services will, therefore, do well. At the same time, companies offering home-based business opportunities or part-time work should also be successful.

There are also huge opportunities for anyone who has capital as they can make a real killing buying up properties and shares at knock-down prices. Not many people understand stocks and shares as well as Warren Buffet, who is acknowledged as being one of the world's most successful investors. He is CEO and major shareholder of Berkshire Hathaway, a leading investment company, and he was ranked by Forbes as the richest man in the world during the first half of 2008 with an estimated net worth of $62 billion. Buffet recently wrote about the opportunities available to investors during a recession. At a time when most investors are panicking and selling off their shares, Buffet says it is time to buy. 'Bad news is an investor's best friend,' he says. 'It lets you buy a slice of America's future at a marked-down price.'

Buffet advises that 'over the long term, the stock market news will be good. In the twentieth century, the US endured a host of problems. They included two world wars and other traumatic and expensive conflicts; the Depression; a dozen or so recessions and financial panics; oil shocks; a flu epidemic; and the resignation of a disgraced president. Yet the DOW rose from 66 to 11,497.'

It can be argued that even with such gains, many investors lost. Buffet explains that 'the hapless ones bought stocks only when they felt comfortable in doing so and then proceeded to sell when the headlines made them queasy.' He says that to find the opportunity in business, one has to adopt the approach of Wayne Gretsky (generally considered to have been the greatest NHL hockey player of all time) who once said, 'I skate to where the puck is going to be, not to where it has been.' That may be the key issue in successfully navigating to the flipside during a recession. Those who win, find the opportunities, anticipate changes and adapt accordingly.

There are significant flipsides to be found in a recession. Difficult times force us to re-evaluate how we live and how we work. We may be pushed out of our comfort zones but, for those who choose to look for them, there are still plenty of opportunities to be had. In the end, a recession will tend to knock a lot of businesses out of the market, leaving those who survive a larger share of the market.

IS ADVERSITY NECESSARY OR GOOD?

'There has never yet been a person in our history who led a life of ease whose name is worth remembering.'

Theodore Roosevelt

Given that adversity can be the precursor to positive outcomes and trauma can lead to personal and spiritual growth, people often ask whether pain and suffering are necessary or good. Certainly, as we have seen, pain and suffering can lead to growth and opportunities that would not have otherwise been found. But is suffering 'necessary' for growth? Professors Tedeschi and Calhoun, the leading exponents of post-traumatic growth, are both clear on this point. 'In no way are we suggesting that trauma is "good",' they say. 'For most trauma survivors, post-traumatic growth and distress will coexist, and the growth emerges from the struggle with coping, not from the trauma itself.'

The doctors go on to emphasize that 'trauma is not necessary for growth'. It is perfectly possible, they say, for people to 'mature and develop in meaningful ways without experiencing tragedy or trauma'. Growth through trauma is never guaranteed and, even though post-traumatic growth is observed in many trauma survivors, life crises, loss and trauma should always be considered undesirable.

Dr Viktor Frankl, founder of Logotherapy, posed the same question: is suffering indispensable to the discovery of meaning? He was also emphatic in the answer; 'In no way,' he said. 'I only insist that meaning is available in spite of – nay, even through – suffering *provided* . . . that the suffering is unavoidable.' If suffering is avoidable, then the meaningful thing to do is to put a stop to it. Unnecessary personal suffering, Frankl says, is 'masochistic rather than heroic'. This might seem obvious but is worth clarifying. When a man called 'Wendell' from America's Deep South appeared on the *Jerry Springer Show* in a wheelchair with both of his lower legs missing, it was clear to the audience that there wasn't much meaning to be found in his condition. Wendell was a strapping man covered in tattoos. When asked how he had lost his legs, Wendell said that he had decided one day that he didn't like them, so he sawed them off. It was clear to all watching that Wendell was of a questionable state of mind. It didn't help his cause that he was wearing a skirt, he was wearing make-up and that he had changed his name to Sandra! There is little doubt that there is not much to be gained, no greater meaning to be found, in self-mutilation. Although, ironically enough, Wendell said he slept better without his legs.

IS OPTIMISM ALWAYS THE BEST OPTION?

'Be an optimist – at least until they start moving animals in pairs to Cape Canaveral.'

Anon.

Despite all of the benefits of optimism and what it brings to our lives, there are times when optimism would not be appropriate. Professor Martin Seligman states that 'if the cost of failure is high, optimism may be the wrong strategy. If you are planning for a risky and uncertain future, optimism will not pay.' Seligman warns that when there is a high cost of failure, optimism needs to be tempered with caution. 'The pilot deciding whether or not to de-ice the plane one more time, or the partygoers deciding whether or not to drive home after drinking, should not use optimism,' he says. 'The risks are too high.'

Optimism would also not be a good strategy when entering a casino (unless you're going to count cards) because, in the long run, the laws of probability will prove that the house is always going to win. Even the most ardent optimist will lose.

Professor Susan Segerstrom offers similar advice. Optimists tend to be persistent, she says, but there are times when giving up is the better option. She gives the example of a man trying to get a date with a woman who he finds attractive, but who does not reciprocate his feelings. The man may ask the woman out two, three, perhaps even four times, but at some point, if she continues to show no interest, he will need to give up – hopefully, Segerstrom says, before the object of the man's affections gets a restraining order against him.

Basically, Segerstrom advises that the chances of success need to be balanced against the cost of failure. If the chances of success are infinitesimally small and the consequences of failure are high, then the best option is to accept defeat. Optimists are high achievers because they are prepared to take risks and invest their resources to achieve their goals. But those risks need to be weighed and balanced against the cost of possible failure. In times of grave or serious risk, it is as well to adopt the Arabic saying: Trust in the Lord, but tie up your camels.

WHAT IS THE ALTERNATIVE TO THE FLIPSIDE?

'Life is change. Growth is optional. Choose wisely.'
Karen Kaiser Clark

When faced with problems, setbacks and adversity, there are two choices; either we start looking for the flipside and build a future, or we stay where we are and cling on to past memories. When life becomes difficult, the flipside gives hope, without it there is a danger of becoming entangled in what is known as the 'Negative Spiral'.

The Negative Spiral is not uncommon among people who are diagnosed with a debilitating or life-threatening illness. Many people diagnosed with cancer or MS or AIDS come to regard their diagnosis as a death sentence. On learning of their situation, negative, pessimistic emotions can propel them into a negative, spiral of increased hopelessness and depression. The spiral turns into a downward freefall that exacerbates the situations which can trigger self-destructive behaviours and cause the person to sink deeper and deeper into an abyss of depression.

Reports show that people who become entangled in the negative spiral are often dead within a shockingly short period of time. By learning to become optimistic and searching for the flipside, patients experience a far superior quality of life and enjoy much longer survival rates. By taking better care of themselves, following treatment regimes, dietary management, and exploring alternative and complementary treatments, even patients who have been diagnosed as being HIV positive can extend their life and, with the rapid rate of medical advances, may live long enough to receive newer, more effective treatments.

EPILOGUE

THE CHANGING-ROOM DOORS slowly swung open and the boy stepped nervously into the pool area. The shouts and screams gradually stopped as, one by one, the other children turned towards him. He could feel everyone's eyes upon him and he could certainly hear some whispers. He struggled to stop his eyes from welling up for the second time that day. He had made a huge mistake. This was exactly what he had feared.

Just an hour earlier, he had been talking to Mr Greenstein about the flipside and they had discussed the critical questions.

- What is good about this?
- What *could* be good about this?
- What could I do, right now, to turn this to my advantage?
- What could I learn from this that would benefit me?
- What could I learn from this that would benefit others?

At first, the boy had said that nothing was good, but when it was put to him, he had agreed that, perhaps this could be an opportunity to show courage, and it could be an opportunity to win the respect of his peers. It might also be an opportunity to find out who his real friends were.

He could also look at this as a personal test, a test to see whether he was strong enough to face his fears or run away from them. If he could overcome this fear, it might help him overcome other fears that he may have to face in the future. And if he could overcome this fear, he might be able to help other people overcome similar fears.

But aside from all of that, this was supposed to be his opportunity to learn to swim and he had to decide whether he was going to let his fear of what the other children might say to him or about him, stop him from learning to swim.

'You cannot lose,' Mr Greenstein promised. 'Whatever happens, if you walk through those doors you'll come out a winner. If you decide not to go, nobody would blame you or think any less of you, but if you can face your fear, you may just find the flipside.'

And so it was with trepidation that he walked through the doors from the changing room and into the school swimming pool. His first thought was, 'What am I doing here?' And then, 'How could I have been so stupid?'

He stood alone. Even though he wore swimming trunks, he felt naked; worse than naked. The red scaly lesions all over his body were there for everyone to see. 'What am I doing?' he mumbled to himself. He decided it had all been a huge mistake. He shouldn't have come, and was about to turn around and run back out.

And then something unexpected happened. His best friend George climbed out of the pool and ran after him. George caught up and threw his arm around him. 'Come on, we need you.' Then some other boys jumped out and ran toward the two boys. 'Yeah. Come on.' Two of the boys grabbed him and pushed him into the pool. George followed and jumped as high as he could into the air, brought his knees to his chest and bombed, making a massive splash.

I can still hear the screams and the laughter, and when I close my eyes I can see the general mayhem in the pool that afternoon. That day I learned about facing and overcoming fears. I learned that I had some courage, and that I was strong enough not to let my fear hold me back. I learned that people don't always see what I see, and sometimes our fears are imaginary. I learned that I had friends, friends I could count on. But most of all, that day I began to understand about the flipside.

As a result of having had psoriasis I became more introspective and more sensitive as a teenager, but I believe that it also helped me to change and become the person I am today. I adopted a healthier diet and lifestyle, and in my mid-twenties I gave up a career in Law and retrained in physical therapies and naturopathic healing sciences.

I opened up a small natural therapy clinic and not long after, I became a regular columnist for the *Nursing Times* and *Health Guardian*, writing about the latest research relating to alternative medicines and complementary therapies.

During my research of alternative medicines for my monthly columns I came across a plant remedy that had been shown in controlled, clinical trials to help over 80 per cent of psoriasis sufferers. To my amazement, the remedy was not commercially available and I later learned that pharmaceutical companies are not interested in natural, plant extracts that cannot be patented. With no patent, a treatment or remedy is not considered worthy of any significant investment and so a natural remedy that was proved to help four out of every five psoriasis sufferers had remained ignored and hidden for years.

As no pharmaceutical company would consider introducing a product without a patent, I decided to set up a company to manufacture it. In 1996, for the first time in the UK, fellow psoriasis sufferers had something natural, free of corticosteroids, that could offer real help.

A few years later I wrote my first book, which was followed

by six more, and you are holding my eighth book in your hands. More importantly, I have some outstanding friends, I married a beautiful woman, I have two wonderful children and, in all that has happened, I have found some meaning and purpose in my life.

So do I ever regret having been afflicted with psoriasis since I was eight years old? Absolutely not! In the words of Oscar Pistorius who, when asked whether he ever wished that he had been born able-bodied with two feet, replied, 'No. If I had legs, I don't think . . . no, I know . . . that I wouldn't be the same person I am today and I'm happy with who I am.'

Too often, we look back with regret and longing for what might have been and in doing so we miss the opportunities that lie in front of us. I hope that this book brings a message of hope and encouragement in times of adversity and change, however traumatic those times may be. Instead of looking back, we can look straight ahead with confidence and expectation for the future, and by asking the right questions, all of us can find the flipside.

NOTES AND REFERENCES

INTRODUCTION

Prior to the 1961 Suicide Act, the act of committing suicide was a crime in the UK and anyone who attempted and failed was liable to prosecution and imprisonment. The 1961 Act made anyone who aids, abets, counsels or procures the suicide of another, or an attempt by another to commit suicide, liable on conviction to imprisonment for a term not exceeding fourteen years.

Part One: Discoveries – Finding the Flipside

1: The Road to Madrid
Julio Iglesias and his story – see www.julioiglesias.com

2: Defining Moments
Peter Jones interview *Skymag*, July 2008, p. 16. See also www.peterjones.tv

Tony Robbins Seminar, Unlimited Power (Nightingale Conant); see also www.tonyrobbins.com

Rhonda Byrne, *The Secret* (Simon & Schuster, 2006) and see interview with Marci Shimoff, www.keepingthesecret.com See also www.thesecret.tv

Harvey Mackay, *We Got Fired And It's The Best Thing That Ever Happened To Us* (Ballentine, 2004)

3: Crises and Opportunities
Sarah Benjamin – see www.simplyrosepetals.com

Simon and Helen Pattinson – www.montezumas.co.uk

4: Life Changes: When Bad Things Happen
Billy Bob Harrell – story reported in *Houston Press News*, 10 Feb 2000 John McGuinness – story reported in the *Mail On Sunday*, 20 April 2008

Joni Eareckson Tada, see http://www.joniandfriends.org

Alan Byrd, see www.alan-byrd.com

Padraig Harrington – see www.nationalpost.com/sports/story.html?id=670086

Douglas Bader – see www.douglasbaderfoundation.co.uk

5: The Two Sides of Trauma
Matthew J. Friedman is Professor of Psychiatry at Dartmouth Medical School and Director of the National Center for Post-traumatic Stress Disorder

Ute Lawrence is co-founder of the Post-traumatic Stress Disorder Association (London, Ontario, Canada)

Paul T. P. Wong, Ph.D, C. Psych., is President of the International Network on Personal Meaning, Coquitlam, BC., Canada

PSTD statistics – According to one study, 90 per cent of the population experience a trauma at least once in their lives. Kessler, R. C., Sonnega, A., Bromet, E., Hughes, M., Nelson, C. B.: Posttraumatic stress disorder in the National Comorbidity Survey. Arch Gen Psychiatry 1995;52:1048–1060

Trisha Meili, *I Am the Central Park Jogger: A Story of Hope and Possibility* (Scribner, 2004). See also www.centralpark jogger.com

Posttraumatic Growth: A New Perspective on Psychotraumatology. Richard G. Tedeschi, Ph.D., and Lawrence Calhoun, Ph.D. 1 April 2004. *Psychiatric Times.* Vol. 21 No. 4

Richard G. Tedeschi, Ph.D., and Lawrence Calhoun, Ph.D. The Paradox of Post-Traumatic Growth. *Boston Globe*, 20 March 2006

Pathways to Posttraumatic Growth. Paul T. P. Wong, Ph.D., C. Psych.www.meaning.ca/archives/presidents_columns/pres_col_may_2003_post-traumatic-growth.htm

From Wounds, Inner Strength: Some Veterans Feel Lives Enlarged by Wartime Suffering. By Michael E. Ruane. *Washington Post* Staff Writer. Saturday, 26 November 2005; Page A01

For Ute Lawrence, author and founder of the Post-traumatic Stress Disorder Association (Canada), see www.ptsd association.com See also Struggling for a Way to 'Just get Over It', *Globe & Mail*, 4 August 2008 and *The Power of Trauma* (iUniverse) by Ute Lawrence

6: Reasons For Optimism

For Professor Charles Carver, see www.psy.miami.edu/faculty/ccarver

Optimism and resources: Effects on each other and on health over 10 years. Susan C. Segerstrom, Dept of Psychology, University of Kentucky. *Journal of Research in Personality* 41 (2007) 772–786

For information on Susan Segerstrom, Associate Professor of Psychology, University of Kentucky, see www.uky.edu/AS/Psychology/faculty/segerstr.html

Optimism and rehabilitation following artery bypass graft surgery was investigated by Scheier, M. F., Matthews,

K. A., Owens, J. F., Schulz, R., Bridges, M. W., Magovern, G. J., Sr., and Carver, C. S. *Arch Intern Med.* 1999; 159:829–835.

Dispositional Optimism and All-Cause and Cardiovascular Mortality in a Prospective Cohort of Elderly Dutch Men and Women. Erik J. Giltay, MD, Ph.D.; Johanna M. Geleijnse, Ph.D.; Frans G. Zitman, MD, Ph.D.; Tiny Hoekstra, Ph.D.; Evert G. Schouten, MD, Ph.D. *Arch Gen Psychiatry.* 2004; 61:1126–1135

Dispositional Optimism and the Risk of Cardiovascular Death. The Zutphen Elderly Study. Erik J. Giltay, Ph.D., MD; Marjolein H. Kamphuis, M.Sc.; Sandra Kalmijn, Ph.D., MD; Frans G. Zitman, Ph.D., MD; Daan Kromhout, Ph.D., MPH. *Arch Intern Med.* 2006; 166:431–436

Optimism, pessimism, and change of psychological well-being in cancer patients. Pinquart, M., Fröhlich, C., Silbereisen, R. K. *Psychol Health Med,* 12(4): 421–32 (2007)

Dispositional optimism: development over 21 years from the perspectives of perceived temperament and mothering. Kati Heinonen, Katri Räikkönen Department of Psychology, University of Helsinki, P.O. Box 9, FIN-00014, Helsinki, Finland

Anda R, Williamson D, Jones D, et al. Hopelessness and heart disease – see Depressed affect, hopelessness, and the risk of ischemic heart disease in a cohort of US adults. *Epidemiology.* 1993; 4:285–294. ISI | PUBMED

Everson, S. A., Goldberg, D. E., Kaplan, G. A., et al. Hopelessness and risk of mortality and incidence of myocardial infarction and cancer. *Psychosom Med.* 1996;58:113–121.

For details of the LOT-R – The optimism questionnaire used in numerous studies on the implications of optimism, see www.psy.miami.edu/faculty/ccarver/sclLOT-R.html Optimism research – Professor Martin Seligman– For more about this optimism research conducted by Professor Seligman, visit the Martin Seligman Research Alliance website at the University of Pennsylvania: www.psych. upenn.edu/seligman/

For Norman Cousins, see *Anatomy Of An Illness as Perceived by the Patient* (Norton, 1979).

'Underpinnings of dispositional optimism and pessimism and associated constructs' – Kati Heinonen. Department of Psychology, University of Helsinki Hsieh Kun-Shan – his incredible works of art can be seen at www.vsarts. org/PreBuilt/showcase/gallery/exhibits/permanent/artists/ kshsieh.html

Lance Armstrong – see www.lancearmstrong.com

Part Two: Pathways – Steps to the Flipside

Epigraph: Charlotte Bühler, 'Basic Theoretical Concepts of Human Psychology', *American Psychologist* XXVI, April 1971

8: Great Expectations: The Strategies of Optimists

Peter Schulman is Research Director, Department of Psychology, University of Pennsylvania

The incorrect notion that optimists set themselves up for disappointment was given credence through an interview given by Admiral Jim Stockdale. Stockdale was reportedly the highest ranking US military officer captured and imprisoned in the 'Hanoi Hilton' POW camp during the Vietnam War. In the eight years that he was incarcerated, he was subjected to physical torture no less than twenty times and, common to all prisoners, from day to day he had no knowledge as to whether he would ever be released.

In the book *Good To Great*, author James C. Collins interviewed Stockdale and one of the questions he asked was how Stockdale managed to cope during those eight years in prison. Stockdale explained, 'I never lost faith in the end of the story, I never doubted not only that I would get out, but also that I would prevail in the end and turn the experience into the defining event of my life, which, in retrospect, I would not trade.'

Then Collins asked Stockdale which type of prisoners didn't survive. Stockdale replied without hesitation, showing that he had already given the issue some thought: 'Oh, that's easy,' he said, the "optimists".' This is a bit like Donald Trump suggesting that the people who never succeed in business are the capitalists!

Stockdale's description of his own outlook draws a portrait of someone who is an extreme optimist, someone who believes that, whatever their situation, they will prevail in the end. However, when Stockdale went on to explain his comment it becomes clear that he was simply confused in his choice of words. He said the people who didn't survive were 'the ones who said, "We're going to be out by Christmas." And Christmas would come, and Christmas would go. Then they'd say, "We're going to be out by Easter." And Easter would come, and Easter would go. And then Thanksgiving, and then it would be Christmas again. And they died of a broken heart.' The type of people he was describing were not optimists (as is commonly understood in modern psychology). The people he was referring to were what many would call 'wishful thinkers' and, ultimately, lost all hope. This is precisely the phenomenon that Professor Martin Seligman describes in his work on Learned Helplessness (see below).

Mike and Bettina Jetter – see www.cancercode.com for the wonderful book *The Cancer Code* and www.mindjet.com for details of the revolutionary software he created while undergoing treatment for CML. Mike and his wife Bettina are currently working on a new project to inspire and empower women. For details, see www.coachingsanctuary.com

Mind-mapping was popularized by the British Psychology author Tony Buzan. For more information see his book *The Mind Map Book* (Penguin Books, 1996)

Optimist International – For those readers interested in encouraging optimism in children, please refer to *Optimist International*, a worldwide organization aimed at helping 'bring out the best in kids' by 'providing hope and positive vision'. Formed in 1919 it has over 100,000 adult members who facilitate in over 3,000 Optimist Clubs in countries all over the world, empowering them to be the best they can. Optimist volunteers continually make this world a better place to live. The organization conducts 65,000 service projects each year, serving six million young people.
The Optimist's Creed is:

To be so strong that nothing can disturb your peace of mind.
To talk health, happiness and prosperity to every person you
  meet.
To make all your friends feel that there is something in them.
To look at the sunny side of everything and make your
  optimism come true.
To think only of the best, to work only for the best and to
  expect only the best.
To be just as enthusiastic about the success of others as you
  are about your own.
To forget the mistakes of the past and press on to the greater
  achievements of the future.

To wear a cheerful countenance at all times and give every living creature you meet a smile.

To give so much time to the improvement of yourself that you have no time to criticize others.

To be too large for worry, too noble for anger, too strong for fear, and too happy to permit the presence of trouble.

For more information, see www.optimist.org

Martin Seligman – see *Learned Helplessness: A Theory for the Age of Personal Control* by Christopher Peterson, Steven F. Maier, Martin E. P. Seligman (Oxford University Press, USA,1995) and *Learned Optimism* (Vintage, 2006)

Optimism research

Applying Learned Optimism. Schulman P. *University of Pennsylvania Journal of Personal Selling & Sales Management* Vol. XIX Number 1 (Winter 1999), 31–7)

CAVEing the MMPI for an Optimism-Pessimism Scale: Seligman's attributional model and the assessment of explanatory style. Colligan, R. C., Offord, K. P., Malinchoc, M., Schulman, P., Seligman, M. E. *J Clin Psychol* 50(1): 71–95 (1994)

Learned Optimism by Martin E. P. Seligman, Ph.D. www.psych. upenn.edu/seligman/index.htm

Finding benefit in breast cancer: Relations with personality, coping, and concurrent well-being. Kenya R. Urcuyo, Amy E. Boyers, Charles S. Carver & Michael Antoni. *Psychology and Health* April 2005, 20(2): 175–92

9: The Entrepreneur's Mindset: Looking for Hidden Opportunities

Regarding Henry (Paramount Pictures, 1991) was written by J. J. Abrams

Clare Newton – to see her Cup Carrier invention visit
http://www.1000inventions.com/detail2.php?id=189
Michael Gerber, *The E-Myth* (HarperBusiness, US, 1988)

10: Reframing Your Life: The Critical Questions

Dan Ariely – *Predictably Irrational* (HarperCollins, 2008); see
also Painful Lessons available for free download at
www.predictablyirrational.com

Gemma Stone – www.rockandruby.com

Jodi Pliszka, *Bald is Beautiful: My Journey to Becoming*
(Nightengale Press, 2007)

NLP – for more information and research, see www.
nlpresearch.org

12: Edison's Legacy: Philosophies to Live By

Unfortunately, not all of Edison's philosophies were beneficent. According to reports, Edison's opposition to alternating
current (AC) led him to conduct a brief but intense campaign
to ban the use of AC or to limit the allowable voltage for safety
purposes. As part of this campaign, Edison's employees
publicly electrocuted animals including stray cats, dogs and
some cattle and horses to demonstrate the dangers of AC. On
4 January 1903 Edison's workers electrocuted Topsy the
elephant at Luna Park, near Coney Island, after she had killed
several men and her owners wanted her put to death. Edison's
company filmed the electrocution. For more information see
www.wired.com/science/discoveries/news/
2008/01/dayintech_0104

Ralph Teetor – see www.cruise-in.com/resource/cismar08.htm
and *Time* magazine, 27 Jan. 1936, 'I see' – www.time.com/
time/magazine/article/0,9171,847646,00.html

The Perfect Circle Corporation – see www.waynet.org/way
net/spotlight/2003/030521-perfectcircle.htm

Steve Heard story – see *Mail on Sunday*, 17 August 2008, p. 53
Sanu Kaji Shrestha – see www.fost-nepal.org
Trevor Bayliss – see www.trevorbaylisbrands.com

13: The Art of Seeing: Doing the Impossible

Amit Goffer – The ReWalk™ is currently undergoing clinical trials and Amit's new company, Agor Medical Technologies, based in Haifa in Israel, hopes to have the ReWalk™ in full scale production by 2010. For more information, see www.argomedtec.com

14: The Paradigm of Possibilities: Hope For the Future

Oscar Pistorius: *The Fastest Man on No Legs*, Channel 5 TV
Natalie du Toit – see www.nataliedutoit.com
For information on Don Rogers, see www.indstate.edu

15: The Three Avenues: The Search For Meaning

Dr Viktor Frankl, *Man's Search For Meaning* (Washington Square Press, 1959)
For What Are We Born to Become? The Logotherapy of Dr Viktor Frankl by Carol Miller SND, D. Min.
Sara Tulcholsky story – see *Chicago Tribune*, 1 May 2008
Randy Pausch, *The Last Lecture* (Hyperion, 2008) 2008
For information on MADD, see www.madd.org

16: The Relationship Factor: Surrounding Yourself With the Right People

For information on Mark Pollock seminars and adventures, see www.markpollock.com
Professor Edward Diener is Professor of Psychology at the University of Illinois
Harold Kushner, *When All You've Ever Wanted Isn't Enough* (Pan Books, 2000)

17: Focusing the Mind: Finding Inner Strength

For information on Richard Turner, see www.richardturner
52.com

For information on W. Mitchell, see www.wmitchell.com

Part Three: Reflections – Thoughts on the Flipside

Nancy Davis – see www.erasems.org

Warren Buffet – article *New York Times*, 17 Oct 2008

ACKNOWLEDGEMENTS

ONE OF THE key characteristics of the flipside that came up time and again was the importance of having a strong support network. The same is true when writing a book. First and foremost, I would like to thank my agent and friend Sara Menguc. Without Sara's support and enthusiasm for the project and continued belief in me as a writer, I doubt that *The Flipside* would have been written. Also, thanks are due to Sara's husband Haluk, who sourced some stories and passed them my way, and to her colleague Amabel Gee.

I must also thank my editor at Headline, John Moseley, who embraced the idea of *The Flipside* and commissioned the book, and also David Wilson, Publishing Director for Non-Fiction at Headline. Both John and David were incredibly supportive and excited about the project from the beginning.

I would also like to thank everyone who has freely given their time to talk or correspond with me about their stories or work in the related fields. Some have become good friends. Special thanks go to Jodi Pliszka, Amit Goffer, Professor Dan Ariely, Professor Charles Carver, Professor Susan Segerstrom, Mike and Bettina Jetter, Gemma Stone, Helen and Simon

Pattinson, Richard Turner, Barnaby Lashbrooke, Krista Grueninger of Optimists International for permission to include the Optimist's Creed, Mark Pollock, and Ken Ross, President of the EKR Foundation, for kind permission to use quotes by Dr Elizabeth Kübler-Ross.

Special thanks also to my lovely wife Karen, who believed in the project even when it was just an idea. As with previous books, her critique and editing vastly improved the final manuscript.

And finally, thank you for reading *The Flipside*. I have tried to make sure that everything contained in the book is correct. If there are any errors, in spite of the input of everyone mentioned, they are all mine.

INDEX

Note: Page numbers in italic denote entries in the Notes and References section.

Abbott, Jim 169–70
Abrams, Jeffrey Jacob, 'J.J.' 138
AC (alternating current) *247*
academic achievement 67
accidents 107, 142, 149, 152, 162, 190
   see also injuries
   bicycles xxii, 140
   broken glass 154–5
   cars xv–xvi, 1–2, 39–40, 155, 192–4
   electrical 54–5
   explosions 132–3
   flying 34–5, 209–10
   hot drinks 115–16
   motorcycles 146–7, 178, 183, 209
   musical record 15
acquired immune deficiency syndrome *see* HIV/AIDS

acting as if optimistic 98–9
adversity, and growth 229–30
Agassi, Andre 7
AIDS (acquired immune deficiency syndrome) see HIV/AIDS
alopecia 119–22, 201
alternating current (AC) *247*
alternative fuels 156–7
amputees 35–6, 55–7, 144, 168–70, 172–81, 199–200, 230
   see also disability
Anatomy of an Illness (Cousins) 86
ankylosing spondylitis (Marie-Strumpell's disease) 83–6
Ariely, Dan 73–5, 100–101, 132–6
Armstrong, Lance 57–8
Army, US 97
arthritis 83–6
athletics 171–2, 173–7

Attraction, Law of 13
automobile industry 151–3

Bach, Richard 3, 213
Bach-y-rita, Paul 166–7
'bad' events *see* life changes
Bader, Douglas 34–6, 171
Bader, Thelma (*née* Edwards) 35
baseball 168–70
basketball 199–200
Bayliss, Trevor 158–9
Baywatch (television series) 113
Bee Gees, The 15–16
Bell, Alexander Graham 161
Benedetti, Fabrizio 62
Benedictus, Edouard 154–5
Benjamin, Sarah 18–19
bicycles, accidents xxii, 140
Binchy, Maeve 128–9
Biondi, Matt 67
birdshot retinochoroidopathy 205
blindness 107–9, 152–3, 164–8,
    195–7, 205–7
    see also disability
Blink! (Gladwell) 128
BLISS (Breathing Life Into Soils
    System) 158
Bloomberg, Michael 11
blue focus 124–6
Bonaparte, Napoleon 161
Braille, Louis 107–9
Braille (system) 107–9
brain damage 137–8
Branson, Richard 9–10
Breaking Murphy's Law
    (Segerstrom) 98
Breathing Life Into Soils System
    (BLISS) 158
Brooks, Garth 143
Buffet, Warren 228–9

Bühler, Charlotte 71
burn injuries 55, 115–16, 132–5,
    142, 209
Burns, George 221
business crises xix, 6, 7–10, 15–23,
    104–5
business ventures
    see also entrepreneurs;
        inventions
    chocolate manufacture 20–23
    Cups Carrier 115–16
    dental treatments xxii–xxiii
    in economic recessions 104–5,
        226–9
    events management 130–31
    financial data exchange 11
    Home Depot, The 12
    Kentucky Fried Chicken (KFC)
        xxi–xxii
    Liquid Paper 109–10
    marmalade 16–17
    Mickey Mouse 114–15
    MicroSolutions 12
    MindManager 79
    rose petals, dried 18–19
    shopping carts 105–6
    Virgin business empire 9–10
Buzan, Tony *245*
Byrne, Rhonda 12–14, 79

Calhoun, Lawrence 43–4, 47, 50,
    229–30
Camus, Albert 203
cancer 57–9, 75–80, 164–5, 232
cardsharps 203–6
career choices, based on statistics
    81–2
Carnage Alley 39–40
cars
    accidents *see* accidents

cruise control 151–3
  drunk-driving 192–4
  hire 227
Carver, Charles 68, 96
Castro, Daniel R. 93
CBT (Cognitive Behavioural
  Therapy) 96
Central Park Jogger (Trisha Meili)
  47–9
children
  death of 192–4
  Optimist International
    (organization) *245–6*
chocolate 20–23
chronic myeloid leukaemia (CML)
  76–7
Churchill, Winston 87
Clark, Karen Kaiser 232
Cleese, John 126–7
climbing 182–3
Clinton, Bill 6–7
CML (Chronic Myeloid
  Leukaemia) 76–7
Coffee, Gerald L. 45–6
Cognitive Behavioural Therapy
  (CBT) 96
Collins, James C. *244*
'Colonel Sanders' xix–xxii
concentration camps 185–7
  see also prisoners of war
correction fluid (typing) 109–10
Cousins, Norman 62–3, 64, 83–7,
  100
Covey, Steven R. 6–7
Crawford, Roger W. II 144, 181
crises (business), as opportunities
  xix, 6, 7–10, 15–23, 104–5
  see also trauma
cruise control (cars) 151–3
Cuban, Mark 12

Cups Carrier (product) 115–16
cycling 57–8

Dalai Lama 198–9
Davis, Geoff 8
Davis, Nancy 223–5
deafness 149–51
Deal Or No Deal (television show)
  124–5
decisions, based on statistics 81–2
dental treatments xxii–xxiii
Diener, Edward 28, 197, 198
Diffey, Joe 143
disability
  see also injuries
  amputees 35–6, 55–7, 144,
    168–70, 172–81, 199–200, 230
  blindness 107–9, 152–3, 164–8,
    195–7, 205–7
  deafness 149–51
  paralysis xv–xviii, 2, 29–31,
    146–7, 162–4, 182–4, 190–91,
    194, 209–10
discount stores 226–7
diseases *see* illness and disease
Disney, Walt 113–15, 161
diving 190
dreams, lost 137–43
  see also goals
  replaced by new dreams 141–2,
    146–8
Dreyfuss, Richard xvi
drinks, hot 115–16
Drucker, Peter F. 111
drunk-driving 192–4
du Toit, Natalie 144–5, 178–80

Eareckson, John 29
Eareckson, Kathy 29–30
Eareckson Tada, Joni 29–31

echolocation 165–6, 167
economic recessions 104–5, 226–9
ectrodactyly 144, 181
Edison, Thomas A. 117, 149–51,
    153–4, 155–6, 160, 226, *247*
education 67
Edwards, Thelma (*married name*
    Bader) 35
electric light bulb 150, 153
electricity, accidents 54 5
Ellett, Porter 199–200
emergency services 147
Engle, Reverend 149
entertainment industry 113–15
entrepreneurs 103–18
    see also business ventures;
        inventors
    Benjamin, Sarah 18–19
    Bloomberg, Michael 11
    Branson, Richard 9–10
    Cuban, Mark 12
    Disney, Walt 113–15
    Fiske, Peter 8–9
    Goldman, Sylvan 103–6
    Graham, Bette Nesmith 109 10
    Hasselhoff, David 113
    Jackson, Adam J 237
    Jetter, Mike 75–80, 200, *245*
    Jones, Peter 5–6
    Keiller, James 16–17
    Marcus, Bernie 12
    mindset 111–12
    Newton, Clare 115–16
    Pattinson, Helen 19–23
    Pattinson, Simon 19–23
    potential in everyone 117–18
    Purchall, Simon xxii–xxiii
    Purchall, Veronika xxii–xxiii
    Sanders, Harland xix–xxii
    Slater, Jan 18–19

Stone, Gemma 129–31
Varsavsky, Martin 112–13
equities (investments) 228–9
euthanasia xvi–xviii
events management industry
    130–31
expectations, influencing
    outcomes 62–3, 73–5
    see also optimism; pessimism
explosions 132–3

Fawlty Towers (television series) 127
fertilizer, alternative 157–8
financial data exchange 11
firings (employment) 10–12,
    129–30
Fisher, Stan 40
Fiske, Peter 8–9
Fitzpatrick, Anna 201
flipside, apparent instances where
    not applicable 221–5
flying accidents 34–5, 209–10
focusing on the positive 124–6,
    128–9, 208
food, expectations influencing
    enjoyment 74
Ford, Harrison 137
FoST (Foundation for Sustainable
    Technologies) 156–7
Foucault, Pierre 108
Foundation for Sustainable
    Technologies (FoST) 156–7
framing events *see* reframing
    events
Frankl, Tilly 185
Frankl, Viktor 47, 185–92, 230
Frederick, Gary 190
Friedman, Matthew J. 38, 46–7
fuels, alternative 156–7
Funt, Allen 86

Garner, James 203
George (friend of author) 236
Gerber, Michael 103, 117
Gettinger, Brian 146–7, 148
Gibb, Barry 15–16
Gibb, Maurice 15–16
Gibb, Robin 15–16
Gilliam, Terry 127
Gladwell, Malcolm 127–8
glass, safety 154–5
goals 143–6
    see also dreams
God 122–3
Goffer, Amit 162–3, 201
Goldman, Sylvan 103–6
golf 33–4
'good' events see life changes
Good To Great (Collins) 244
Graham, Bette Nesmith 109–10
Gray, Elisha 161
Gray, Peter 168–9
Great Depression 104–5
    see also economic recessions
Greenstein, Mr (tutor) xii–xiii, 236
Gretsky, Wayne 229
Guadalupe Peak 182–3

hair loss 119–22, 201
happiness, science of 197–8
Harrell, Billy Bob 26
Harrington, Padraig 33–4
Hasselhoff, David 113
Haüy, Valentin 107
Headline It! (product) 121
health see illness and disease
Heard, Steve 157–8
heart disease 59–60, 128–9
helplessness (Learned
    Helplessness theory) 91–3
HIV/AIDS 158–9, 232–3

Holtman, Mallory 189–90
Home Depot, The 12
hot drinks 115–16
Hsieh Kun-Shan 54–7
human immunodeficiency virus see
    HIV/AIDS
Humpty Dumpty supermarket
    chain 103–4
Hurley, Chuck 194

IBM 154
Idle, Eric 127
Iglesias, Julio 1–3, 138–9, 148
Ilchenko, Larissa 178
illness and disease
    see also trauma
    alopecia 119–22, 201
    arthritis 83–6
    cancer 57–9, 75–80, 164–5, 232
    heart disease 59–60, 128–9
    leading to blindness 107, 164–5,
        195–6, 205
    multiple sclerosis 222–5, 232
    and optimism 58–64
    Parkinson's disease 62
    and pessimism 59–60
    positive emotions, therapeutic
        effects of 84–5, 86
    psoriasis xii–xiii, 237–8
    and statistics 86–7
impossibilities, made possible
    161–70
injuries 140
    see also accidents; disability;
        trauma
    brain damage 137–8
    burns 55, 115–16, 132–5, 142,
        209
    leading to amputations 34–5, 55,
        168, 178, 199

leading to blindness 107, 152
leading to deafness 149
leading to paralysis xv–xvi, 2,
    29–30, 146–7, 162, 183, 190,
    194, 209–10
slipped disc 20
sporting 33–4, 173, 189–90
teeth xxii
insurance sales people 65–6
inventions 149–60
see also business ventures;
    inventors
Braille 107–9
cruise control 151–3
Cups Carrier 115–16
electric light bulb 150, 153
fertilizer, alternative 157–8
fuels, alternative 156–7
Headline It! 121
Liquid Paper 109–10
marmalade 16–17
mind-mapping software 77–9
others by Edison 150
phonograph 150–51
Post-it notes 154
ReWalk 162–3, *248*
safety glass 154–5
shopping carts 105–6
tactile vision 166–7
wind-up radio 158–9
inventors 149–60
see also entrepreneurs;
    inventions
Bach-y-rita, Paul 166–7
Bayliss, Trevor 158–9
Benedictus, Edouard 154–5
Braille, Louis 107–9
Edison, Thomas A. 117, 149–51,
    153–4, 155–6, 160, 226, 247
Goffer, Amit 162–3

Goldman, Sylvan 103–6
Graham, Bette Nesmith 109–10
Heard, Steve 157–8
Jetter, Mike 75–80, 200, *245*
Keiller, James 16–17
Keiller, Janet 17
Newton, Clare 115–16
Pliszka, Jodi 119–22
Shrestha, Sanu Kaji 156–7
Silver, Spencer 154
Teetor, Ralph 151–3
investments 228–9
Iwerks, Ub 114–15

Jackson, Adam J, psoriasis xi–xiii,
    235–8
JAF (Joni and Friends) Ministries
    30–31
James, William 69
Jerry Springer Show 230
Jetter, Andi 76
Jetter, Bettina 76, 77, 79–80, 200,
    245
Jetter, Mike 75–80, 200, *245*
jobs, losing 10–12, 129–30
Johnson, Doug 143
Jones, Peter 5–6
Joni and Friends (JAF) Ministries
    30–31
Joyce, James 109
Joyce, Leonard 35

Kaiof, Radi 162
karma 122–3
Keiller, James 16–17
Keiller, Janet 17
Keller, Helen xi, 1, 137
Kennedy, John F. 15
Kentucky Fried Chicken (KFC)
    xxi–xxii

KFC (Kentucky Fried Chicken)
xxi–xxii
Kingpin (film) 100
Knight Rider (television series) 113
Kushner, Harold 202

L.A. Kings 7
Laffoon, Ruby xx
Lamb, Cindi 193–4
Lamb, Laura 194
Lao Tzu 32
Lashbrooke, Barnaby 227
laughter, therapeutic effects of
84–5, 86, 100
Law of Attraction 13
Lawrence, Ute 39–42
Lean On Me (Davis) 225
Learned Helplessness theory 91–3
Learned Optimism theory 93–5
Lennon, John 82
Lennon, Julia 82
Levy, Becca R. 60
Lewis, C.S. 139
life changes ('bad' and 'good'
events) 24–37
see also trauma
lottery winners 25–8
reframing 119–36
Taoist philosophy 32–3
life choices, based on statistics
81–2
light bulb, electric 150, 153
Lightner, Candace 192–4
Lightner, Cari 192–3
Lightner, Steve 192–3
Lin Yeh-chen 56, 57
Liquid Paper (product) 109–10
Locatelli, Elio 175
logotherapy 188–92
Long, Jerry 190–91

lottery winners 25–8
Louw, Ampie 176
low points, shaping future success
5–14
see also trauma
business crises xix, 6, 7–10,
15–23, 104–5
jobs, losing 10–12, 129–30
Lozano, Lucila 208

McCain, John 131–2
McGuinness, John 27
McHale, Des 81
Mackay, Harvey 12
MADD (Mothers Against Drunk
Drivers) 193–4
Magdaleno, Eladio 2
Man's Search For Meaning (Frankl)
185, 186
Marcus, Bernie 12
Marie-Strumpell's disease
(ankylosing spondylitis) 83–6
marmalade 16–17
martial arts 206, 207–8
meaning to life 185–94
Three Avenues theory
(logotherapy) 187–92
medication
expectations influencing
effectiveness 62–3, 75
placebos 61–4
Meili, Trisha (Central Park Jogger)
47–9
mental power, constructive 147
mental stimulation, optimistic
99–102
Merritt, LaShawn 171
Mickey Mouse (cartoon character)
114–15
MicroSolutions 12

mind-mapping 77–9
MindManager 79
Mintz, Charles 114
Mintz, Margaret (*née* Winkler) 114
mistakes, as learning experiences 153–4
Mitchell, W. 208–12, 219
modelling, optimists' strategies 96–9
Montezuma's (shop) 22
Morrell, Kade 199
Mothers Against Drunk Drivers (MADD) 193–4
motorcycles, accidents 146–7, 178, 183, 209
MS (multiple sclerosis) 222–5, 232
multiple sclerosis (MS) 222–5, 232
musicians and singers
    Bee Gees, The 15–16
    Iglesias, Julio 1–3, 138–9, 148
    Rinaldi, Elaine 139–41, 148
    Williams, Kim 142–3

Nancy Davis Foundation for Multiple Sclerosis 224
Napoleon Bonaparte 161
Native American Indians 99
Negative Spiral 232
Nepal 156–7
Nesmith, Michael 109
Neuro Linguistic Programming (NLP) 7, 96–9
Newton, Clare 115–16
NLP (Neuro Linguistic Programming) 7, 96–9
Norman, Greg 7
Nunn, Bill 137
Nupponen, Erik 124

Obama, Barack 131–2
Olympic Games 67, 179–80
    see also Paralympics
Only Fools And Horses (television series) 127
optimism 53–68, 214
    see also expectations; pessimism; positive emotions; positive things
    conflict with pessimism 99
    developing 93–102
        acting as if optimistic 98–9
        Cognitive Behavioural Therapy 96
        Learned Optimism theory 93–5
        mental stimulation 99–102
        modelling optimists' strategies 96–9
    and health 58–64
    and human potential 64–7
    inappropriate 231–2
    life strategies 94–9
    as opposed to wishful thinking *243–4*
    origins of 90–91
    testing levels 65–7, 87–9
Optimist International (organization) *245–6*
Orchestra Miami 141
Oswald the Lucky Rabbit (cartoon character) 114
outsourcing services 227

Palin, Michael 126
Paralympics 174, 177, 179, 180
    see also Olympic Games; wheelchair sports
paralysis *see* disability
Parkin, Kate 163

Parkinson's disease 62
Patten, Cassie 177–8
Pattinson, Daisy 19
Pattinson, Helen 19–23
Pattinson, Poppy 19
Pattinson, Simon 19–23
pessimism
  see also expectations; optimism
  conflict with optimism 99
  and health 59–60
  and human potential 66
  Learned Helplessness theory
    91–3
  life strategies 95
  origins of 90–91
  self-fulfilling prophesy 73–4
  testing levels 87–9
Peter, Laurence J. 147
phonograph 150–51
pistol shooting 97
Pistorius, Carl 176
Pistorius, Henke 172
Pistorius, Oscar 171–7, 181–2
Pistorius, Sheila 172, 174, 177
placebo effect 61–4
Pliszka, Jessica 120
Pliszka, Jodi 119–22
Pollock, Mark 195–7
positive emotions, therapeutic
  effects of 84–5, 86
  see also optimism
Positive Psychology 198
positive things, focusing on 124–6,
  128–9, 208
  see also optimism
positive thinking see optimism
Post-traumatic growth 42–4, 49–52
Post Traumatic Stress Disorder
  Association 41–2
Post-traumatic stress disorder

(PTSD) xvii, 40–42, 43
Post, William 'Bud' 26–7
Post-it notes 154
POWs see prisoners of war
Predictably Irrational (Ariely) 74
prisoners of war (POWs) 45–7,
  243–4
  see also concentration camps
prosthetic limbs 36, 55–6, 173–7
  see also amputees
psoriasis xii–xiii, 237–8
Psychiatric Times 43
psychotherapy 187–8
PTSD (Post-traumatic stress
  disorder) xvii, 40–42, 43
Purchall, Simon xxii–xxiii
Purchall, Veronika xxii–xxiii

radios, wind-up 158–9
rape victims 48, 49
recessions, economic 104–5, 226–9
redundancy see jobs, losing
reframing events 119–36
  blue focus 124–6
  'why me?' question 122–4
Regarding Henry (film) 137–8
relationships, importance of 50–51,
  195–202, 217
religious beliefs 51, 122–3
resources, sustainable 156–7
retinoblastoma 164–5
ReWalk (product) 162–3, 248
Rinaldi, Elaine 139–41, 148
Rinaldi, Leo 140
road traffic accidents see accidents
Robbins, Anthony 5, 6–8, 97, 195
Rock And Ruby Event
  Management 130–31
Rogers, Don 183–4
Roosevelt, Eleanor 141

Roosevelt, Theodore 229
rose petals, dried 18–19
Ruben, James 164
rugby 173

Sackstein, Rosalina 139, 140, 141
safety glass 154–5
sailing 145–6
sales people 65–6
Salomon Brothers 11
Sanders, Harland ('The Colonel')
    xix–xxii
SASQ (Seligman Attributional
    Style Questionnaire) 65–7
Saving Private Ryan (film) 99–100
Scheier, Michael F. 60
Schmutz, Robin 147
Schulman, Peter 73, 99
Schweitzer, Albert 80
Secret, The (Byrne) 13–14, 79
Segerstrom, Suzanne 98–9, 231–2
self-mutilation 230
Seligman Attributional Style
    Questionnaire (SASQ) 65–7
Seligman, Martin 65–7, 91–4, 198,
    231
Shakespeare, William 31
shares (investments) 228–9
Shaw, George Bernard 106
shooting (pistols) 97
shopping carts 105–6
Shrestha, Sanu Kaji 156–7
Silver, Spencer 154
Simply Rose Petals 19
Sinclair, Donald 126–7
singers *see* musicians and singers
Slater, Jan 18–19
slipped discs 20
SmileSavers xxiii
softball 188–90

Solomon, King 85
spiritual beliefs 51, 122–3
sport 7
    athletics 171–2, 173–7
    baseball 168–70
    basketball 199–200
    climbing 182–3
    cycling 57–8
    diving 190
    golf 33–4
    martial arts 206, 207–8
    Olympic Games 67, 179–80
    and optimism 66–7
    Paralympics 174, 177, 179, 180
    rugby 173
    sailing 145–6
    softball 188–90
    swimming 66–7, 177–80
    wheelchair sports 182–4
sporting injuries 33–4, 173, 189–90
statistics 81–2, 86–7
Stockdale, Jim *243–4*
stocks and shares 228–9
Stone, Gemma 129–31
strategies
    optimists 94–9
    pessimists 95
suffering, and growth 229–30
Sugarman, Joseph xv
suggestion (mental stimulation)
    99–102
suicide xvi–xviii, *239*
Sullivan, John 127
supermarkets 103–6
sustainable resources 156–7
swimming 29–30, 66–7, 177–80

tactile vision 166–7
Tada, Joni *see* Eareckson Tada
Taoism 32–3

Taylor, Angelo 171
Tedeschi, Richard G. 43–4, 47, 50,
   229–30
teeth, injuries xxii
Teetor, Ralph 151–3
Teilhard de Chardin, Pierre 119
Theresienstadt concentration
   camp 185–7
Thorpe, Ian 179
Three Avenues theory
   (logotherapy) 187–92
TimeEtc Limited 227
Topsy (elephant) *247*
Tour de France 57–8
Tracey, Brian 68
traffic accidents *see* accidents
trauma 38–52
   see also crises; illness and
      disease; injuries; life changes;
      low points
   creation of goals 143–4
   not essential to growth 229–30
   Post-traumatic growth 42–4,
      49–52
   Post-traumatic stress disorder
      xvii, 40–42, 43
   Third Avenue theory
      (logotherapy) 190–92
Travis, Randy 143
Tucholsky, Sara 189–90
Turner, Richard 203–7
Turner, Ted 111
typing 109–10
Tyson, Mike 7

Underwood, Aquanetta 164–5
Underwood, Ben 164–8
US Army 97

Valdez, Miguel 207–8

Varsavsky, Martin 112–13
Versveld, Gerry 173, 174, 176
Vietnam War 45–6, *243–4*
Virgin business empire 9–10

warfare
   prisoners of war 45–7, *243–4*
   World War Two 35–6, 99–100,
      185–7
Watson, Tom 154
Watt, William W. 82
*We Got Fired And It's The Best Thing
   That Ever Happened To Us*
   (Mackay) 12
'Wendell' (self-mutilator) 230
wheelchair sports 182–4
   see also disability; Paralympics
Whitney, King, Jr. 24
WhizzGo (company) 227
Whose Life Is It Anyway? (play)
   xv–xvi
wigs 121
Williams, Kim 142–3
Williamson, Darold 171
Williamson, Marianne 6
wind-up radios 158–9
Winkler, Margaret (*married name*
   Mintz) 114
wishful thinking 243–4
   see also optimism
Wong, Paul T.P. 42
World War Two 35–6, 99–100
   concentration camps 185–7
Wright, Orville 161
Wright, Wilbur 161
Wu Ah-Sun 56

Young, Fred 105, 106

Ziglar, Zig 53